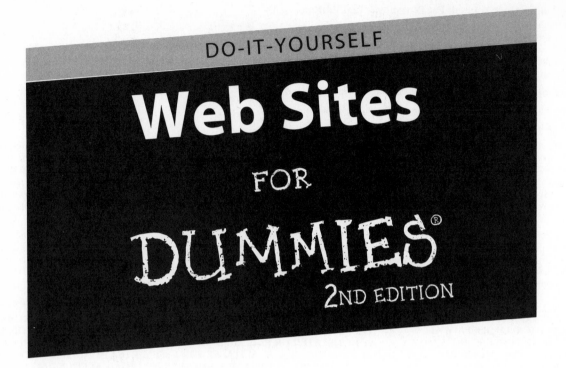

DO-IT-YOURSELF

Web Sites

FOR

DUMMIES®

2ND EDITION

by Janine Warner

WILEY

Wiley Publishing, Inc.

Web Sites Do-It-Yourself For Dummies®, 2nd Edition

Published by
Wiley Publishing, Inc.
111 River Street
Hoboken, NJ 07030-5774
www.wiley.com

WILEY

About the Author

Since 1996, **Janine Warner** has authored more than a dozen books about the Internet, including every edition of *Dreamweaver For Dummies*, *Creating Family Web Sites For Dummies*, and the last 5 editions of *Teach Yourself Dreamweaver Visually*.

She's also the host of a series of training videos about Web design for Total Training, including programs on Adobe Dreamweaver and Microsoft Expression Web. Highlights of her videos are featured on both the Microsoft and Adobe Web sites.

An award-winning journalist, her articles and columns have appeared in a variety of publications, including *The Miami Herald*, *Shape Magazine*, and the Pulitzer Prize-winning *Point Reyes Light* newspaper. She is also a regular columnist for *Layers Magazine*.

Janine has been a part-time faculty member at both the University of Miami and the University of Southern California Annenberg School for Communication. She has also developed online training programs for the Western Knight Center, a joint project of USC and UC Berkeley funded by the Knight Foundation.

Janine has extensive Internet experience working on large and small Web sites. From 1994 to 1998, she ran Visiontec Communications, a Web design business in Northern California, where she worked for a diverse group of clients including Levi Strauss & Co., AirTouch International, Beth's Desserts, and many other small and medium-size businesses.

In 1998, she joined *The Miami Herald* as their Online Managing Editor. A year later, she was promoted to Director of New Media and managed a team of designers, programmers, journalists, and marketing staff who produced the Web sites for *The Miami Herald*, *El Nuevo Herald*, and Miami.com. She left that position to serve as Director of Latin American Operations for CNET Networks, an international technology media company.

Since 2001, Janine has run her own business as a writer, speaker, and consultant. She is a popular speaker at conferences and events throughout the United States, and her fluency in Spanish has led to many speaking engagements in Latin America and Spain. She served as a judge for the *Arroba de Oro* Latin American Internet awards from 2001 to 2005. As part of that project, she helped to create an Internet literacy program for students in Central America called *Operación Red* (Operation Network).

Janine earned a degree in journalism and Spanish from the University of Massachusetts, Amherst, and spent the first several years of her career in Northern California as a reporter and editor.

She lives with her husband in Los Angeles.

Dedication

I love teaching Web design because it's so much fun to see all the great Web sites people create. I dedicate this book to everyone who aspires to share their ideas, stories, views, photos, business products and services on the Internet. Don't ever fear that Web design is too hard. You can do this, you can create your own Web site. In this book you find everything you need to create, design, publish, and promote your own Web site. I wish you all the best with your Web designs!

Author's Acknowledgments

More than anyone, I want to thank my husband, David LaFontaine, for his patience, love, delightful sense of humor, and all his help in the research and production of this book. Among his many contributions, he authored Chapters 1, 11, and 12. Dave, your intelligence and creativity inspire me, and your love brings me more joy than I could have imagined.

Thanks to my dear friend and mentor David Mitchell who helped me get started in my writing career many moons ago when he served as publisher of the *Point Reyes Light* newspaper.

Thanks to all four of my fabulous parents, Malinda, Janice, Helen, and Robin, for your love, support, and encouragement. Thanks to my brothers Brian and Kevin, and to Kevin's delightful wife Stephanie, and their amazing children Mikayla, Savannah, Jessica, and Calahan (you'll find their photos in the sample site in the Family Web sites chapter). Thanks also to all my extended family, which now includes David's large and wonderful collection of relatives, including Gail, Dave, Linda, Mark, Beth, Sarah, and everyone else in the LaFontaine, Roos, and other clans.Thanks to Jeff Noble for his contributions to Chapter 10 and for his careful tech editing and testing of all the lessons in this book. Thanks to the entire editorial team at Wiley Publishing, especially my acquisitions editor Bob Woerner, my development editor Becky Huehls, and everyone who helped to edit, produce, and develop this book.

And finally, let me thank my lucky stars that this book is finally done. Complete. Finished. That's it. (And don't even tell me those aren't complete sentences.)

Publisher's Acknowledgments

We're proud of this book; please send us your comments at http://dummies.custhelp.com. For other comments, please contact our Customer Care Department within the U.S. at 877-762-2974, outside the U.S. at 317-572-3993, or fax 317-572-4002.

Some of the people who helped bring this book to market include the following:

Acquisitions and Editorial

Project Editor: Rebecca Huehls

Executive Editor: Bob Woerner

Sr. Copy Editor: Teresa Artman

Technical Editor: Jeff Noble

Editorial Manager: Leah P. Cameron

Editorial Assistant: Amanda Graham

Sr. Editorial Assistant: Cherie Case

Cartoons: Rich Tennant (www.the5thwave.com)

Composition Services

Project Coordinator: Patrick Redmond

Layout and Graphics: Carrie A. Cesavice, Jennifer Henry, Erin Zeltner

Special Art: istockphoto.com

Proofreaders: Joanne Keaton

Indexer: BIM Indexing & Proofreading Services

Special Help: Jennifer Riggs

Publishing and Editorial for Technology Dummies

    Richard Swadley, Vice President and Executive Group Publisher

    Andy Cummings, Vice President and Publisher

    Mary Bednarek, Executive Acquisitions Director

    Mary C. Corder, Editorial Director

Publishing for Consumer Dummies

    Diane Graves Steele, Vice President and Publisher

Composition Services

    Debbie Stailey, Director of Composition Services

Contents at a Glance

Table of Contents

Introduction

If you're feeling left out of the mad scramble to establish a presence on the Internet, relax — you're not alone. And it's not too late.

Despite the hype, many small businesses, clubs, and families still don't have Web sites. And, even if you already have a site, you're not alone if you're still trying to figure out how to make it better or more profitable, or you've come to the realization that it's time to redesign.

These days, it seems that every TV commercial, movie trailer, magazine insert, and grocery store bulletin board warns that any serious business owner needs to have a Web site, and most families, clubs, and even pet snakes do, too.

Although that's increasingly true, building a presence on the Internet isn't something you should do just because everyone else is doing it, and it isn't all bad if you've waited this long to make the Web a priority. Too many people have raced to put up Web sites without taking the time to consider how the Web fits in with their other goals and how they can best take advantage of what the Web has to offer.

If you've waited until now, you may even be better off because the Internet has matured, its audience has matured (it isn't populated solely by teenagers and academics anymore), and building a Web site has become easier than ever. If you're ready for a redesign of your first site, you have the advantage of being able to benefit from your own and everyone else's mistakes.

About This Book

This book is designed to help you progress through the entire process of creating a site, from registering a domain name, to creating a compelling design, to attracting just the right audience.

But you don't have to read this book from cover to cover, and you certainly don't have to memorize it. *Web Sites Do-It-Yourself For Dummies* was written to help you find the answers you need when you need them. Consider this book a quick guide and a reference you can return to. Each part stands alone, giving you easy answers to specific questions and step-by-step instructions for common tasks. If you want to find out how to choose a hosting service, optimize images, or add video to your site, just jump right in and go directly to the section that most interests you. And don't worry about spilling coffee on the pages if you bring the book to breakfast — I promise it won't complain!

I designed this book using what I consider the best technologies for someone who wants to create their own, custom Web site. If you picked up this book, I assume that you're not an advanced programmer and that you don't want to hire a team of expensive Web consultants. You want to do it yourself.

To help you create the best site you can without your having to invest a million dollars, or a million hours, I based the step-by-step tasks in each chapter on the technologies that I think offer all the features you need yet are relatively easy to figure out with a little guidance. For images, you find instructions for using Photoshop Elements, a popular and competitively priced image program that you can use to create, edit, and optimize images so that they download quickly. If you already have Adobe Photoshop, you can use that program instead; the instructions work for both programs. For the pages of your site, you find step-by-step instructions for Adobe Dreamweaver, as well as a variety of templates you can download for free to go along with this book so you can create a professionally designed Web site quickly. If you want to use other programs or services, you find alternatives in handy sidebars near the relevant step-by-step tasks. For example, if you want to use Microsoft Expression Web instead of Adobe Dreamweaver, no problem, you'll find templates on the companion Web site that will work with both programs and instructions for using both.

About the Templates and Web Site for this Book

To help you get the most from this book, I created a special section at my Digital Family Web site with files and templates you can download and use as you follow along with the step-by-step tasks. You also find a FAQ (*f*requently *a*sked *q*uestions), links, additional resources, and updates. To get all these goodies, just enter the following address in your Web browser:

```
www.digitalfamily.com/diy
```

You need a password to get into this protected site, but if you have this book with you when you log on, you have everything you need to answer a simple question on the Web site and gain access right away.

After you are authorized to enter the Web site, you'll find instructions for downloading the images and templates, which give you a head start in creating a full-fledged site of your own. Along with this book, you get a collection of templates designed to create an online profile, an artist portfolio, a business site, and a family or hobby site. And, you can customize the look and feel of all these templates to use them to create any type of site for your corner of the Web.

Throughout this book, you find references to the Web site and the templates and other goodies that go with the step-by-step tasks.

Conventions Used in This Book

Keeping things consistent makes them easier to understand. In this book, those consistent elements are *conventions*. Notice how the word *conventions* is in italics? That's a convention I use frequently. I put new terms in italics and then define them so that you know what they mean.

When I type URLs (Web addresses) or e-mail addresses within regular paragraph text, they look like this: `www.jcwarner.com`. Sometimes, however, I set off a URL on its own line, like this:

```
www.jcwarner.com
```

That's so you can easily spot URLs on a page if you want to type them into your browser to visit a site. I also assume that your Web browser doesn't require the introductory `http://` for Web addresses. If you use an older browser, remember to type this part before the address. (Also make sure to include that part of the address when you're creating links.)

Even though programs like Dreamweaver make knowing the HTML code unnecessary, you may want to wade into the HTML waters occasionally. When I include HTML, such as the following code to link a URL to a Web page, I set off the HTML in the same monofont type as I use for URLs:

```
<A HREF="http://www.jcwarner.com">Janine's Web Site</A>
```

When I introduce you to a new set of features, such as options in a dialog box, I set these items apart with bullets so that you can see that they're all related. When I want you to follow instructions, I use numbered steps to walk you through the process.

Foolish Assumptions

Although this book is designed to help you create a professional-looking Web site, I don't assume that you're a pro — at least not yet. In keeping with the philosophy behind the *For Dummies* series, this easy-to-use guide is designed for readers with a wide range of experience. Being interested in Web design and wanting to create a Web site is the key, but that desire is all I expect from you.

How This Book Is Organized

To ease you through the learning curve associated with any new program, I organized *Web Sites Do-It-Yourself For Dummies,* 2nd Edition, to be a complete reference. This section provides a breakdown of the four parts of the book and what you can find in each one.

Part 1: Laying the Groundwork

Part I gets you started in creating a Web site and helps you lay a solid foundation for your site. In Chapter 1, I introduce you to the many ways you can create a Web site to help you find the best template, technology, and software you'll need for your project. In Chapter 2, I walk you through the planning process, which can save you a lot of time in the long run. In Chapter 3, you find out how to register a domain name, and I give you tips for selecting the best Web server hosting service. And then in Chapter 4, I introduce you to just enough Web technologies, including HTML, CSS to give you a head start on your Web site.

Part II: Putting the Pages Together

In Chapter 5, I move on to graphics, with an introduction to creating graphics for the Web, an overview of the differences in formats (GIF, JPEG, and PNG files), and a selection of tips for optimizing images so that they download quickly. In Chapter 6, you find an introduction to Dreamweaver, and in Chapters 7, 8, and 9, you get step-by-step instructions for personalizing the many templates that come with this book. In Chapter 10, you discover the Dreamweaver testing and publishing features so that you can publish your pages to the Internet as soon as you're ready.

Part III: Going Web 2.0

In Part III, I go beyond basic Web design, by giving you instructions for creating a blog in Chapter 11 and for recording and publishing a podcast in Chapter 12. In Chapter 13, you find a review of the many audio, video, and animation formats and instructions for how to add multimedia to your Web site. In Chapter 14, I "show you the money" with instructions for including advertising and affiliates on your pages as well as for adding e-commerce options to sell products and services.

Part IV: The Part of Tens

Chapter 15 includes ten cool Web services that can help you add advanced features to your site without having to know how to program. Finally, Chapter 16 features ten ways to promote your site, because after you do all the work of creating an outstanding Web site, you want to make sure to attract a good audience.

Icons Used in This Book

This icon reminds you of an important concept or procedure that you should store away in your memory banks for later use.

This icon indicates a tip or technique that can save you time and money — and headaches — later.

This icon warns you of any potential pitfalls — and gives you the all-important information on how to avoid them.

Part I
Laying the Groundwork

The 5th Wave   By Rich Tennant

"Just how accurately should my Web site reflect my place of business?"

Chapter 1

Exploring the Best Ways to Create Web Sites

Creating a Web site can open doors for you that you never knew existed. Every day, thousands more people connect to the Web for the first time, and those who are already online get more adept at using online tools and services. The effect of all these people reaching out to each other to play, laugh, argue, buy, sell, trade, collaborate, invent, experiment, research, learn, and just chat about the mundane details of what constitutes a perfect cup of coffee — are transforming the world.

Thanks to the ever-simpler, easier, and less expensive Web technologies that you discover in this book, you can create a Web site today that just a few years ago would have required a crack team of programmers, the computing power of a room full of servers, and a budget of hundreds of thousands of dollars.

Today's Internet is a friendlier place where programs like Dreamweaver and WordPress make it so easy that even celebrities and politicians can run their own sites. And if they can do it, believe me, you can, too! For just a few dollars per month, you can host your site on a professional Web server. At that price, almost any old businesses can afford to try new tricks, and new businesses can launch with little investment.

Whether you're new to Web design or want to take your Web skills to the next level to create a world-class Web site or blog, it's often best to start by taking a step back to better understand your options before you dive in to the details of building and publishing a Web site. That's what this chapter is for: to start you out with an overview of the different kinds of Web sites and blogs, to help you appreciate how templates work for different kinds of sites, and to introduce you to the tools and technologies you can use to create your own Web site.

I'm not offering any "get-rich-quick" schemes in this book, but if you're ready to share your talents with the world, the Web is a better place than ever. And because I know you probably don't want to spend all your time creating your Web site, I've gathered everything you need in this book to make it easy for you.

Checking Out Examples of Success on the Web

Before I get into the technical details in this chapter, here are a few Internet success stories to inspire you and give you an idea of what you can do on the Internet today:

- Three friends in Chicago started `www.threadless.com` as an entry into a contest, hoping to win $1,000. The business took off when designers flocked to the site to submit their artwork to be printed on t-shirts, and millions of people started placing orders. In a case study, the Harvard Business School cited Threadless as an example of a "perfect business," one that has made its founders millionaires, thanks to the Web.

- Two creative Chefs blended Korean barbecue with Mexican tacos and created Kogi, which they sold out of a lunch truck in Los Angles. When they started posting the schedule and location of the truck on Twitter.com (the popular micro-blogging Web site), crowds started lining up in advance for their fabulous food. Word spread and Kogi became a breakout hit. Today, in addition to the Web site shown in Figure 1-1, they have more than 42,000 rabid followers, and three state-of-the-art trucks roaming Los Angeles and catering Hollywood parties. You can learn all about their great food and thriving business at `www.kogibbq.com`.

Figure 1-1: The Kogi lunch truck in Los Angeles developed a loyal following and a growing business thanks to their tasty Web site and smart use of www.Twitter.com.

✔ A truly fanatical hockey aficionado who writes under the pseudonym "Eklund" built HockeyBuzz.com from a tiny fansite dedicated to the game he loved into the core of a media empire that employs more than 50 bloggers and launched a show on XM Radio.

✔ One of the most popular personalities on YouTube, Fred is a 14-year-old kid in Nebraska who parlayed a cheap video camera and YouTube into a multimillion dollar career. If you're old enough to drive, you've probably never even heard of him, but his videos are watched by millions of giggling kids every week at www.youtube.com/user/Fred.

✔ Gossip writer Perez Hilton built a career through his blog where he's known for his snarky comments. His celebrity-filled site at www.perezhilton.com is now read by more people than the tabloid magazines in the supermarket check-out aisles, and he charges thousands of dollars to make personal appearances at events.

✔ A woman who just loved to shop and find bargains built Outblush.com into a must-read beauty, fashion, and makeup advisor for millions — and a successful business for herself. Her site, featured in Figure 1-2, is now as influential as many glossy fashion magazines, and her product reviews can make or break a new line of products.

Figure 1-2: The creator of www.outblush.com made a name for herself with a well-researched collection of product reviews.

What all these Web success stories have in common is that their creators were able to use technologies that are cheaper and easier to use than ever before to do what they do best in front of a bigger audience. And that's one of the most powerful ways to use the Internet.

How much does a Web site cost?

The first question many people ask Web designers is one of the hardest to answer: "How much does a Web site cost?" Just because the answer is, "Well, it depends . . ." does not mean that we're trying to be evasive. (Well, maybe some people are intentionally evasive.) The truth is that the answer is complicated.

Building a Web site is often compared to building a house because the cost depends on what materials you want to use and how much experience and fancy tools you have. Like a house, a Web site can range from a Spartan hut with bare walls and a dirt floor, to an opulent mansion tricked out with the finest marble, to a secure fortress with layers of security guards demanding, "Identification, please."

In the land of the Internet, these buildings might compare with a simple profile site, a multimedia showcase, or an e-commerce business site with shopping cart features.

The good news is that thanks to the advances in Web technology, you can build any of these kinds of Web sites for about the cost of this book and a little of your own time. All the software featured in this book is available for free (or at least a free 30-day trial). If you use the templates you can download from this book's companion Web site, you should be able to create a Web site in just a few days. And if you want advanced features, like e-commerce or video, don't worry. You find instructions in these pages for using some of the newest and best online services, including Google Checkout, which makes it easy (and economical) to add a shopping cart to your Web site, and Vimeo's video hosting service, which makes it possible to offer high-resolution video on your site without an expensive Web server.

You find links to all the online services, templates, and software featured in this book on my companion Web site at www. DigitalFamily.com/diy.

Creating Web Sites with the Templates in This Book

My goal in this book is to help you create not just a Web site but an online presence that truly serves your goals, whether you want to launch a new business on the Internet, promote an organization you've loved for years, or stay in touch with distant family members and classmates.

Here are a few of the kinds of Web sites you can create with the templates and instructions included with this book:

✔ **Portfolio:** Photographers, graphic designers, and artists are quickly realizing that one of the best ways to show off their work and win new (and better-paying) clients is to have a snazzy online portfolio. In Figure 1-3, photographer Jasper Johal showcases his photos in an online gallery that makes it easy to view a collection of images on his home page and in a series of galleries on his site. A consulting firm could also use this type of site template to showcase a series of case studies, or by a carpenter or landscape architect to share photos of completed projects. You'll find templates for this design on the companion Web site, and instructions for customizing it to create your own site, in Chapter 7.

✔ **Online profile:** It used to be that "who you know" was the key to getting ahead. Now it's "who knows you." A Web site is a great way to introduce yourself, your business, or your club to the world, and it's also an important way to make it easy for other people to introduce you when they make a referral.

Consultants, authors, attorneys, dentists, and other professionals are well served by an online profile site that includes biographical information, a list of services or specialties, references, awards, testimonials, and links to completed projects and descriptions of your work. The template shown in Figure 1-4 is included with this book, and you find instructions in Chapter 7 that will help you to create a variety of profile designs.

✔ **Club or organization:** Better than a bumper sticker, a Web site is an excellent way to showcase your favorite clubs, charities, after-school activities, hobbies, and more. The Web enables you to easily notify everyone of meeting dates and times, or post pictures and descriptions of recent awards and triumphs. A well-designed Web site can save organizers from having to make dozens of phone calls just to see whether everyone is good to take the soccer team out for ice cream after practice next week, or to coordinate fundraisers for worthy causes. You can use any of the templates featured in Chapters 7–9 to create a Web site for a club or organization.

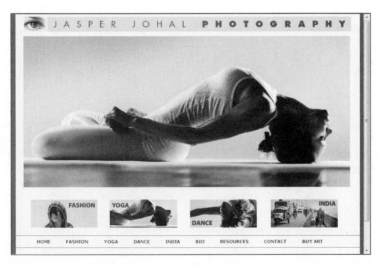

Figure 1-3: Portfolio sites can showcase photos or artwork, like this photo gallery on Jasper Johal's Web site.

Figure 1-4: You can use a template, like this design for a professional profile, to create a variety of designs. Change the templates a little, or a lot, to make them your own.

✔ **Small business:** Whether you want to share your professional services, like the massage therapist featured in Figure 1-5, or you have a growing business taking care of pampered pooches, like Pamela's Pet Services in Chapter 2, creating a Web site can make all the difference in your success, online and off. You can edit any of the templates in Chapters 7–9 to create a business Web site, but the designs in Chapter 8 are especially well suited to business needs.

✔ **Family and wedding:** Before couples say "I do," more and more of them are building wedding Web sites that feature invitations, directions, guest registries, and more. And, as a family grows, building a Web site is a helpful way to help the doting grandparents impress their friends without having to carry a wallet bulging with baby pictures. You can use the template featured in Chapter 9 to create any kind of site you want, but it's especially well suited to creating a site for the entire family, much like the one I created for my brother and his family, shown in Figure 1-6.

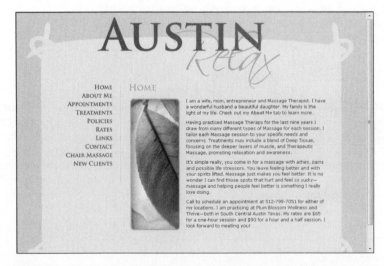

Figure 1-5: The use of a big image in the background of this Austin massage site help create the feeling of a design that fills the page.

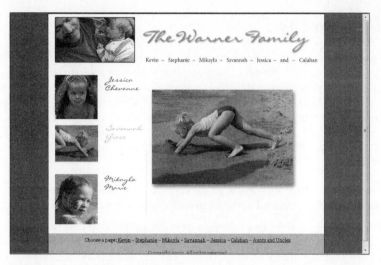

Figure 1-6: Showcase your family, wedding, and new baby photos, and stay connected with all those you love.

Comparing Web Design Options

The first step to building a site is choosing what kind of site you want to build. So, before you get too far into creating your own site, it can help to start with a general introduction to how different features are built on the Web.

To start, know that Web sites fall into two very broad categories: *static* Web sites, which are generally built with a program like Adobe Dreamweaver, and *dynamic* Web sites, which use advanced programming to create advanced, interactive features, like those used in a WordPress blog. Keep in mind that you can add multimedia, video, audio, animation, and so on to either type of site.

Static Web sites are made up of a collection of individual pages with the `.html` or `.htm` extension. You might think that all Web sites are made up of individual pages (and in a way they are), but with static sites those pages are saved as separate files. With a dynamic site, as you discover a little later in this section, the pages you view in a Web browser are created dynamically as they are delivered to the browser, so they're not saved as individual pages but as pieces of pages that can be mixed and matched. That gives dynamic sites many advantages, but it also makes them a lot more complicated to create.

The upshot is this: Because dynamic Web sites are more complicated to create, if you're just creating a simple profile or small business site, dynamic sites are often not worth the extra effort. The big exception comes in with blogs, because thanks to specialized blogging tools like WordPress, creating a dynamic site with the common features of a blog is relatively easy (as you learn in Chapter 11).

As a result, many people create both a static Web site for their profile or small business and a blog where they can easily add posts and other updates.

Static Web pages

Static pages are easier to design, and they work well for small- and medium-sized Web sites, such as a professional profile or an online gallery. Because static Web pages are written in plain text, you can create them in a program as simple as Notepad or SimpleText although tools like Adobe Dreamweaver and Microsoft Expression Web make it a lot easier and save you having to remember all the cryptic XHTML tags.

A static Web site offers a few advantages, especially if you're just starting out, including the following:

- **Easy to learn to develop:** Anyone who can resize a photo has a head start on the skills needed to create and arrange graphic elements on a static page.

- **Gives you complete control over design of each page:** You can tweak the size, colors, fonts, and arrangement of the elements on each page individually, and you can edit templates for these kinds of sites more easily than the templates for dynamic sites.

- **Easy to build, test, and publish to a Web server:** You can create and test static Web pages on any personal computer and then host them on any commercial Web server and you only need FTP access (which is built into programs like Dreamweaver) to publish pages to the Internet.

Dynamic Web pages

The technical aspects of dynamic sites get complicated quickly, but the gist of it is that instead of creating a collection of individual pages, you store all your content in a way that makes it easy to display text, images, and other data in a variety of combinations. That's what makes it possible for shopping sites like Amazon.com to keep track of your last order and recommend books when you return.

A site can even gather information from different sources to create complex pages dynamically. For example, you can combine information about customers' shopping habits with a list of your overstocked items on sale and create a page tailored to each visitor.

Dynamic sites are generally created on a Web server by combining CSS (Cascading Style Sheets, introduced in Chapter 4) and XHTML (which is more or less HTML that complies with today's standards, also explained in Chapter 4) with more advanced technologies, such as PHP, ASP.NET, or ColdFusion. That brings up another of the big challenges of working on dynamic sites: You have to build and test dynamic pages on a computer that runs a Web server, which is a lot more complicated than simply installing a Web browser on your personal PC to test your pages, as you learn in Chapter 10. Launching a dynamic site on a commercial Web server is also far more complicated than publishing a static page site to a Web server.

That said, the advantages of dynamic Web sites are significant, and most big sites on the Web are created this way, but most of the big sites on the Web also have a team of experienced programmers behind them. Unless you have advanced programming skills or a big budget, the challenges of creating a dynamic Web site mean that most small- and medium-sized Web sites are still better served with static Web sites.

The big exception is blogging. Although blogging tools, such as WordPress and Blogger, create dynamic Web sites with all these advanced capabilities, they do it in a way that makes it relatively easy to launch and update. As you discover in the section on WordPress templates that follows, it's easy to create a blog but not so easy to edit the templates for a blog — another reason to consider creating a static site with a program like Dreamweaver. And remember: You can always create one of each, to get the best of both worlds.

The gardening Web site `www.GardenstoTables.com` (featured in Figure 1-7), was created with a program called Joomla!. Similar to WordPress, Joomla! offers many types of templates and add-ons to make it easier to create a dynamic Web site. These tools are ideal if you plan to create a large, complex site, especially one that you expect to grow to have hundreds or thousands of pages over time.

The advantages of a dynamic site include

- ✔ **Easily updated:** When you want to put new content into a dynamic Web site, you can simply add a new product or image to the database, and it automatically appears in all the corresponding pages in the site.

- ✔ **Consistent look:** When you create a dynamic site, you have to use templates, which help create a consistent look across a Web site. No matter how you build a site, being consistent is good practice when it comes to navigation buttons, banners, and other essential elements you want your visitors to find no matter which page they visit.

- ✔ **Easier to redesign:** All great Web sites grow and change over time, and as they get bigger, they become even more complex to redesign. With a dynamic site, you can simply update the templates, and the content will automatically be included in the new version of the site.

Figure 1-7: Online blogging and content management programs, such as WordPress and Joomla!, make it easier than ever to create magazine-style sites like Gardens to Tables.

Multimedia: You like to move it-move it . . .

I use the catch-all title "multimedia" to describe anything that moves on a Web page, but that's a lot of different things these days, and most people have trouble identifying the different ways you can make characters sing and dance on the Web. Multimedia should be considered distinct from static and dynamic sites because video, audio, and images can be added to both static and dynamic Web pages.

Today there are many ways to add multimedia to a Web page, and the same series of animated images could be created using video as an animation in Adobe Flash or as a simple animated GIF. One of the newest ways to add interactivity to a site is to use a technology called AJAX, which combines JavaScript and XML and is growing in popularity.

Fortunately, you don't have to worry too much about all the technical details to add multimedia to your Web pages. As you learn in Chapter 13, you can easily add many different kinds of audio and video formats using Adobe Dreamweaver, and you can even upload videos to a site like YouTube or Vimeo, and then insert them into any Web page with copy-and-paste ease.

Working with Different Kinds of Templates

The term *template* is used in many different ways for many different kinds of design work (on and off the Web), but essentially, a template is a shortcut in the design process. Think of a template as a set of design specifications that you can use to control the look and feel of your Web page. Templates can be used to set the background colors, how many columns (if any) your Web pages have, what font sizes and colors are used, how links are handled, and so on. Just about any aspect of the design or functionality can be set or adjusted by working with templates.

But not all templates are created equally. Although they all share those basic characteristics, many different kinds of templates are in use on the Web today. For example, most of the templates featured in this book were designed to create static Web sites with Dreamweaver, but they are quite different from the kinds of templates you would use if you were creating a blog with WordPress. You learn how to create a WordPress blog in Chapter 11, but before you start using any of these templates, I think it's helpful to better understand how they are different.

The templates featured in this book are

- **Dreamweaver templates (extension `.dwt`)**

    Dreamweaver templates offer many advantages without requiring advanced programming skills. When you create Dreamweaver templates with the `.dwt` extension, you can use XHTML and CSS to create relatively simple static Web sites that include high-end features found on dynamic sites, such as the ability to create new pages quickly and to update every page in your site with the click of a button.

    Although you can use Dreamweaver to create templates that use advanced programming like PHP or Java, the `.dwt` Dreamweaver template is a much simpler option that is ideal for small- to medium-sized Web sites, which is why I used this template style for the profile, portfolio, small business, and family sites featured in Chapters 7–9.

You can even create your own Dreamweaver templates by following the instructions in Chapter 6, and you can download Dreamweaver templates from many different Web sites (some for free, others for a fee). If you have this book, you have everything you need to download the collection of templates specially designed for the tutorials in Chapters 7, 8, and 9. Just visit `www.DigitalFamily.com/diy` and follow the simple instructions to download the Dreamweaver Templates and image files included with them.

✔ **WordPress templates (extension:** `.php`**)**

Templates such as the ones you get with a blogging program like WordPress use the extension `.php` because they are written in the PHP (Hypertext Preprocessor) programming language. WordPress templates offer many of the same benefits as Dreamweaver templates, except that templates for blogs like WordPress draw their content from a database. As a result, they include XHTML and CSS like the Dreamweaver templates, plus much more complicated programming in the PHP programming language.

When you design a blog or any other kind of *dynamic* site (explained in greater detail in the previous section), it's important to understand that the technology behind the scenes gets complicated very quickly. This may seem counterintuitive because creating a blog on a site like WordPress.com is so easy, and updating a blog with new posts after it's been built is super easy.

But here's the rub: It is easy to create a basic blog with a WordPress template, but it's not easy to edit a WordPress template. Thus, if you want to be able to change the design of your blog pages, alter the fonts, colors, and other design features, things get complicated really quickly.

What kind of templates should you use?

Which templates are best for you depends on your goals and your technical skills, but it comes down to this. If you're creating a relatively small Web site (less than 50 pages), you'll probably have an easier time with Dreamweaver templates and the instructions in Chapters 7–9 for creating profile, portfolio, and small business sites.

Matching templates and technology

In addition to the WordPress and Dreamweaver templates featured in this book, there are many other kinds of templates in use on the Web. For example, if you download a template designed for Adobe Flash, you'll need a program that supports Flash to edit the pages. Flash templates end in the `.swf` extension, and you wouldn't be able to use a Flash template with WordPress blog, for example.

Other kinds of templates in use on the Web today include templates for Microsoft ASP and ASP.NET sites, which use the `.asp` and `.aspx` extensions, respectively.

If a site is created using the Java or Pearl programming languages, the templates should end in `.jsp` or `.prl`, respectively.

The big lesson is this: Make sure you have the right kind of template for the kind of site or blog you are creating.

If, however, you want to create an online journal or magazine that you will update often and expect to grow to hundreds or even thousands of pages, then creating a blog with WordPress is well worth the extra effort.

And here's where it gets really fun. Many people create both a Web site, say for their business portfolio, and a blog where they can add posts and other updates over time. Linking a blog and a Web site together is easy, and with this book, you have everything you need to create both.

Reviewing Web Design and Graphics Programs

I've chosen the most popular and powerful tools for you in this book. After years of testing Web design programs and building many different kinds of sites, I have found these to be the best options for the kinds of sites featured in this book. But that doesn't mean you can't substitute another program you prefer (or already have lying around your hard drive). For example, if you already have the full professional version of Adobe Photoshop, you can definitely use it with the lessons in the book. But because that program alone costs around $600, I choose to feature Photoshop's little sister, Photoshop Elements, which has all the basic features you need, but with a simpler user interface (and a price tag of less than $100).

When it comes to creating Web sites with XHTML and CSS, my first choice is Adobe Dreamweaver. If you're a Microsoft fan, I have to say I've also had good success with Microsoft Expression Web, and you can use that program to create all the sites featured in this book as well.

Both Dreamweaver and Expression Web sport graphic user interfaces that allow you to accomplish tasks through clicking and dragging instead of writing complicated CSS and XHTML tags. To help you appreciate the differences between these programs, you'll find a few more details in the last section of this chapter.

Although I believe that Photoshop Elements and Dreamweaver are the best programs for do-it-yourselfers just getting started on the Web, I include this general description of a few popular Web design and graphics programs on the market today to help you better appreciate your options. (You find descriptions of the most popular blogging programs, such as WordPress and TypePad, in Chapter 11.)

Comparing Web design programs

In the early days of the Web, people were using lots of different visual HTML editors. Today only a few major ones are in common use on the Web: Adobe Dreamweaver and Microsoft Expression Web. Both programs are available for download as trial versions.

> ✔ **Adobe Dreamweaver:** By far the most popular choice among professional Web designers, this award-winning program offers high-end development tools, excellent design features, and valuable support for all the latest Internet technologies. Dreamweaver features a wide collection of customizable palettes,

floating dialog boxes, and toolbars, which makes it look more like an image editor than a word processor. If you're serious about Web design, this is *the* tool to use, which is why I chose Dreamweaver to feature in this book.

If you don't have a copy of Dreamweaver, you can download a fully functional 30-day trial version for free by visiting www.adobe.com/dreamweaver.

You find an introduction to Dreamweaver in Chapter 6 and step-by-step instructions for customizing the various templates featured in this book in Chapters 7, 8, and 9. When you're ready for more advanced design with Dreamweaver, you find a collection of online tutorials at www.Digital Family.com/dreamweaver (shown in Figure 1-8), including excerpts of my book *Dreamweaver CS4 For Dummies* (Wiley).

✔ **Adobe Contribute:** Contribute is designed to make it easy for anyone to "contribute" to a Web site. This reasonably priced program is easy and intuitive to use, but it's not a stand-alone program. Contribute isn't designed to create Web sites but to help you easily *update* an existing site. You need a program like Dreamweaver to create a Web site using the templates in this book, but if you want to enable others who know little or nothing about the Web to update the site, Contribute is a great option. You can download a free trial version at www.adobe.com/contribute.

✔ **Microsoft Expression Web:** Just because I loved Dreamweaver first doesn't mean I don't respect Expression Web. Microsoft has a lot to be proud of with this relatively new professional design program. Expression Web offers strong CSS support and follows standards better than FrontPage ever did. You can create XHTML and CSS with Expression Web, and you'll find special features for creating dynamic sites with ASP.NET. If you generally prefer Microsoft products and/or work with a developer who uses Visual Studio, you should appreciate the compatibility between Microsoft Visual Studio and Expression Web. You can download a free trial version at www.microsoft.com/expression.

Figure 1-8: You can find more tutorials for Dreamweaver and Expression Web on my Digital Family Web site.

Comparing image editing programs

You can find many choices in the world of image editing programs, from high-end programs, such as Adobe Photoshop, to "prosumer" (*pro*fessional con*sumer*) products, like Photoshop Elements, to simple programs that you can download for free over the Internet, such as Irfanview. Here's a quick comparison of image editing programs:

- ✔ **Adobe Photoshop:** By far the most popular image editing program in the history of computer design, Photoshop lets you create, edit, and manipulate images in myriad ways. It's a professional tool with a professional price tag (around $600), so unless you have a big budget or you're a serious photographer or designer, Photoshop is probably more than you need (or want to pay for). You can download a 30-day free trial version at www.adobe.com/photoshop.

- ✔ **Adobe Photoshop Elements:** Photoshop Elements features many of the same powerful tools as Photoshop, but it's easier to use and costs less than $100. Elements provides more than enough power for almost anything you need to do on a Web site, including optimizing images in the JPEG, GIF, or PNG format so that they download faster over the Internet. You find an introduction to Elements and instructions for creating and optimizing graphics for the Web in Chapter 5.

The difference between Photoshop and Photoshop Elements boils down to this: The expensive version is used by magazine editors and high-fashion photographers, for example, to perform painstaking, exacting work on their photos, to make flawless images that can be turned into four-color separations to run on million-dollar printing presses. (Given enough time, you can use Photoshop to make a mule look like a supermodel.) For the rest of us, who just want to edit photos or perhaps create the impression that Uncle Ernie's basset hound is driving the lawnmower, Photoshop Elements is all you need. You can download a 30-day free trial version at www.adobe.com/elements.

- ✔ **Adobe Fireworks:** Fireworks was designed specifically for creating and optimizing images on the Web. Fireworks is a favorite among many professional Web designers because you can create a complete page layout in Fireworks, and then use the program's slicing tool to optimize and export images for the Web while Fireworks automatically creates the necessary XHTML code for you. It's not a perfect science, but it's pretty impressive. And because Fireworks is integrated with Dreamweaver, you can move back and forth between the two programs, which makes it easier to make changes to designs that use lots of images. You can download a 30-day free trial version at www.adobe.com/fireworks.

- ✔ **Free image editing programs:** Search the Web for *free photo editor,* and you find many listed but only a few that are even worth downloading. If you're willing to settle for a more limited program to save money, consider the online editor at www.irfanview.com or download the popular GIMP (GNU Image Manipulation Program). You can find this open-source editor (available for Windows, Unix, and Linux) at www.gimp.org.

Chapter 2

Planning Makes Web Design Easier

・・

In This Chapter

▶ Pinpointing your Web site goals

▶ Understanding the benefits of developing a plan

▶ Stepping through a project plan

▶ Accommodating new ideas while sticking to your plan

▶ Creating an organized, consistent design

・・

If a potential partner approached you with a "great new business idea" guaranteed to make you money, you'd probably ask a lot of questions before you even considered writing a check to get things started. You'd probably also develop a business plan, or at least explore in detail how the new business would work, how much it would cost you, and how much money you could expect to make in return.

If you're considering creating a Web site, or redesigning the one you already have, I recommend taking the same cautious approach. After all, a good Web site is an extension of your business — and, in many cases, a new product, service, or storefront that deserves the same level of planning as any other serious business venture. Even if you're creating a site for a hobby, vacation photos, or pictures of your family, the principles covered in this chapter will help ensure that developing your site goes smoothly and the final result gains you all the approval and praise you deserve.

This chapter is designed to help you carefully consider the many aspects of planning a Web site before you start building. You'll also find a series of questions to help guide you through the early stages of the development process.

 If you can complete the exercises in this chapter with a business partner or someone you trust to provide a reality check, I recommend it. You know what they say about decisions made in a vacuum: They generally suck. If you're reading this book, you're probably already convinced that you should create a Web site, and you may even have a pretty good idea about how you want to design it. Before you dive in, talk through the process with someone else who can provide a fresh perspective and help you consider aspects you may have overlooked. It's also a lot more fun to go through the exercises in this chapter and answer the questionnaires with a partner. Don't worry, though, if you're on your own (or you're determined to keep your project a secret until it's done). Consider me your virtual partner and let my questions and planning tips in this chapter serve as a guide to get you started.

Developing a Project Plan

As with most project plans, a good Web site plan is made up of a series of tasks, a budget, a timeline, and a list of the resources and materials you need. Taking the time to create a detailed project plan gives you a structure within which you can work with greater confidence, and a much better chance of meeting your original goals on time and on budget.

The following list provides a step-by-step approach to creating a project plan:

1. Define the goals and objectives of your site.
2. Create a content list.
3. Create a task list.
4. Set a timeline.
5. Establish a budget.
6. Assemble a team.
7. Create a site design and navigation structure.

In the sections that follow, you find out the details involved in each of these steps (with the exception of Step 7). Creating your design and navigation is such a big step that it gets a section all its own later in this chapter, "Designing Your Web Site."

In the sections that follow, you find out the details involved in each of these steps.

Defining goals and objectives

The series of questions in this section are designed to help you assess how a Web site can best serve you, your business, or organization. Taking the time to answer each question should help you define the goals of your site and create a guide that you can use as you organize and prioritize the development.

Before you start sketching out the *home page* (also called the *front page*), define the most important aspects of a Web site to identify what you really need. Remember that you can always start small and develop a Web site over time. And there's no rush to get the site up as fast as possible — the Web isn't going anywhere, and the best uses of the Web are the ones that will be around for a long time.

Before you even start, make sure that you and your staff (or friends and family) are clear about why you're creating a Web site and what it will take. Spend a little time answering each of the following questions, and use your responses to shape the planning and implementation of your Web site. Creating an outstanding Web site takes effort, and that effort can take time away from other things that are important. The more you plan, the more you have time left over for a little fun and relaxation (at least once in a while).

✔ **Why is having a Web site important to you?**

Separate the pipe from the dream and get clear on your true motivation.

✔ **What are your objectives?**

Determine whether you will use your Web site to promote your business, sell products or services, cut costs, showcase clients, provide customer support, stay in touch with friends and family, or do something that no one else has ever done.

As you go through the planning and development process, write down your top goals and refine them until you have two (at most, three) clear objectives for your site. Then keep your list somewhere that you're forced to look at your objectives regularly, like the edge of your computer monitor or the bathroom mirror. Whenever you have a question about any aspect of the design, content, or development of your site, refer to your list of goals and make sure that your decisions remain true to your objectives.

✔ **How will you measure success?**

You won't achieve success with your Web site project unless you can effectively measure its results, so be sure that you can voice your objectives in measurable ways. The more specific and quantifiable you can be, the better. For example, rather than just state, "The goal is reducing the telemarketing staff," assign an amount and a timeframe to make an objective quantifiable, such as, "The goal is reducing the telemarketing staff by 20 percent in six months." Doing so helps you make sure that you're taking the necessary steps to achieve that goal.

✔ **Whom do you want to visit your Web site?**

Consider your audience above all else. If you're creating a sales site for real estate investors, you should probably take a different design approach than if you're creating a game site for 12-year-olds. If you're not sure what 12-year-olds want on a Web site, round some up and ask them.

Clarifying the target audience of your Web site should be a key factor in how you plan and develop your site, from the vocabulary you use to how public you make the information. For example, a site for doctors might include complex medical terms, whereas a site for patients needs more common language. Similarly, an architect might create a Web site with a public section where potential clients can view photos of completed projects and testimonials, and also create a password-protected section where current clients can view plans as they're being developed.

✔ **What do you want a user to gain from visiting your Web site?**

One of my favorite benefits of a Web site is instant information at 1 a.m. without having to talk to anybody or wait on hold. Take time to consider what you want your visitors to learn from your site, and then make sure that the information is front and center in your design and development plans.

✔ **What do you want users to do after or on visits to your Web site?**

The more specific you can be about what you want visitors to do on your site, the better. Do you want visitors to buy a product, hire you to perform a service, join an association, call and ask for an appointment, sign up for a newsletter, or just tell their friends and family how cool your Web site is? Whatever you desire, you want your site's design to encourage visitors to take that action and to make it as easy as possible for them to do so.

✔ **How does your idea for a Web site compare with others?**

Taking the time to research what other people have done with their Web sites before you get too far into developing yours is an important part of the planning process. An afternoon spent surfing the Web for related businesses, and even unrelated businesses that have similar features, can help you identify things you may want to include on your own site and help ensure you're not starting a Web site in a category that's already so competitive you'll need to really distinguish yourself to attract an audience.

✔ **Do you expect to make money on your Web site?**

If your answer is, "Of course I do!" that goal should shape everything you do as you design the way visitors will use your site. Pay special attention to the section "Establishing a budget," later in this chapter, to help ensure you see a return on your investment.

Besides being potential cash generators, Web sites can help you be more competitive, advertise your store or services, schedule and inform staff, and reduce travel and other types of expenses. Web sites are a great way to introduce yourself to the world and help other people introduce you when they make a referral. Some of the most successful Web sites are designed to save money by reducing long distance phone charges and other customer support expenses.

Creating a content list

All the text, graphics, and multimedia that you want to display on the pages of your Web site are commonly referred to as the *content* of your site. To help guide your work and planning, your content list should include all the photos, graphics, biographies, product descriptions, maps, video files, and any other items that you might want to feature on your site.

The best way to start creating a content list is to brainstorm all the things you think you might want to include, such as contact information, product descriptions, logos, pictures of the staff, and biographies.

Pamela's Pet Services defined goals

To help you appreciate how the planning process for a Web site could work, I'll use the fictitious business, Pamela's Pet Services, as an example. After you complete the initial questionnaire earlier in this chapter, you should create a list of goals that looks something like this:

✔ Promote Pamela's dog walking, grooming, and other services.

✔ Describe and showcase Pamela's pet services.

✔ Help customers easily find Pamela's contact information, hours, and location.

✔ Encourage site visitors to register their pet's names, ages, and special needs.

✔ Sign up visitors for Pamela's Pet Tips e-mail newsletter.

Pamela's Pet Services content list

Continuing with Pamela's Pet Services as an example, a content list might look like this:

- ✔ Company logo
- ✔ Contact information
- ✔ Biography and photo of Pamela
- ✔ Photos of Pamela dogs and some of her client's pets
- ✔ Descriptive paragraph about each of her pet services: grooming, walking, and so on
- ✔ Pricing and scheduling information
- ✔ Credit and payment information and policies
- ✔ Photos that provide a tour of the grooming salon
- ✔ A map to the grooming salon
- ✔ A welcome message for the home page
- ✔ Description of the newsletter and invitation to sign up
- ✔ Company description for the About Us page
- ✔ Testimonials from current clients

Even if you think you already know what you want on your site, you may be surprised when you start brainstorming by the ideas you come up with, such as gathering testimonials from happy customers. Creating a detailed content list is well worth the time because it will serve as a valuable tool that you can refer to as you develop your project plan, site map, and task list. As you continue to develop the project plan and ultimately the site, you'll probably discover more things that you want to add to the content list, so make sure to create it in a way that's easy to add to and edit as you progress.

A program like Microsoft Word (or, if you prefer, Excel) is an excellent tool for this task because you can easily make additions and move content around as you develop your list.

Use the content list as you create the site map (covered later in this chapter, in the section "Creating a site map"), and you're likely to think of additions to the content list as you work on that step. For example, as Pamela creates the About Us page for her Pet Services site, she might realize that she wants to add a picture of her own dogs and a map to her grooming salon.

Creating a task list

The task list — the heart of your project plan — is a list of tasks that must be accomplished to meet your goals and launch your Web site. Your task list should include everything from registering your domain name to promoting your site after it's launched.

You can create a task list in many ways, including a few software programs designed to help with project management. If you're creating a relatively simple Web site and you're working alone or on a very small team, you might not need much more than a list with a few notes and dates attached to each task. If you're working on a more complex project with a team, you might want to further define the task list by using a program like Microsoft Project, which includes a variety of features designed to make it easy to plan and track tasks.

When you create your task list, keep in mind that gathering your content is one of the most time-consuming aspects of any Web site project. Most people underestimate how much time they'll spend taking pictures (or finding the ones they already have); gathering digital versions of logos and other graphics; and writing all the text descriptions, biographies and other elements for their Web site. Creating a comprehensive content list at the beginning can serve as a great first step and an excellent guide to help you gauge how long it will take you to gather, create, and review all the contents of your site. Here are a few suggestions for breaking down the complex task of gathering the materials you'll need in your site:

- **Gather existing content.** You might already have much of the content you need in brochures, press releases, or other materials related to your company or organization. Start with the easy stuff; it will give you a sense of accomplishment right away and help you determine how much more you'll need to do.

- **Digitize your text.** If you're including existing content in your site, you might still have to do some work to get it all in *digital format,* where text is converted into a word processing or other text file. For example, you may have to retype text files to be able to use them on your Web site. If you have a lot of text, consider scanning the documents and using Optical Character Recognition (OCR) software to transform the scanned text into editable text.

- **Digitize images.** If you already have photos, a logo, or other graphics you want to use, those images might have to be scanned. Even if you already have digital photos, before you can add them to a Web page, they must be in the correct format and *optimized,* a process that helps them to be downloaded as quickly as possible over the Internet. (You can find step-by-step instructions for preparing and optimizing images for the Web in Chapter 5.)

- **Create new content for your site.** You might want to create a photo tour of your shop (to feature on the home page) or write or update biographies of key personnel.

If you hired a graphic designer to create your logo or brochure, you may want to go back to that person to ask for digital copies of the text and graphics, but don't expect to get it overnight. Plan ahead and request any materials you may need from other people early in the process so you'll be less likely to have to delay launching your site because you're still waiting for them.

Setting a timeline

With your task list ironed out, you're ready to create a timeline. Several popular task-management programs can help. Microsoft Project can help you define a task, specify how long it should take, and then associate it with other tasks on a timeline. If you don't want to spend the money on Microsoft Project or take the time to learn this somewhat complex program, you can create a simple project plan in any calendar program or even in a spreadsheet or word processing program. It's even okay to use the old-fashioned approach of writing your tasks on a printed calendar page. (I rather like having them up on the wall in my office for easy reference.)

Pamela's Pet Services task list

The following includes many common tasks you'll likely want to include in your own list.

✔ Register a domain name for the Web site.

✔ Evaluate and select a Web site–hosting company.

✔ Create a list of all the main sections and subsections of the site.

✔ Create and gather photos and graphics.

✔ Request photos or graphics other people (graphic designer, clients, and friends).

✔ Write the first e-mail newsletter to send to those who sign up.

✔ Request testimonials from current clients.

✔ Create a site map that details how the main sections and subsections will be linked.

✔ Download the templates from Janine's Web site that goes with this book (www. DigitalFamily.com/diy).

✔ Optimize images, graphics, and multi-media files to prepare them for the site.

✔ Use templates to create the home page, each main section front, and any special internal pages.

✔ Build out the pages of the site, adding content into the page templates.

✔ Test, test, and test some more.

✔ Publish your site on the Web.

✔ Tell everyone you know that your site is online and start working on the details of your marketing plan.

Your main goal is to create a timeline that can be adjusted if someone misses a deadline or if a project takes more (or less) time than expected.

Be sure to give yourself a realistic timeframe to do a good job, and factor in a little more time than you think you need, especially if you're new to Web design. Setting and enforcing deadlines can help you stick to your timeline: Even if you're working on a Web site by yourself, or with a very small team, setting deadlines can be one of the most important parts of your project plan — and your best chance of finishing. Most good Web sites are never-ending projects because you can always add more content and develop them further although you shouldn't let that keep you from getting your site launched. Set a deadline for at least the first phase of development, and then hold yourself to it.

Tying a deadline to a special event or occasion, even if you're creating a personal site, can help make you stick to the date. For example, set a launch date for a family Web site on an occasion like your grandma's birthday so that you can make it a surprise for her. Or, plan to publish the redesign for your small business site in time for a trade show or annual sales event. When a deadline has a specific date and a clear goal associated with it, it's easier to take the deadlines seriously.

Establishing a budget

"How much does a Web site cost?" is often the first question asked by someone who decides that they want a Web site. But, if you think about it, it's a little like asking how much it costs to build a house: "It depends." The answer depends on how many rooms you want, whether you want a marble or cement staircase, and whether you want a swimming pool in the backyard. You may have no idea how much it costs to build a home. After all, different contractors provide different price quotes based on how experienced they are or the kinds of materials they plan to use. If you're planning to build the house yourself, it becomes your job to figure out whether the features you want are reasonable and affordable.

Fortunately, most Web sites (at least the kind you're likely to build yourself with the templates and instructions provided in this book) don't cost nearly as much as a house (or even a dog house). Before you can set a realistic budget, though, you need to break down the project into pieces (by following the steps outlined earlier in this chapter) and then start adding prices to the task list in your project plan. Determining the cost of each element of a Web project helps you manage the cost and scope and estimate the overall costs. Among the key costs you can expect are the ones in this list:

- ✔ **Web hosting:** This service can cost as little as a few dollars per month or as much as a couple of hundred dollars (if you plan to include high-definition video files, which require more space on a server and more bandwidth to download). E-commerce features can also add to the cost of monthly hosting. (You find suggestions for choosing the best hosting service for your site in Chapter 3.)

- ✔ **Domain names:** A domain name costs between $8 to $20 per year, depending on the registration service you use and any special features you request, such as private registration, which is a lot like having an unlisted phone number. You can even register more than one domain name for the same site, but only if the name hasn't already been registered by someone else. (You find tips about, check the availability of domains, and register your own domain names in Chapter 3.)

- ✔ **Software programs:** The tools used to create a Web site can range from free to expensive. At the very least, consider getting an image editing program like Adobe Photoshop ($650) or Photoshop Elements ($99; a fine alternative if you're not a professional graphic designer). For Web design, I find that Adobe Dreamweaver ($399) is well worth the price. However, Microsoft Expression Web is also a great Web design program, and Microsoft lowered the price of its most recent version to just $149. You can use any of these programs with the templates and lessons in this book. You find a more detailed comparison of the options to help you find what's best for your site in Chapter 1.

- ✔ **Your time:** If you're building a site yourself, one of your biggest costs is likely to be the time you spend working on it. Don't underestimate the value of your own time if you run your own business. It may be well worth hiring a student or an assistant to help with time-consuming tasks, such as adding text and images to all the pages of your site, or scanning lots of photos and graphics.

- ✔ **Consulting services:** Another major cost for do-it-yourselfers is any consulting service you use to augment your own skills. For example, you might hire a graphic designer to create a logo; an editor to review text; or a programmer to create complex, interactive features, like a password-protected section where you keep clients informed as you work on their private projects.

- ✔ **Shopping cart and e-commerce transaction features:** If you want a shopping system, compare the costs of a few and then include a rough estimate until you make a final decision. (You find recommended services in Chapter 15.)

- ✔ **Traffic reporting services:** Most Web hosting companies provide basic traffic statistics about visitors to your Web site, but you will almost always get more detailed reports if you use a dedicated traffic service, such as Google Analytics, covered in Chapter 10.

As you put together your budget, start with the clear-cut costs, like paying for a domain name and hosting, and then move on to other items specific to your needs and include your best estimate. After you have a price quote for each element and begin putting the pieces together, you can distinguish the more expensive features and better decide which ones you can afford now and which ones you may want to add later.

Assembling a team

Don't go it alone! The best Web sites are developed by a team of people with a variety of skills, including writers, designers, programmers, and multimedia producers. If you're developing a relatively small, simple Web site, you might not need a lot of people with specialized skills on your team, but the more you can divide the work among experts, the better. Although the instructions and templates included with this book are designed to help you do it yourself, you occasionally still have to seek out specialists — like a good editor to ensure that your text is well written, or a programmer who can create advanced features, like password-protected sections of a Web site.

Throughout this book, I've worked hard to give you the best and easiest ways to create a Web site on your own, but I would be remiss not to point out that hiring a specialist or two once in a while can be a helpful way to complement the work you do yourself. Don't be afraid to ask for help if you need it.

Designing Your Web Site

No matter how technically sophisticated a Web site is or how creative its writing, most people notice a site's design first. If you want to make the most impact with your Web site, make sure that you leave plenty of time or reserve funds in the budget to develop (or buy) professional-looking graphics.

The best design is one that suits your audience — and that may or may not mean lots of fancy graphics and animations. To pinpoint the right design for your site, follow these guidelines:

- ✔ **Before you develop the design, think about whom you want to attract to your Web site.** A gaming Web site geared toward teenagers should look much different from a Web site with gardening tips or an online banking site for adults.

- ✔ **Review other sites designed for your target market.** A good way to determine what might work best for your audience is to study similar sites, taking note of how they use images, set up navigational links, and organize information. You don't want your site to look exactly like your competition because you want your site to stand out (and you shouldn't just copy someone else's design), but you can certainly gain useful ideas from reviewing other people's sites.

- ✔ **Consider the limitations of mobile devices.** Increasingly, people are visiting Web sites from cellphones, looking for things like a new restaurant for lunch while they're running errands or the address of a business they want to visit while they're driving there. Mobile devices are a great way to find what you need, when you need it, but only if the Web site you're trying to visit is designed to work on a mobile phone. As you create the design for your site, keep in mind the limitations of small screen sizes and how much harder it can be to click links without a mouse. Today, you have two options if you care about visitors using mobile phones. Keep things relatively simple so they work on most devices or create a second, simplified version of your sites specifically for the mobile phone. To learn more about designing Web sites for cellphones and other mobile devices, read my upcoming book *Mobile Web Design For Dummies* (Wiley).

✔ **Keep in mind how your design decisions might affect download times.**
Consider your audience's time constraints, attention span, and (most importantly) goals. If you design your site to provide information to busy businesspeople, you want fast-loading pages with limited graphics, video, or other multimedia. If you design your site for entertainment, your audience is likely to wait a little longer for videos and other interactive features.

Creating a consistent design

Most Web sites work best, and are easiest to navigate, when they follow a consistent design. Here's a case in point: Most readers take for granted that books don't change their design from page to page and that newspapers don't change headline fonts and logos from day to day. Consistency is one of the primary tools used in books and newspapers to help readers easily distinguish different elements and follow a story or theme.

As you lay out your Web page, keep related items close to one another and be consistent about how you design similar content elements. Viewers should instantly understand which pieces of information are related to each other.

Here are a few good ways to distinguish different kinds of information:

✔ **Design:** To ensure a consistent style, define a set of colors, shapes, or other elements that you use throughout the site and then stick to them. Choose two or three fonts for your Web site and use them consistently. For example, a common practice is to use the Arial font for headlines and Times for the text in paragraphs. Then you might use a special font for a logo or for advertising so that it stands out on the page. Using too many fonts makes anything harder to read and confusing.

You can easily get dazzled by all the special effects you can add to a Web page. Don't fall into the trap of using fancy features just because you can. ("Look, Ma — I made the text on my Web page blink in neon pink!") Keep in mind that the most important thing is to make your photos and Web pages look good and download quickly on the Internet. A clean, classic design will almost always look more professional than a busy design loaded with blinking or animated images.

✔ **Location:** The position of elements on a page can strongly affect the amount of attention they receive. Many Internet studies have shown that text and images toward the top of the page get the most attention, which is why putting your most content toward the top of the page is best. Some things are commonly placed at the bottom of Web pages, including copyright information and links to legal notices, such as privacy information or terms and conditions.

✔ **Prominence:** Give elements of similar importance the same weight on a page, and change the prominence based on priority. If all your headlines are the same size, it's hard to tell what's most important, which is why most news sites and print publications use larger text for the biggest news stories and smaller and smaller headlines for less important news.

Here's the exception to the rule. Strive for consistency in your designs *except* when you're trying to be unpredictable. A little surprise here and there can keep your Web site lively. A touch of red or a special icon can bring attention to a special section or newly updated information.

Mapping the structure: Organization, navigation, and links

Helping visitors find their way around your site is a critical part of your site's design. As you start planning the organization of your home page and the main sections of your site, consider these questions:

- ✓ When visitors arrive at your home page, how will they find what's most important to them?
- ✓ How can you divide the information in your site into sections?
- ✓ How will visitors move from one section of the site to another?
- ✓ How will you encourage visitors to find the information that you most want them to find or to take the action you want them to take (such as buying a product or ordering your services)?

A good way to help answer these questions is to imagine that you're a typical user of your site. For example, you might say, "If I were a busy attorney who came to my site looking for a new couch for my living room, what would make it easy for me to find the color and style I want in my office?" Or, "If I had a shaggy dog that needed a haircut every week, how could I easily find the scheduling and pricing information for the grooming salon?"

As you plan what appears on the first page of your site, draw on your answers to these questions, and revisit the exercise throughout the design process to make sure that your most important visitors can easily find what they need. In fact, here's a great practice professional designers use: Create a few profiles of typical users and then return to these profiles as you design the site.

Designing the home page and main sections

One of the biggest mistakes in Web design is cramming your home page so full of information that it's hard to find anything. Studies show it's better to guide people through a series of simple choices with two to five options each, than to overwhelm them with all options at once.

As you consider what information you want to appear on the home page and how to organize the information in your site into subsections, think about guiding your most important visitors through a series of choices. For example, Pamela's Pet Services site might include a few general service categories on the home page, such as grooming, boarding, and walking, and then link to subsections that offer more specific information, organized by the kind of pet or grooming service.

As you plan your initial site structure, think also about where you're likely to add content down the road. Be sure to include these considerations in the planning process by asking questions, such as these:

> ✔ **For a site that sells products:** What will you do when you have more products to add? Where will you put new lines of products? How will you locate new product information pages or more detailed descriptions? How will you handle price changes or inventory fluctuations?

> ✔ **For an online magazine:** How will you handle breaking news? Where will you add new stories on a regular basis? How will you archive old stories? How will you connect related stories over time?

> ✔ **For a service site, like my fictional Pamela's Pet Service:** Where will you add new services? How will you add new photos of pets? Where will you include seasonal specials or discounts?

Whatever you do, never let users "get stuck" on a page because the link is broken or labeled `Under Construction`. Good Web sites are *always* under construction. Let visitors know that new treats are coming by putting notices on pages that already have content. You find more about creating links in Chapter 6 and tips about finding and fixing broken links in Chapter 10.

Setting up navigation links

After you determine how you're going to organize your information into sections on your site, you've done most of the work needed to create the navigational structure of your site. Creating a menu bar — or *navigation bar* — that includes links to each main section of your site is one of the most important ways you can make your site easy to navigate. Adding that same navigation bar to every page on your site makes it easy to access all of the main sections from anywhere within the site.

Here's an example of a navigation bar you might create with a row of links to the main sections of a small business site:

> Home Page ~ About Us ~ Products ~ Services ~ Contact Info

A good Web site is designed so that users can easily access key information from more than one place in the site and can also move back and forth between the main sections.

As you plan the navigation of your site, make sure that visitors can

> ✔ **Follow different paths to the same important information.** Providing more than one link to the same page can seem repetitive but makes it easier for visitors to find their way around your site. For example, if you have a family history section, you might link to that page from pages throughout your site, such as the page about your daughter's wedding as well as the page about your grandparents.

✔ **Move back and forth between pages and sections.** Links that help users move forward and backward through a series of related pages can be especially useful in a slide show or an image gallery.

✔ **Search your site.** If your Web site is packed with content, users are likely to appreciate the ability to search through your pages. One simple solution is the Google Search tools, which you use for free by signing up at Google.com and copying a little bit of code from their site to yours. (You find instructions for adding Google AdSense to your pages, which works much like Google Search, in Chapter 14.)

Follow the *three-clicks rule,* which states that no important piece of information should ever be more than three clicks away from anywhere else on your Web site. And the most important information — such as contact information — should never be more than one click away.

Chapter 3

Securing a Domain Name and Web Host

A schoolteacher once asked me: "When you talk about 'there' on the Internet, where's 'there?'" I knew immediately what she meant, but I've pondered her question ever since.

If you're still trying to understand "where" your Web site will live when you're ready to share it with the world — and how domain names and Web servers fit into your Web site plans — you've turned to the right chapter. Simply put, a *domain name* is the address for your Web site, and a *Web server* (often provided by a *hosting service*) is a computer with special software that makes it possible for you to publish your site on the Web.

Although many companies offer both domain registration and Web servers, registering a domain name is very different from setting up a server to host your Web site. In this chapter, you find out how these two important aspects of Web development work and how to get the best domain and hosting service for your Web site.

In the first part of this chapter, you discover how domain name registration works, where you can search for domain names to see what's available, and what to do if the name you want is already taken. In the second part of this chapter, you find tips about choosing the best Web server so you can publish your site online.

Whether you're creating a Web site for your business, hobby, or family, you'll want to follow the steps in this chapter to register a domain name and select a Web server. Taking care of the preliminary steps in this chapter before you start creating your pages in Part II will help ensure that everything is set up when you're ready to launch your new Web site.

Finding and Registering Domain Names

The address for a Web site is its *domain name,* also called the URL or Uniform Resource Locator. For example, Wiley Publishing, the company that published this book, has a Web site with the domain name `www.wiley.com`. The company also has a Web site with the domain name `www.dummies.com`, for the *For Dummies* book series.

Even before you start building a Web site, I recommend that you register your own domain name. The process is simple and painless and costs less than $10 per year at most domain registration services. If you don't register a domain name, your Web site's address will probably look something like this:

```
www.serviceprovider.com/users/yourname
```

If you register a domain name, your address should look more like this:

```
www.wiley.com
```

Choosing a good domain name

Your domain name is your calling card, and the best ones are short and sweet and easy to spell. If your Web address is too long or complex, it's hard for anyone to remember or type accurately on a keyboard. The best domain name for your site will be easy to remember and easy to convey: It can be said in one simple sentence.

A shortened version of your business name may seem like a better choice because it requires less typing, but if your customers know you by your full name, they may be confused. For example, I would never recommend a domain such as `am-airlines.com` for American Airlines. The official site for American Airlines is `www.aa.com`, which is a great domain because the company's initials are well known, and you couldn't possibly get a much shorter domain name. Because `www.aa.com` is an abbreviation, American Airlines was smart enough to recognize it might be confusing to visitors and to register more than one name (it's easy to do); if you type `www.americanairlines.com`, your browser goes to the same site.

When you're tossing around ideas for a domain name, keep these rules in mind:

✔ **Domain names aren't case sensitive.** For example, you can get to my Web design training site by entering `digitalfamily.com` or `DigitalFamily.com`. (See Figure 3-1.) I prefer to capitalize the *D* and *F* in my domain name when I print it on business cards or other collateral because it makes the domain name easier to read.

Figure 3-1: Both `DigitalFamily.com` and `digitalfamily.com` take you to the same Web site.

TIP

✔ **Any characters that appear *after* a domain name extension are case sensitive** (the dot-com or dot-org part of the address, for example). Thus, `www.DigitalFamily.com/books` isn't the same address as `www.DigitalFamily.com/Books`.

✔ **Use of the leading www depends on how the domain is configured on a server.** You can set up a domain on a Web server to work with or without the `www`, or you can set it up to work either way. You can also set up subdomains if you own a domain. For example, you can find my personal profile at `http://JCWarner.com`, and you can find the Spanish version at `http://spanish.JCWarner.com`.

✔ **The use of the `http://` that appears at the very beginning of a domain name is optional.** Most people no longer type these initial characters when entering a Web address because they're unnecessary, but it is helpful to include them when you're writing an address that doesn't include the `www`. Throughout this book, when I write a domain that does not include the 3ws, I include the `http://` to avoid confusion.

✔ **Although you can use a hyphen or an underscore in a domain name, it's generally simpler to use a combination of words run together.** For example, you can register `www.digital-family.com`, but that's harder to convey verbally because you have to explain the hyphens in the middle. If you simply use `www.digitalfamily.com`, you can say, "My address is *Digital Family dot com,* all one word."

✔ **Domain names cannot contain special characters.** You can't use spaces, periods, apostrophes, or other punctuation or special characters, but you can use numbers and dashes.

✔ **Make sure that your domain name doesn't violate a trademark.** You can do a simple trademark search at `www.uspto.gov`. If you're starting a business or concerned about violating someone's trademark, consult an attorney.

Register your name

I tell all my friends that they should register their own names as domain names because "owning" your name is a key part of protecting your online reputation. A personal Web site serves as a great way to promote yourself, whether you're job hunting, developing a consulting business, or simply want to share your story with the world. And because search engines tend to give priority to keywords that match domain names, your site should score high when someone searches your name if you've registered the domain. And even if you don't plan to use your domain name right away, registering it will prevent anyone else from setting up a site with your name.

I registered my own name, JanineWarner.com, years ago. When I realized that many people misspell my first name, though, I decided to register a simpler alternative. The domain jwarner.com was already registered by a gentleman named John Warner when I got the idea, but he's been nice enough to keep a link on his site for me. I finally settled on JCWarner.com because it's easier for people to spell the domain using my middle initial than using my full first name. I know that even if someone misses the C in my domain, they still have a good chance to find my site thanks to the link on John's site. (Thanks, John!)

Searching for an available domain name

You can register any domain name that hasn't already been taken by someone else. Finding out whether a name is already in use is easy — and free. To see whether a domain name is already registered, do a simple search at any domain registration Web site. All domain registrars check the same master databases that track all domain names on the Web. Hundreds of sites offer the service; the following steps use Domain.com as an example, but most work the same way:

1. **Use a Web browser to visit a domain name registrar.**

   In this example, I'm using Domain.com (`www.domain.com`).

2. **In the Search area on the registrar's site, type the name you want to register.**

   In Figure 3-2, I'm searching for `www.petservice.com`.

3. **Click to begin your search.**

   The results of your search are displayed. (If you use Domain.com, for example, you'll see a list that includes the name you searched for, as well as a list of variations. Most common names and phrases have already been registered, so it's no surprise that the status next to the name `petservice.com` shows that it's already taken. If you scroll down the list of alternatives shown in Figure 3-2, you see that `petservice.us` is still available, as is `thepetservice.net`.

4. **If the name you want isn't available and you don't like the alternatives offered, you can enter another name to see whether it's available.**

   Domain registrars don't limit the number of names you can search for in any given search session.

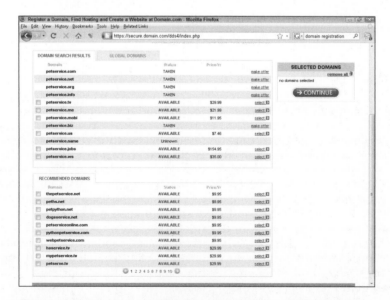

Figure 3-2: If the name you want isn't available, most registrars, such as Domain.com, offer a list of recommended alternatives.

Don't get frustrated if you find that the domain name you want is already taken. You can almost always find a name that will serve you well if you get creative and try a few variations. Here are a few tips for finding a suitable variation:

- ✔ **Add a word or phrase that indicates geographic location or makes the name more specific.** For example, if www.news.com is taken, consider using www.PointReyesNews.com or www.WestMarinNews.com.

- ✔ **Sometimes a different name that has similar meaning can work.** For example, if every variation of news is taken, consider registering a similar name, such as www.PointReyesReports.com.

- ✔ **Try looking for playful names.** For example, www.Accountant.com is taken, but you might still find www.FunnyAccountants.com or www.FrugalAccountants.com.

Before you choose a close variation (or any domain name, for that matter), *always* check for sites whose names are similar to yours. It's generally not a good idea to choose a name that's too close to someone else's if that person is a competitor or runs a site you would be embarrassed to be associated with. Similarly, consider whether others have already set up sites with your domain name but a different domain name ending. It may seem like a good alternative to register FrugalAccountants.net if the .com version is already taken. However, because the .com ending is more common, you're likely to lose customers to FrugalAccounts.com if they offer a competitive service. If you really want a domain name that's been taken, check out the sidebar, "Disputing a domain name," later in this chapter, which explains how you can purchase a domain name that has already been registered from the owner (if he or she is willing to negotiate).

Understanding top-level domains

When you search for a domain name, you need to determine not only the first part of the name but also the ending, commonly called the *top-level domain,* or TLD. Table 3-1 provides a list of the most common domain name endings, their intended purposes, and their restrictions.

The .com domain has emerged as the most valuable because it's the best recognized and the one that people are most likely to remember. However, all these domains work the same way in terms of directing users to a Web site address. For example, www.smith.com, www.smith.net, and www.smith.org work the same way on the Internet and are used by three different Web sites.

The number of domain endings has been growing, and there are proposals to make the options nearly unlimited. Table 3-1 provides a list of the most common domain unrestricted names as well as the original list of restricted names. (ICANN controls all domain names and; only an entity that's approved to use a restricted ending can set up a domain name with that ending.)

Table 3-1	Domain Name Endings	
Top-Level Domain	**Used By**	**Restrictions?**
.com	Commercial organizations; by far the most popular domain ending	No
.net	Internet services; used increasingly by people who don't get the .com names they want	No
.org	Nonprofit organizations	No
.biz	Businesses; a newer domain, used increasingly by businesses that don't get the .com domain names they want	No
.name	Individuals	No
.info	Informational sites	No
.mobi	Mobile sites	No
.aero	The air-transport industry	Yes
.coop	Cooperative associations	Yes
.museum	Museums	Yes
.gov	The United States government	Yes
.edu	Accredited colleges and universities	Yes
.mil	The United States military	Yes

Comparing country domains: .tv, .us, and .ws

Nearly every country in the world now has its own domain, such as .us for the United States, .am for Armenia, .br for Brazil, .uk for the United Kingdom, and .zw for Zimbabwe.

A few foreign country codes have become popular in the United States because they represent common acronyms, such as .tv. Many folks mistakenly assume that .tv stands for *television,* but it's really the domain name for the country of Tuvalu. Similarly, .ws is often assumed to mean *Web site* (and is even listed that way on some registrar sites), but it's really the country code for Western Samoa. You can register a name with the .ws or .tv domain even if you don't live in one of those countries, but some countries have restrictions, and country domains are generally more expensive to register than names that use .com, .net, or .org.

Registering your domain name

The specifics of registering a domain name vary among the services, but the basic domain registration process is similar. Typically, after you perform your search, you're given instructions for registering the name, as well as offers to buy other kinds of services, such as Web hosting. You should never *have* to purchase additional services to register a domain name, but many companies offer discounts if you order multiple services. Common types of services, in addition to registration, are

- ✔ **Hosting:** Many registration services also offer Web site hosting (covered later in this chapter).

- ✔ **E-mail:** Typically, you have the option of creating one or more e-mail addresses associated with your domain name, but e-mail set-up is often better handled through your Web hosting service.

- ✔ **Privacy:** Most services allow you to choose whether your contact information as the owner of this domain name is readily available to others through a search on the Whois database (`http://www.whois.net`). Most services charge a fee for private registration, which is kind of like having an unlisted phone number.

Disputing a domain name

What if your name — either your personal name or your company name — is already taken, and you want to have it (or don't like what someone else is doing with it)?

Unless the owner has opted for private registration, you can find out who owns a domain name by searching the Whois database, a central registry of all domain registrants on the Internet. Most domain registration sites include a More Info link in the results page if you search for a domain name that is already taken. Registration listings in the Whois database include the street address, phone number, and e-mail address of the person or business that registered the domain name in addition to information about the server or service provider that hosts the domain.

If you have your heart set on a domain name that is already registered, you can contact the owner and try negotiating. Many people have registered names that they aren't using, and if you find one that's registered but not in use, the owner might be willing to sell. I know many people who have picked up great domain names for $500 to $1,000, but some names have sold for as much as $1 million.

There is no clear set of rules about the value of a domain name, but there are services at registrations sites, such as www.godaddy. com and www.1and1.com, that will appraise a domain name or even broker an offer to the current owner.

To date, the courts seem to be applying the same laws to domain names that they apply to trademarks. For example, if you have a legal trademark such as Levi, and someone registers www.levi.com before you do, you can probably go to court and force the person to give you the domain name, although domain name disputes can be lengthy and expensive. If you don't have a trademark, you may have no alternative than to try to buy it from the person or choose another name instead.

If you think you have a case against someone who has taken your name, don't bother the registration service with your complaint. Domain registrars don't handle domain name disputes; they just register names on a first-come, first-served basis. Instead, talk to the guilty party directly. If that doesn't work, take the matter to court. If you can get a judge to rule that you're right, the domain registration service revokes the name and lets you have it.

In addition to registering your main domain name — the one you plan to hand out to colleagues and clients or friends and family — my best advice is to register every variation and misspelling of your name that you can think of and direct those domain names to your Web site. Just because some people didn't do well in the third grade spelling bee doesn't mean that they don't have money to buy your products or services online.

Directing more than one domain name to the same Web site is a relatively simple technical detail that you can arrange through your Internet service provider (ISP) or the company where you register the name. And, it's not that expensive. At the time of this writing, GoDaddy (`www.godaddy.com`) charges $9.99 per year, Network Solutions (`www.networksolutions.com`) charge, $14.99 per year, and 1&1 (`www.1and1.com`) charges $5.99 per year.

Also consider registering the same name with different domain endings, such as `.org`, `.net` — and, most important, `.com`. The educational Web site Whyville, for example, registered `whyville.org` (the domain ending used by most nonprofits), but it also registered `whyville.com` because many people will assume that's the address. Owning these additional domains can also prevent you or your visitors from potential embarrassment or misrepresentation.

Most people consider the `.com` version of a name the most valuable, but if the `.com` version is unavailable, registering the `.net`, `.biz`, or `.info` versions may be a fine alternative. Just make sure that the site that has the `.com` version isn't a direct competitor or a site that you would be embarrassed by if your visitors found it accidentally.

Technically, when you register a domain name, you are leasing it, not purchasing it, which means that it's possible to lose a domain name. Make sure that your registration remains valid by renewing it when your registration service requires. Many registrars offer auto-renewal options and discounts for registering a name for two or more years in advance.

Choosing a Web Hosting Service

Choosing a Web host is a little like choosing a cellphone company or a long distance carrier. In theory, all phone companies provide the same ability to make a phone call, but in practice, they offer different rate plans and different levels of service.

For the purposes of this book, I'm going to assume that you don't want to run your own Web server, which would be kind of like starting your own phone company when all you need is long-distance service. Unless you're running an extremely large Web site, you should definitely look for what's called "managed hosting."

Essentially, when you sign up with a Web host, you're renting a small portion of a big computer (a *Web server*) that's connected to the Internet. The host gives you access to your part of that computer's hard drive, and when you transfer your Web pages to their computer, they are "served" to the Internet.

Although you can use the same service to host your site that you used to register your domain name, I've had better experiences with companies that make Web hosting their top priority. For example, Liquid Web (as shown in Figure 3-3) offers 24/7 phone support, a service you won't find at all Web hosting companies.

Figure 3-3: Look for a company that makes Web hosting a priority and offers good technical support.

If you're looking for one of the cheapest Web hosting services, consider 1&1 or GoDaddy, both offer domain registration and a variety of low-cost Web hosting options, for as little as 4.99 per month. If you want to use one of the best hosting companies I've found to date and you're willing to pay between $25 and $100 per month for an account, consider `www.rackspace.com`.

So how do you find a Web host with the features you need for your Web site? And, how do you even know what to ask?

Before you select a Web host, consider what you want on your Web site and make sure that you find a service that meets your needs. Your goal is to find the provider with the best collection of services within your budget. The following sections highlight a few questions to ask as you explore your Web hosting options.

Finding the best host for your site

My best advice is to get a good start on the development plan for your site before you shop around for a service provider so that you know which kinds of services you need. (You can find more information about planning a Web project in Chapter 2.) You might decide, for example, that you want 24-hour technical support so that you can get help at night after work, but you don't want to pay extra for secure financial transactions because you don't plan to sell products online.

Here are a few of the common features to consider as you select a Web hosting service:

> ✔ **Bandwidth:** *Bandwidth* measures the carrying capacity of a connection on the Internet. Compare bandwidth with a garden hose and its capacity to transport water: the larger the diameter of the hose, the more water it can carry. Bandwidth works the same way: the greater the bandwidth, the faster the transmission of

information. Bandwidth gets expensive if lots of people visit your site because more visitors mean more use of the connection. If you want to offer streaming video or audio files, they can also use up a lot of bandwidth — and that means you'll have to pay a premium for hosting.

✔ **Disk space:** The bigger your site — the more images and especially the more sound files, video, and animation files you include — the more you'll pay for the disk space to host it. Because video files are much larger than images or text files, video takes up much more hard disk space and requires more bandwidth to be viewed. As a result, providing many hours of video on your site can be expensive.

✔ **E-commerce:** Some Web hosting packages include secure e-commerce capabilities and sophisticated programming options. Unless you're planning to sell products or services on your site or to publish large amounts of video or sound files, you'll probably do fine with the simplest or lowest-level Web hosting package your service provider offers.

✔ **Blogs and other third-party services:** You can install blogging software, such as WordPress (covered in Chapter 11) on almost any Web server, but many hosts include a feature that makes it easy to install blogging and other software. Some call this *one-click services;* others use a program called Fantastico, which is included in your Web hosting service. The advantage is that it makes it easy to set up a blog (and many other programs) on your own server, which is something that can get complicated if you have to do it yourself.

✔ **Unix, Linux versus Microsoft Web hosting:** Some service providers use Linux server software; others use Microsoft. If you use the templates included in this book, either type of server should work fine, but if you create a WordPress blog or other service or system that requires programming language, you'll want to make sure your server supports it. The most common technologies used in the Web these days are PHP, JSP, and Perl, which work well on Linux servers, and ASP or ASP.NET, which work only on Microsoft servers.

✔ **Streaming media:** If you want to offer audio, video, or Flash animations on your Web site, check whether your hosting service features the ability to stream your multimedia files. It's a nice option: Streaming is what enables site visitors to start playing a video or audio file while it is downloading, instead of having to wait for the entire file to download before it can start. Keep in mind, however, that you can use a third-party service to host your video, avoiding the potential cost and challenges of hosting video on your own server. YouTube offers free hosting for short videos and it's easy to insert videos hosted on YouTube on your own pages. You'll find a slightly higher-level service from Vimeo (www.vimeo.com). (You find more information about these and other services in Chapter 13.)

If your Web host sets a limit on bandwidth usage, you can end up with a big, unexpected bill if a video or audio file on your site becomes very popular. For example, I have a client on a premium Web host that offers excellent service but sets a limit on the bandwidth included in their monthly fee. If just one of their high-quality videos got popular enough to attract a million visitors in one month (which is not so unusual on the Web), they could get hit with a $12,000 bill, just for that month of video hosting. That's why I recommend a dedicated video host for anyone who does video on their Web site. With www.vimeo.com, one of the most popular video services, you upload your videos to Vimeo and then simply copy a piece of code to your own site and then it plays within the page on your Web site. (You learn more about video hosting services, such as Vimeo and YouTube, in Chapter 13.)

Setting up e-commerce service

Many Web hosting services, such as those provided by Yahoo!, as shown in Figure 3-4, provide e-commerce features in addition to hosting and domain registration all in one place. If you're thinking of starting a business or taking your existing retail business online, you want to make sure your service provider can handle e-commerce transactions. If you plan to sell a lot of products, I also recommend using a *shopping cart* system, which is a program that enables visitors to add products to a checkout page that tracks and tallies selected items as a visitor moves through your site. You can buy shopping cart systems separately, but many service providers (such as Yahoo!) include shopping cart features as part of their online store services. (You can find more information about selling products on the Web in Chapter 14.)

Figure 3-4: Some Web hosting services, such as Yahoo!, provide e-commerce capabilities.

Hosting multiple sites with different domain names

As you compare options, you might notice that some providers charge more for packages that enable you to host multiple domain names. You might choose a package that supports multiple domain names if you want each member of the family to be able to register their own domain name and set up their own site separately or if you run multiple companies or information sites. For example, you can set up `www.JeanDoherty.com`, `www.JoshDoherty.com`, and `www.TheDohertyFamily.com` as separate sites on the same account if it supports multiple domains. Although a Web hosting package that supports multiple domain names is generally more expensive, it might save you money compared with the cost of setting up a different Web hosting account for each Web site you want to create.

Note the difference between hosting multiple domain names that point to different Web sites, as in the example in the preceding paragraph, and pointing two or more domain names to the same site. If you want two names (such as `www.TheDohertyFamily.com` and `www.TheDohertys.com`) to direct visitors to the same site, you can manage that situation with your domain name registrar and save the cost of a premium Web server account that supports multiple domain names. Check with your domain name registrar for more information on how to forward multiple domain names to the same Web server.

Chapter 4

Understanding Web Design

· ·

· ·

In the early days of the Web, designers were limited to a few simple page layout options — you could center your text and images, or leave it all aligned to the left. As HTML evolved, creating great, more complex Web designs became possible, but finding the best solution became a lot more confusing.

If you've done any Web design in the past, you may have used tables, frames, or layers to create page layouts. Today, all those options are considered outdated and are generally no longer recommended except in very special cases.

Today, most professional designers agree that the best way to create a Web page design is to use XHTML (eXtensible HyperText Markup Language, a strict form of HTML) with Cascading Style Sheets (better known by the acronym CSS).

If you're starting to worry that this book is getting a lot more technical than you expected, relax. I assure you, you don't need to learn any advanced programming to create a Web site with the templates included with this book. That said, I find that many people like to know more about how all this works, and that's what this chapter is about — helping you better understand the choices, why CSS is better than almost any other design option and how CSS and XTHML work together.

If you're ready to dive in and start building your Web site right away, feel free to jump ahead to the chapter and templates for the site design you want to create. You can always come back here for more details later.

HTM-what? Exploring HTML and XHTML

Contrary to popular belief, HTML isn't a programming language. Rather, it's a *mark-up* language: That is, HTML is designed to "mark up" a page, or to provide instructions for how a Web page should look. HTML is written by using *tags,* markup instructions that tell a Web browser how the page should be displayed. For example, to make a section of text italic, you use the HTML tag <em>, which stands for *emphasis.* Most tags in HTML include both an opening tag and a close tag, indicated by the forward slash /. Thus, to make the name of this book appear in italics, I would write the code like this:

```
<strong>Web Sites Do It Yourself For Dummies.</strong>
```

Building, testing, and publishing a Web site

In a nutshell, building a Web site involves creating a *home page* (often called the *front page*) that links to other pages representing different sections of the site. Those pages, in turn, can link to subsections that can then lead to additional subsections or individual pages. After you create a Web site, you can test all the links on your own hard drive and then upload the pages to a Web server when everything is ready and working well. You can read more about Web servers in Chapter 2 and how to upload your pages to a server in Chapter 10.

XHTML is a more strict version of HTML that is the recommended language to use to meet the highest standards of Web design today. Among the differences between the two languages, XHTML must be written in lowercase letters; in HTML, it doesn't matter whether tags are upper or lowercase. Similarly, XHTML requires that all tags include a close tag (more on that later in this chapter.) Rest assured all templates and code examples in this book follow the XHTML standard.

To see what the code behind a Web page looks like in most browsers, choose View⇨Source. If you're using Dreamweaver, as shown in Figure 4-1, you can click the Split button (upper-left corner of the workspace) to see the code and the design areas of the program at the same time in *Split view*.

Split view in Dreamweaver is a useful way to keep an eye on what's going on behind the scenes and, as a bonus, you can learn a lot of XHTML as you go along.

Dreamweaver offers three view options:

- **Code:** In Code view, you see only the XHTML and other code.
- **Split:** In Split view, the page is divided so you can see the code in one part of the workspace, and a view of the how the page should be displayed in a Web browser in the other part.
- **Design:** In Design view, you only see the page as it should be displayed in a Web browser.

In Dreamweaver's Split view, Code and Design views are completely integrated, so if you select something in Design view, like the headline you see in Figure 4-1, the same text is highlighted in Code view, making it easy to find your place in the code.

If at first glance you think that XHTML code looks like hieroglyphics, don't give up too quickly. With just a little training, you can start to recognize at least some common tags, like the <h1> tag (heading 1 tag) that was used to format the headline on the page shown in Figure 4-2.

To help distinguish the code in a Web page from the text, Dreamweaver displays the tags in a contrasting color, usually blue. You can change the size, color, font, and other features of the code in Dreamweaver's preferences.

. . . to view this
index.html*
Source Code
common.css
front.css
urchin.js
snap_shots.js
Code
Split
Design
Live View
Title: DigitalFamily.com | Free tutori
149 ¶
150 ····<h1>Welcome·to·my·Digital·Family</h1>¶
151 ····<p><img·src=
"Janine-Warner/Janine-Warner-Total-Training.gif"·alt="Janine·
Warner"·width="191"·height="180"·class="fltrt"·/>Hi,·I'm·
Janine·Warner,·author·of·more·than·a·dozen·books·about··the·
Digitalfamily.com
Home
Bookstore
Videos
Dreamweaver
Expression Web
Free Tutorials
What do you want to learn today?
Welcome to my Digital Family
Hi, I'm Janine Warner, author of more than a dozen books about the Internet and a growing collection of training videos and free tutorials.
On this site, you'll find:
Adobe Dreamweaver
<body> <div#container> <div#mainContent> <div#dreamweaver> <h1>
100%
760 x 331
193K / 28 sec Unicode (UTF-8)
Select this . . .

Figure 4-1: Use the Split view option in Dreamweaver to display the page design and the code behind the page.

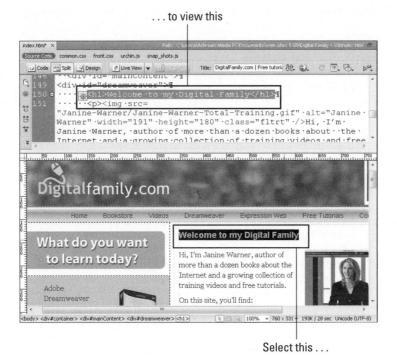

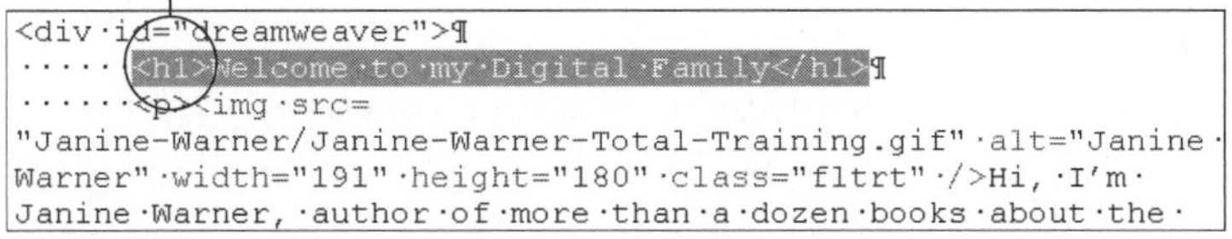

H1 tag
<div·id="dreamweaver">¶
·····<h1>Welcome·to·my·Digital·Family</h1>¶
······<p><img·src=
"Janine-Warner/Janine-Warner-Total-Training.gif"·alt="Janine·
Warner"·width="191"·height="180"·class="fltrt"·/>Hi,·I'm·
Janine·Warner,·author·of·more·than·a·dozen·books·about·the·

Figure 4-2: A heading 1 tag highlighted in Dreamweaver Code view.

A few points to help you better understand XHTML:

- **In XHTML, all tags must include the closing slash.** A few tags can stand alone, such as the `<br />` tag, which adds a line break. XHTML tags must have a closing tag, even if there is only one tag, and close tags always contain a forward slash (/). As a result, the line break tag in HTML looks like `<br>`, but in XHTML, it looks like `<br />`.
- **XHTML includes many tags that are designed to be hierarchical.** Examples are the `<h1>` through `<h6>` (heading 6) tags, which are ideally suited to formatting text according to its importance on a Web page. Reserve the `<h1>` tag for the most important text on the page, such as the top headline. `<h2>` is ideal for subheads or secondary headings, `<h3>` for the third level of headings, and so on. A headline formatted with the `<h1>` tag looks like this:

```
<h1>This is a headline</h1>
```

How Web browsers work

Web browsers such as Internet Explorer, Firefox, Chrome, and Safari are designed to decipher HTML, XHTML, CSS, AJAX, and other code and display the corresponding text, images, and multimedia on a computer screen. Essentially, browsers read the code in a Web page and interpret how the page should be displayed to visitors. Unfortunately, because Web browsers are created by different companies and the code they display has evolved dramatically over the years, not all Web browsers display Web pages the same way. Differences in browser display can lead to unpredictable (and often frustrating) results because a page that looks good in one browser may be unreadable in another. For more information on browser differences and testing your pages to make sure they look good to all your visitors, see Chapter 10.

✔ **Some tags are more complex, and the open and close tags don't always match.** More complicated tags, such as the tags used to create links or insert images into pages, are more challenging to use because they include link information, and the close tag doesn't always match the open tag. For example, the code to create a link to another Web site looks like this:

```
<a href="http://www.digitalfamily.com">This is a link to
          DigitalFamily.com</a>
```

At its heart, XHTML is just text, and believe it or not, you can write XHTML in a plain-text editor as simple as Notepad, SimpleText, or TextEdit. If you ever try it, however, you have to be careful to type all the code perfectly because there is no room for error or typos in XHTML. After writing code yourself, even to create a simple page, you're sure to quickly appreciate programs — such as Dreamweaver — that write the code for you.

One of the great advantages of using Dreamweaver is that you can specify formatting by clicking buttons or using menu commands, and Dreamweaver takes care of writing the XHTML code for you. For this and many other reasons, I chose to use Dreamweaver in this book.

If you prefer to use Expression Web, a similar program created by Microsoft, you can apply most of the instructions in this book to that program, although some of the menu items and other features are located in different places. If you do choose to use Expression Web, you can download specially created templates and instructions for creating all the template designs in this book on the companion Web site at www. DigitalFamily.com/diy.

Comparing Tables, Frames, and Layers

If you've already done a little Web design, you may be wondering what happened to some of the old ways of creating Web page layouts. For years, Web designers used the HTML feature called Tables to create page layouts. Then, Frames came along, and many people were excited by the ability to display multiple pages in one browser window, which is possible when using Frames and iFrames. Then came Layers, which were especially popular among designers because they seemed to offer precise design control.

Over the years, all these options have become less desirable except in a few special cases. In this section, you find a quick review of when Tables, Frames, and Layers may still be useful.

Creating page designs with HTML Tables

In the early days of Web design, most page layouts on the Web were created with tables. By merging and splitting table cells, and even adding background images, you can create complex Web designs with tables. CSS expands upon this concept by adding many new design options, including the ability to precisely add margins and padding around elements, and better control how and where background images appear.

Cascading Style Sheets, better known by the acronym CSS, also enables you to keep formatting information separate from content, making it possible to use less code and create pages with smaller file sizes that download more quickly. Using CSS also makes pages easier to update because you can change formatting in a more stream-lined way. You can read more about CSS in the upcoming section, "Designing with Cascading Style Sheets."

Figure 4-3 provides an example of an old-school site created with the HTML `table` tag. To help you appreciate how this page was created, I altered the original design to display the table borders although most designers turn off table borders when using tables to create cleaner layouts. Setting the table border to `0` (instead of `2` as I did here to show you the borders), makes it possible to turn off the border of a table so that it doesn't interfere with the design.

If you visit the site at `www.chocolategamerules.com`, you can see how this same page was created using `div` tags and CSS. (I explain how `div` tags work within CSS in "Designing with Cascading Style Sheets" later in this chapter.)

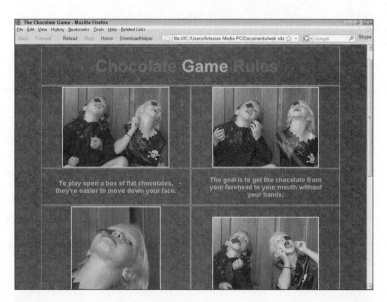

Figure 4-3: In the old days, the only way you could create a complex Web page design was to use an HTML table to control text and image placement.

Although tables are no longer recommended for creating page layouts, they're still considered the best way to format tabular data like you'd find in a spreadsheet program. That means that you can use tables to format a consistent collection of information, such as the photos and names in the list of winners from the Chocolate Game Rules site shown in Figure 4-4.

Although I recommend that you redesign sites like the one shown in Figure 4-3 with CSS and `div` tags, I do understand that many designers still find it easier to create layouts with tables, and not everyone has time to redesign their Web sites right away. I have to admit, I've been guilty of leaving a few sites online designed with tables long after I knew better. That said, I recommend using only CSS today for all your Web page layouts except when you are creating a layout for tabular data. Even then, I still urge you to use CSS to add any styling, such as background colors or padding, that you might want in your tables.

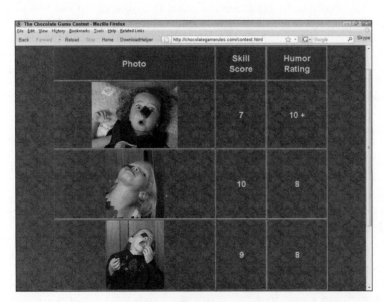

Figure 4-4: Tables are still considered the best way to display tabular data like the information on this contest page.

Considering design options with HTML frames

You won't find any instructions in this book for creating Web sites that use frames, such as the Pink Flamingos site shown in Figure 4-5. Frames enable you to display multiple Web pages in one browser window. Among Web designers, Frames are a little like those plastic pink flamingos stuck in the front yards of so many homes in South Florida; some people love how kitsch they are, and others just think they are tacky. Although Frames are still used on the Web, most designers don't like them because they can make navigation confusing.

Frames are also problematic because when you use frames, the URL at the top of a Web browser does not change, even when you click links and change the pages displayed within frames. As a result, you can only bookmark, or create a link to, the first page of a site that uses frames. Worse yet, frames make it harder for search engines to index a site properly, which can diminish your search engine ranking.

Figure 4-5: Frames enable you to display multiple Web pages in one browser window.

Using Layers (or AP Divs) to create designs

Dreamweaver MX, MX 2004, and 8 had a button for the layer feature, and it offered an easy way to click and drag boxes using divs that were positioned with precision on a page. In later versions of Dreamweaver, the name was changed to AP Divs. *Divs* are simply XHTML tags that serve as *dividers* in a page. Essentially, they create boxes around content that make it easier to position sections of text or images independently. Don't be confused by the fact that I (and most other Web designers today) recommend using Div tags with CSS to create your page layouts. We just don't recommend that you do so with the AP Divs.

AP Divs, as the name implies, are Div tags that include styling information that adds absolute positioning. That means that when you place an AP Div in a Web page, it stays where you put it, no matter how much space you have in the browser window. That may seem like a good idea at first, and AP Divs were popular among some designers for a while because they are so easy to use and so similar to many of the features in desktop publishing programs (such as Adobe InDesign). But because layers create such inflexible layouts, they don't adapt well to the changing environment of the Web where different sized monitors and other display variations can lead to text getting cut off and other undesirable results.

To cut down on the confusion caused by the term *layers,* Adobe changed the name of this feature from layers to AP Divs (short for Absolutely Positioned Div tags) in later versions of Dreamweaver, including CS3 and CS4. Many designers use AP Divs on occasion to add fixed position elements to a layout, but creating an entire design with this feature is no longer recommended.

Designing with Cascading Style Sheets

The concept of creating styles has been around since long before the Web. Desktop publishing programs (such as Adobe InDesign) and even word processing programs (such as Microsoft Word) have long used styles to manage the formatting and editing of text on printed pages. When using styles in a word processor, you can create and save styles for common features, such as headlines and captions. In print design, styles are great timesavers because they enable you to combine a collection of formatting options (such as Arial and bold and italic) into one style and then apply all those options at once to any selected text in your document by using only a single style. The advantage is that if you change a style, you can automatically apply the change everywhere you've used that style in a document.

On the Web, you can do all that and more with CSS because you can use style sheets for even more than just text formatting. For example, you can use CSS to create styles that align images to the left or right side of a page, add padding around text or images, and change background and link colors. You can even create more than one style sheet for the same page — say, one that makes your design look good on computers, another for cellphones, and a third for a printed page.

For all these reasons (and more), CSS has quickly become the preferred method of designing Web pages among professional Web designers. One of the most powerful aspects of CSS is how you can use it to make global style changes across an entire Web site. Suppose, for example, that you create a style for your headlines by redefining the `<h1>` tag to create large, blue, bold headlines. Then one fine day, you decide that all your headlines should be red instead of blue. If you aren't using CSS, changing all your headlines could be a huge undertaking — a matter of opening every Web page in your site to make changes to the font tags around your headlines. But, if you're using CSS in an external style sheet, you can simply change the style that controls the headline in the style sheet, and *voilà!* Your headlines all turn red automatically. If you ever have to redesign your site (and believe me, every good site goes through periodic redesigns), you can save hours or even days of work if you created your design with CSS.

Appreciating the advantages of CSS

A Web site designed with CSS separates content from design. Keeping the site content (such as the text and headings) separate from the instructions that tell a browser how the page should look benefits both the designers and your site visitors:

  ✔ **CSS simplifies design changes.** For example, instead of formatting every headline in your site as 24-point Arial bold, you can create a style for the `<h1>` tag that contains all the formatting information in one place and then apply that style to the text in an XHTML file. CSS styles can be saved in the header section at the very top of an XHTML page, or they can be saved in a separate file that can be attached to multiple XHTML pages. One of the advantages of styles is that if you can use the same style to format many headlines and then you decide later that you want all your headlines to use the Garamond font instead of Arial, all you need to do is change the style for the `<h1>` tag once, and it automatically applies everywhere you've used the `<h1>` tag to format your headlines.

✔ **Separating content from design enables you to create different style sheets for different audiences and devices.** In the future, separating content from design is likely to become even more important as a growing number of people view Web pages on everything from giant, flat-screen monitors to tiny, cellphone screens. One of the coolest features in Adobe Dreamweaver is *Device Central,* where you can preview your page designs in a variety of handheld devices and cellphones to see just how different they can look when displayed on these small screens.

As you get more advanced with CSS, you can even create multiple style sheets for the same Web page. For example, you can create one that's ideally suited to a small screen like the one shown in Figure 4-6, another one that works best when the page is printed, and yet another designed with a larger font size for anyone who may have trouble reading the small print that is so common on Web pages.

✔ **Using CSS makes your site comply with the current standards.** Today, the *W3C,* which sets standards for the Internet, recommends using CSS for nearly every aspect of Web design because the best CSS designs are accessible, flexible, and adaptable.

Figure 4-6: Designing Web pages with CSS can help you create designs
that display well on large or small screens.

✔ **Web sites designed in CSS are accessible to more visitors.** Today, there's a growing movement among some of the best designers in the world to get everyone to follow the same standards, create Web sites with CSS, and make sure they're accessible to everyone.

When Web designers talk about *accessibility,* they mean creating a site that can be accessed by anyone who might ever visit your pages — and that includes people with limited vision who use special browsers (often called *screen readers*) that read Web pages aloud, as well as many others who use specialized browsers for a variety of other reasons.

If you work for a university, a nonprofit, a government agency, or a similar organization, you may be required to create accessible designs. In Chapter 6, you find instructions for you alternative text with images and other features that can improve Web site accessibility. Even if you're not required to design for accessibility, it's still good practice because pages that meet accessibility standards also tend to score better in search engines because they're designed in a way that makes it easy for search engines to access and interpret their content.

Combining CSS and XHTML

Most professional Web designers today recommend creating Web page designs by combining XHTML and CSS. How the two work together can get a bit complicated, but you essentially:

1. Use XHTML to create the structure of a page with tags, such as division (div), heading (h1, h2), and paragraph (p).

2. Create styles in CSS that specify the size of these elements, where they appear on a page, and a variety of other formatting options.

Similarly, you use XHTML to insert images and create links, and then add styles to change formatting options, such as removing the underline from your links or changing the color that appears when someone rolls a cursor over a link.

Following standards

Following standards has become increasingly important as Web design has become more complex over the years.

Web technology has evolved to include new features, such as CSS, that provide greater design control than ever. Unfortunately, Web browsers (such as Internet Explorer and Firefox) don't always display the features of Web sites in the same way. As a result, the same Web page can look quite different from one browser to another, especially in older browsers. (Find more about browser differences and testing your designs in Chapter 10.) Enter standards, which help minimize the browser differences and enable Web pages to do their job of connecting people across the Internet. Today, it's easy to agree that if everyone who designed Web sites and everyone who created the browsers that displayed them followed the same rules, or standards, we'd all have a much easier time designing sites for the Internet.

All the templates featured in this book are written in XHTML and formatted with CSS, following modern Web standards. In Chapters 7– 9, you can find specific instructions for using Adobe Dreamweaver to edit the templates and customize them. I did every-thing I can to make these templates as versatile — and easy to use — as possible , but the more you understand about CSS and XHTML, the better you can customize the templates without changing them in a way that violates current standards or that will cause them to not display well in most Web browsers.

Creating page layouts with CSS and XHTML

The key to understanding how CSS works in page layout is to think in terms of designing with a series of infinitely adjustable containers, or *boxes*. Indeed, this approach to Web design is commonly referred to as the *box model*. Think of the box model this way: First you use HTML tags, such as the <div> (*div*ision) tag or <p> (*p*aragraph) tag, to create a box around your content. Then you use CSS to style each box, using attributes to control the position and alignment of each box, and specify such settings as margins, padding, and borders.

Although you can use any XHTML tag as part of your page layout, the <div> tag is used most often to create the boxes for main sections of a page, such as the banner area, main content area, sidebars, and footer of a page. Think of <div> as a generic container — designed to hold text, images, or other content — or to make a divi-sion on the page, to separate one section of content from another. Unlike other HTML tags, <div> has no inherent formatting features. Unless CSS is applied to a <div> tag, it can seem invisible on a page, yet the tag has a powerful purpose because any content surrounded by opening and closing <div> tags becomes an object (or a box) that can be formatted with CSS.

I used the box model to create all the templates in this book. As a result, to change the size or positioning of a section of a Web page in one of the templates featured in Chapters 7–9, you need to edit the corresponding style. When you create or edit a style that corresponds to a <div> tag ID, you can specify properties such as align-ment, border, margin, height, and width to control how the <div> tag is displayed on the page. In the template chapters, you find step-by-step instructions for adding your own images and text to these templates, and for making minor changes to the styles of the page. To edit the styles that control the positioning, width, and other display options of the <div> tags that make up these pages layouts, read Chapter 6, where you find instructions for editing a CSS layout.

Each <div> in the page templates has an ID, which corresponds to a style in the style sheet. The ID appears in the HTML within the <div> tag brackets so that the browser knows which style to use to control the formatting of that <div> when it displays the page. For example, all the templates have a <div> with the ID container that controls the overall size of the design area. If you look at the code, the <div> looks like this:

```
<div id="container"></div>
```

In the corresponding style sheet, which you can easily access through the CSS Panel in Dreamweaver, you'll find a style called #container, which controls the width and other settings for that <div>. If this all seems a bit confusing, don't

this stage. When you put all this theory into practice with the
ters 7–9, it makes a lot more sense, and you find more detailed
diting CSS layouts in Chapter 6.

bout CSS, you can find many more lessons on how to create, define,
n my book *Dreamweaver CS4 For Dummies* (Wiley).

tanding style selectors

One of the first things you need to understand when you create new styles is
which selector to use for which job. The selector determines the kind of style you
will create. Each selector option has different naming restrictions and purposes.
If you're completely new to working with styles, this may not make much sense
yet, but this is a fundamental part of work with styles, and I encourage you to read
through all these descriptions of selectors so that you can appreciate your options
before you move on.

Don't feel you have to memorize all this. Instead, consider folding down the corner
on this page so you can refer to this list of selectors when you create and edit styles
later.

Class selectors

The class selector is the most versatile selector option. *Class styles* can be used to
format any element (from text to images to multimedia), and they can be used as
many times as you like on any page in a Web site.

Class style names always begin with a period, and you can create class styles with
any name as long as you don't use spaces or special characters. ***Note:*** Hyphens
and dashes are okay. Thus, you could create a style called *caption* for the text that
appears before your pictures.

```
.caption
```

Dreamweaver helps you with the opening period (or a dot). If you choose class
as the selector type and forget to include a dot at the beginning of the name,
Dreamweaver adds one for you. ***Note:*** Don't include any space between the dot and
the style name, though.

One other thing that can make styles confusing is that when you *apply* a class style
to text or another element, the dot doesn't appear in the name when it's added to
your HTML code. Thus, if you applied the .caption style to a paragraph tag to
format the text under an image, it would look like this:

```
<p class="caption">This is a photo of an Egret in flight.</p>
```

Class styles must be applied to an element, such as the paragraph tag shown in this
example. Class tags can even be added to elements that are already defined by other
styles.

When you create a class style in Dreamweaver, the style is displayed in the CSS
Styles panel on the right side of the workspace (shown in Figure 4-7). You can apply
class styles by using the CSS drop-down list, also shown in Figure 4-7.

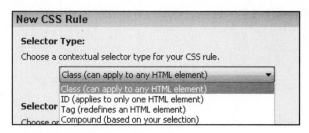

Figure 4-7: Styles created with class selectors are available from the CSS drop-down list and can be applied to any element and used as many times as you like on any page.

One more thing about styles for now: It's common to create styles to align images and other elements to the right or left of a page, and styles with the names `.float-right` and `.float-left` are included in all the templates included with this book. These styles commonly include margin spacing to create a little white space between an image and text when text is wrapped around the aligned image, as shown in Figure 4-7.

For more details and step-by-step instructions for creating and applying styles with class selectors, see Chapter 6.

ID selectors

Think of ID styles as the building blocks of most CSS layouts. What's special about ID styles is that they should be used only once per page. This makes them ideally suited to formatting `<div>` tags and other block-level elements that are used to create distinct sections in a design and only appear once per page.

ID styles must begin with a pound (#) character. Similar to class styles, Dreamweaver adds # to the beginning of the style name automatically if you forget to include it. And, like with a class style, don't include a space between # and the style name.

The ID selector option is a new addition to the CSS Rule dialog box in Dreamweaver CS4. (In CS3, you had to choose the Advanced option to create an ID style.) Similar to class styles, you can name ID styles anything you like as long as you don't use spaces or special characters (again hyphens and underscores are okay). An ID style used to identify the sidebar section of a page could look like this:

```
#sidebar
```

Similar to class styles, # isn't used in the HTML code when a style is applied to an element, such as a `<div>` tag like this:

```
<div id="sidebar">Between these tags with the sidebar ID style,
        you would include any headlines, text, or other
        elements in your sidebar.</div>
```

In the predesigned CSS layouts included in Dreamweaver, all the designs are created by combining a series of `<div>` tags with ID styles using names like `#container`, `#header`, and `#footer` to identify the main sections of the design. In Figure 4-8, you can see how a collection of ID and class styles are displayed in the CSS Styles panel after they're created.

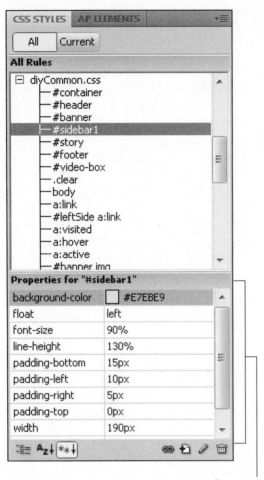

Property Inspector

Figure 4-8: Styles created with the ID selector should be used only once per page and are ideal for creating a CSS layout.

Tag selectors

The tag selector is used to redefine existing XHTML tags. Select this option if you want to change the appearance of an existing XHTML tag, such as the <h1> (heading 1) tag or the <ul> (unordered list) tag.

In many cases, redefining existing XHTML tags with CSS has advantages over creating new styles. For example, content formatted with the heading 1 tag is well recognized on the Web as the most important text on a page. For that reason, many search engines give priority to text formatted with the heading 1 tag. Similarly, the hierarchical structure of the <h1>–<h6> tags helps ensure that, even if a visitor to your site changes the text size in his Web browser, text formatted with the heading 1 tag is still larger relative to text formatted with an heading 2 tag, which is larger than text formatted with the heading 3 tag, and so on.

The ability to change the appearance of headings and other tags with CSS makes it possible to retain these advantages while still being able to use the font, size, color, spacing, and other formatting options that you prefer in your Web design. When you use the tag selector, the style definition is applied automatically to any text or other element that's been formatted with the corresponding tag. Thus, if you've formatted a headline with an <h1> tag and then create a new <h1> style, the formatting you used to define the style will apply automatically to the headline as soon as the style is created.

When you choose a tag selector type, all the XHTML tags become visible in a drop-down list in the New CSS Rule dialog, making it easy to choose the tag style you want to create, such as the H1 tag shown in Figure 4-9.

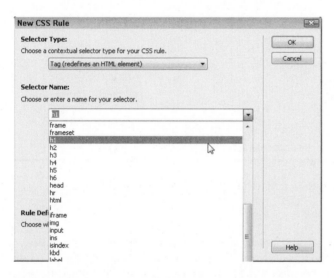

Figure 4-9: You can redefine the appearance of any XHTML tag
by creating a style with a tag selector.

Creating compound styles

The compound selector can be used to combine two or more style rules to create a style definition that displays only when one style is contained within another. Compound styles are useful when you want to do something like use the heading 1 tag multiple times to format headlines in different ways on the same Web page. For example, you could create one style for headlines that appear in the main story area of a page and then create another style for headlines that appear in the sidebar on the page and still use the heading 1 tag to format both.

Compound styles are created by combining ID, class, or tag styles and look like this:

```
#sidebar1 h1
```

See Figure 4-10 for an example of how an <h1> style defined like this within a #sidebar1 ID style looks in the New CSS Rule dialog box. Note that you must include a space between each name or tag in a compound style and that you don't include the brackets around tag in a style name. In this example, the style definition will apply only to <h1> tags that appear within another element, such as a <div> tag with an ID style #sidebar1.

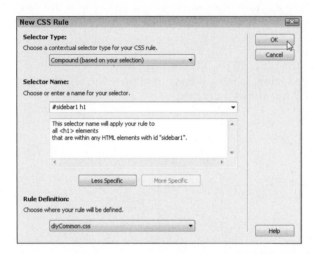

Figure 4-10: Use the compound style selector to combine styles.

If a compound style combines more than one tag, it's written like this:

```
#sidebar1 h1 a:link
```

Again, you must include a space between each name or tag. In this example, you see a style that defines the appearance of the active link tag only when the link is located inside an element formatted with the <h1> tag that's also inside an element formatted with the #sidebar1 ID. A compound style like this makes it possible to create links that look different when they appear in a headline in the sidebar of a page than when they appear in another part of the sidebar.

After you figure out the differences among these style selector options and when they're best used, you're well on your way to mastering the art of creating Web pages with CSS in Dreamweaver. (Find more information about compound styles in Chapter 6.)

Understanding rule definition options

In CSS, you have the option of creating internal, external, or inline styles. You can even use a combination of these options, or attach multiple external style sheets, to the same Web page. Here's an explanation of these options:

✔ **Internal styles:** If you create internal styles, the CSS code is stored in the <head> area at the top of the HTML page you're working on, and the styles can be applied only to the page in which they were created. If you're just creating a one-page Web site or you're creating styles that will be used only on one page, an internal style sheet is fine, but for most sites, external style sheets offer many advantages.

✔ **External styles:** If you save your styles in an external style sheet, they're stored in a separate file with a `.css` extension. External style sheets can be attached to any or all the pages in a Web site in much the same way that you can insert the same image into multiple pages. You can also attach multiple external style sheets to the same page. For example, you can create one style sheet for styles that format text and another for layout styles. You can also create external style sheets for different purposes, such as one for print and one for screen display. One of the biggest advantages of external style sheets is that they make it faster and easier to create new pages, and they make it possible to update styles across many pages at once.

✔ **Inline styles:** Inline styles are created within a document at the place that a style is used and only apply to the element they're attached to in the document. These are generally considered the least useful of the three style sheet options because any changes to the defined style must be made to the code that contains the element, which means you lose many of the benefits of styles, such as the ability to make global updates and create very clean, fast-loading code. For example, creating one style for all your headlines and saving it in an external style sheet is more efficient than applying the style formatting options to each headline separately.

At the bottom of the New CSS Rule dialog box, shown in Figure 4-11, you find a Rule Definition drop-down list. Use this list to specify where and how you want to save each new style that you define. The options are

✔ **This Document Only:** Create an internal style that can only be used in the open document.

✔ **New Style Sheet file:** Create the new style in an external style sheet and create a new external style sheet simultaneously.

✔ **An existing external style sheet:** Choose any existing external style sheet attached to the page by selecting the name of the style sheet from the Rule Definition drop-down list. In Figure 4-11, I am selecting an existing style sheet with the name `main.css`.

If you're creating a style that you'll likely want to use on more than one page in your site, saving the style to a new or existing external style sheet is your best choice. If you save a style in an internal style sheet and later decide you want to add it to an external style sheet, you can move the style by clicking and dragging the style into the external style sheet list in the CSS Styles panel.

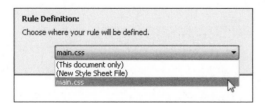

Figure 4-11: When defining a new CSS rule, save it in an internal or external style sheet.

Why so many fonts?

Although you can specify any font you want for text on your Web pages, you don't have complete control over how that font appears on your visitor's computer because the font you apply is displayed properly only if your visitors have the same font on their hard drives. To help ensure that your text appears as you intend, Dreamweaver includes collections of the most common fonts on Windows and Macintosh computers, grouped together in families, such as Arial, Helvetica, sans serif, and Georgia, Times New Roman, Times, and serif.

Here's how it works. When you apply a collection of fonts like these, the browser displays the formatted text in the first font available in the list. For example, if you choose the font collection that starts with Georgia and your visitors have Georgia on their hard drives, they'll see your text in Georgia. If they don't have Georgia, the text is displayed in the next font on the list that your visitors do have — in this case, Times New Roman. If they don't have that font either, the text is displayed in Times; and if they don't even have Times (which would be very unusual), the browser looks for any serif font. (In case you're not familiar with font terms, *serif* describes fonts, such as Times, that have those little curly things

on the edges of letters; *sans serif* means no curly things, which is what you get with a font like Arial.)

You can create your own font collections by selecting the Edit Font List option from the bottom of the Font-Family drop-down list in the Property inspector or the Type category of the CSS Rule definition dialog box. In the Edit Font List dialog box, shown here, use the plus and minus buttons at the top of the Edit Font List dialog box to add or remove a font collection. To add individual fonts to a collection, select the font name from the bottom right of the dialog box and use the double-left arrows to add it to a font list. (Use the double-right arrows to remove a font from a collection.)

The only way to ensure that text appears in the font you want is to create the text in a graphic in a program, such as Photoshop or Fireworks, and then insert the graphic with the text into your page. That's not a bad option for special text, such as banners or logos; but it's usually not a good option for all your text because graphics take longer to download than text and are harder to update later.

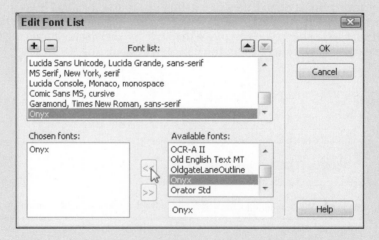

Looking at the code behind the scenes

Even if you *prefer* not to look at the code behind your Web pages, it's helpful to at least have some familiarity with different kinds of tags, CSS, and other code that Dreamweaver creates for you when you design Web pages. The following examples show what the CSS code in an internal or external style sheet would look like in Dreamweaver for the following styles:

✔ An ID style created with the ID selector, that is named `#container`, and is defined as 780 pixels wide with the left and right margins set to auto (a cool trick for centering a CSS design, covered in Chapter 6).

✔ A style created with a class selector, that is named `.caption`, and is defined as Verdana, Arial, Helvetica, sans serif, small, italic, and bold.

✔ A style created with a tag selector to redefine the HTML tag <h1> — as Arial, Helvetica, sans serif, large, and bold. (*Note:* Because the heading tags already include bold formatting, it's not necessary to include bold in the style definition.)

```
#container {
        width: 780px;
        margin-right: auto;
        margin-left: auto;
}
.caption {
        font-family:  Verdana, Arial, Helvetica, sans-serif;
        font-size: small;
        font-style: italic;
        font-weight: bold;
}
H1 {
        font-family: Arial, Helvetica, sans-serif;
        font-size: large;
}
```

Part II
Putting the Pages Together

The 5th Wave   By Rich Tennant

"Well, shoot—I know the animation's moving a mite too fast, but dang if I can find a 'mosey' function in the toolbox!"

Chapter 5

Editing and Creating Web Graphics

Tasks Performed in This Chapter

✔ Getting to know Photoshop Elements

✔ Cropping images

✔ Resizing images

✔ Optimizing photos as JPEGs

✔ Optimizing graphics in GIF format

✔ Combining photos and text in a new image

✔ Editing images with multiple layers

In this chapter, you discover some of the extraordinary things you can do with a program like Photoshop Elements. You find out how to create images (like banners and buttons) for Web pages and then resize, crop, and edit those images.

Perhaps most important in this book about creating Web sites, you find step-by-step instructions for creating and optimizing graphics that download quickly over the Web.

You can use a number of competing image-editing programs to complete the tasks in this book. I recommend Adobe Photoshop Elements because it's based on the industry standard in image editing, Adobe Photoshop, but is a lot easier to use and a lot less expensive. In this book, I use Elements 8, but if you use any of the last few versions of Photoshop or Photoshop Elements, you should have no trouble following along with the features covered in the step-by-step tasks.

Introducing Photoshop Elements

Although Photoshop Elements is a stripped-down version of its big-sister program, Adobe Photoshop, it's still a powerful tool. The workspace, shown in Figure 5-1, is clean and simple yet features many tools and panels — and it has loads of options for editing images and saving them for the Web. Adobe designed the interface of this program to keep the tools around the edge of the screen and to give you the largest possible workspace in the middle, although you can open and close panels and move them around the screen to suit your preferences.

When you first launch Photoshop Elements, you're greeted by a Welcome screen featuring six choices. To access the program's main editing features, which are covered in the following sections, choose Edit and Enhance Photos.

Figure 5-1: Photoshop Elements displays a wide range of tools and panels around the perimeter of the main workspace, where you can create and edit images.

To help you become familiar with the program before you start on the tasks, the following sections introduce you to the way the workspace in Elements is organized and its main features: the Toolbox, Options bar, menu, and panels.

The Toolbox

One of the first things you have to get used to when you use graphics programs like Photoshop Elements is that before you can do anything, like crop an image, you have to select the correct tool from the Toolbox. This feature works much like the toolbox you may have in your garage: You choose a hammer when you want to pound a nail, or a screwdriver when you want to turn a screw.

Selecting a tool from the Toolbox is easy: Just click the icon that represents the tool you want, such as the T icon (for adding text to an image). The tricky part is knowing which tool to use for the job (which is similar to understanding the difference between flat-head and Phillips-head screwdrivers). Some tools are easy to identify: The Brush tool is for painting, for example. Other tools, such as the Clone Stamp tool, may seem confusing at first.

The list of tools shown in Figure 5-2 is designed to help you appreciate all your options in the Toolbox.

The Toolbox can appear in one long list down the side of the Workspace (refer to Figure 5-1), or you can drag it anywhere on the screen and adjust it to appear in two columns (see Figure 5-2).

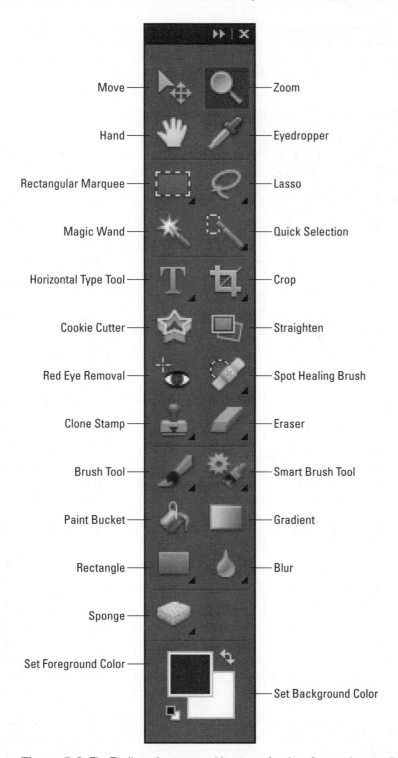

Move —

Zoom

Hand —

Eyedropper

Rectangular Marquee —

Lasso

Magic Wand —

Quick Selection

Horizontal Type Tool —

Crop

Cookie Cutter —

Straighten

Red Eye Removal —

Spot Healing Brush

Clone Stamp —

Eraser

Brush Tool —

Smart Brush Tool

Paint Bucket —

Gradient

Rectangle —

Blur

Sponge —

Set Foreground Color —

Set Background Color

Figure 5-2: The Toolbox gives you a wide range of options for your image editing arsenal.

Here's a hint: Some tools are hidden underneath other tools. If a Toolbox button has a small triangle in its lower-right corner, it means that multiple tools are accessible from the same button. To view these alternative tools, simply click and hold the visible tool until a small fly-out menu appears, as shown in Figure 5-3.

Figure 5-3: The fly-out menus reveal more options under some of the Toolbox items.

Although you use many of these tools in the step-by-step tasks in this book to create and edit images for the Web, I can't possibly cover all the ways you can use these great features in this introduction to Web graphics. In this book, I focus on the tools and features that are most important in Web design. If you want to find out more about creating and editing images, check out *Photoshop Elements 8 For Dummies,* by Barbara Obermeier and Ted Padova, or (for more advanced techniques) *Photoshop Bible,* by Laurie Ulrich Fuller and Robert C. Fuller (both from Wiley Publishing).

The Options bar

Running across the top of the Elements workspace is the Options bar, shown in Figure 5-4. The Options bar includes drop-down lists, check boxes, and radio buttons that you can use to adjust the settings for any selected tool. For example, when you select the Brush tool, options are available for changing the size and shape of the stroke that you make when you click and drag the Brush tool over an image. If you switch to the Text tool, the Options bar changes to feature font and size options.

The art of Undo and Redo

With all the features, filters, and editing options in Photoshop Elements, trial and error is often your best strategy — and it's easy when you can use Undo, Redo, and even Revert to restore any image to its last-saved version.

If you make a change to an image and then change your mind, just choose Edit➪Undo to undo it. If you aren't quite sure whether you made an improvement, try Undo and then Redo (Edit➪Redo) so that you can compare the image before and after the effect. Photoshop Elements includes many levels of Undo, so you can go back many steps and experiment until an image is just the way you want it.

If you're a keyboard shortcut fan, press Ctrl+Z to use Undo in Windows (or ⌘+Z on the Mac); for Redo, press Ctrl+Y (or ⌘+Y).

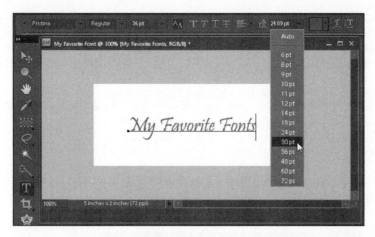

Figure 5-4: The Options bar provides easy access to settings for each tool, such as the font and size options that correspond to the Text tool.

The menu bar

No program is complete without a menu bar at the top of the workspace (shown in Figure 5-5). When you click the menu names, you can choose from a list of commands and editing options. If an ellipsis (. . .) follows the command name, the option launches a dialog box where you can apply a variety of features. Otherwise, the command kicks in automatically as soon as it's selected.

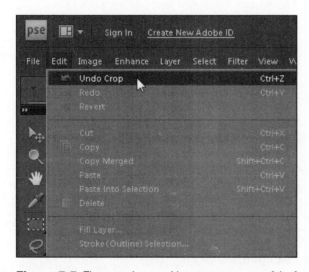

Figure 5-5: The menu bar provides access to most of the features in Photoshop Elements, including my personal favorite, the Undo option, which can get you out of all kinds of problems.

The panels

As in every Adobe application, the Elements workspace is filled with *panels*, which are small windows that hold formatting options and other settings. The various panels provide tools to help you edit and examine images. To open a panel, choose it from the Window menu. For example, choosing Window⇨Color Swatches opens a panel with color options. Note that each panel has a More button; clicking More displays a list of additional commands.

A panel can remain in its column on the right side of the workspace, or you can drag panels anywhere on the screen, which is a handy way to get them closer to where you're working. To move a panel, click it and then drag it by its tab, and then release it where you like. After you detach a panel from the main application window, it gains its own title bar, which allows for easier moving and identification.

In Figure 5-6, I'm using the Layer Styles in the Special Effects panel to add a drop shadow to my text, a common way to add depth and make text appear to float on a page.

Figure 5-6: You can move a panel so that it's closer to whatever you're working on.

If you ever want to get back to the original workspace layout in Photoshop Elements, just choose Window⇨Reset Panels, and all the panels and bins magically rearrange themselves to their original positions.

Creating and opening images in Elements

You can open existing images in Photoshop Elements or create completely new images, and you can have multiple images open at a time, which makes it easier to combine images and create complex designs. When you create a new image, you can specify many settings, including size, resolution, and color.

To create a new document, choose File⇨New, and in the New File dialog box that appears, specify the height, width, resolution, color mode, and background color. You can alter any of the settings after you create an image.

To open an existing image, choose File⇨ Open, find the image you want on your hard drive, click to select it, and then click Open. The image appears in a new window, ready for you to edit.

If you try to open an image and don't see it in a folder on your hard drive when you know that it should be there, change the Files of Type field (at the bottom of the Open dialog box) to All Formats. Every image in the folder should now appear in the file list.

Cropping an Image

Because photos on the Web are generally small, one way to ensure that important features are visible is to crop out any material that's not essential. The best strategy when cropping an image for the Web is to focus on the key elements in the image. You can cut off the top, bottom, or sides, as much or as little as you like, with the adjustable edges of the Crop tool.

In this step-by-step task, you see how using the Crop tool to remove the background helps focus attention on the subject.

Whenever you crop, edit, or resize an image, it's good practice to first save a copy of the image to edit. That way you can always go back to the original image if you're not happy with the results of your edits.

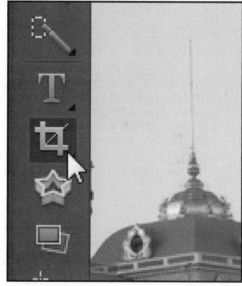

1. With an image open in Elements, select the Crop tool from the Tools panel. Because you can't retrieve cropped parts of an image after you save and close the image file, you likely want to work with a copy of your original image.

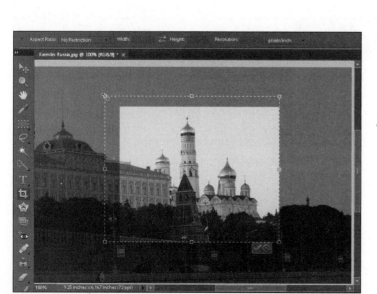

2. Click and drag within the image to define the area you want to crop. As you drag, a crop box appears. Everything outside the crop box is removed when you complete the crop. To increase or decrease the size of the crop box, drag the handles at the corners or edges of the box.

3. To complete the crop, double-click in the middle of the selected area or click the Commit icon (the green check mark) in the lower-right corner of the crop box. To cancel the Crop tool without cropping the image, click the Cancel button (the red circle with a line through it).

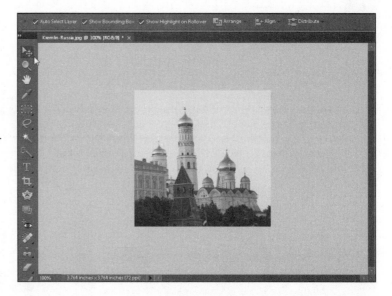

4. When you complete the crop, the areas of the image outside the crop box are removed, and the overall size of the image is reduced proportionately. The Crop tool remains active until you select a different tool from the Toolbox.

Repeat Steps 2 through 4 to make an additional crop. Choose Edit➪Undo Crop to restore the image if you're unhappy with the crop. When you save the image, your changes become permanent.

Resizing an Image

Stuff You Need to Know

Toolbox:
- Adobe Photoshop Elements (or a similar program)
- A digital image

Time needed:
Less than half an hour

Resizing is important for two reasons: The images must be small enough to display well on a computer monitor, and you want them to download quickly to a user's computer. The smaller the image is, the faster it will download. There are two steps to reducing the size of an image you want to use on the Web.

The first step is to reduce the physical size of an image by reducing its dimensions. You want to size your images to fit well in a browser window and to work within the design of your site. And remember, the smaller you make the image, the faster it downloads to a user's computer.

The second step is a bit more complex to understand at first. It has to do with reducing the resolution of an image, which changes the number of pixels in the image, but won't alter the size the image appears on a computer screen. When you're working with images for the Web, you want to reduce the resolution to 72 pixels per inch (or ppi). (If you're wondering why 72, see the sidebar that's appropriately named "Why only 72 ppi?")

Follow these steps to reduce the size of an image and lower the resolution:

1. With an image open in Elements, choose Image⇨Resize. If you don't want your original image to lose quality, make a copy of it by choosing File⇨Save As and giving the copy a new name. Then resize the *copy* for your Web site.

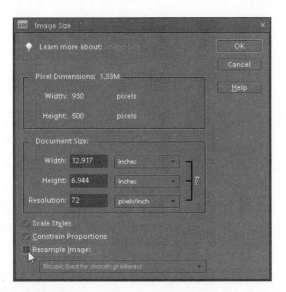

2. Before you change the resolution of an image, make sure to deselect the Resample Image check box at the bottom of the Image Size dialog box (you should always make sure the resample check box is deselected when you change resolution). Then highlight the number in the Resolution field and replace it by typing in the number 72. (Note that with the Resample Image check box deselected, you can't change the Pixel dimensions.)

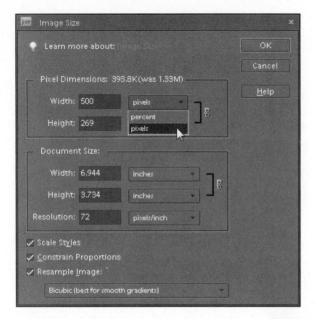

3. Before you change the dimensions of an image, make sure to select the Resample Image check box (you always want the Resample box selected when you resize), and also select the Scale Styles and Constrain Proportions check boxes to maintain the height and width ratio in the image. In this example, I am changing the width of this image to 500 pixels, and the height automatically adjusts to 269 pixels to maintain the proportions. When you're resizing an image for the Web, it's best to use the fields in the Pixel Dimensions area, at the top of the dialog box. Using these options, you can alter the height and width of an image to a specified size in pixels or enlarge or reduce the image by any percentage.

4. Click OK to resize the image. If you want to return the image to its previous size, choose Edit⇨Undo. When you save the image, the changes become permanent. Notice that the file size is reduced from 1.33MB to 393.8K.

Why only 72 ppi?

When you save images for the Web, you should save them at a resolution of 72 pixels per inch (better known as *ppi*). Most computer monitors display no more than 72 ppi, so any number higher than that is wasted on the Web because you're making your visitors download more pixels than they can see. However, if you want to print an image, you want all the pixels you can get, usually at least 200 ppi or higher, which is why most images you see on the Web look terrible if you try to print them in a large size.

Optimizing Photos as JPEGs

The JPEG format is the best choice for images with many colors, such as photographs or images that include shading or gradients. You can save any image in GIF, PNG, or JPEG format by using the Save for Web dialog box, but you produce the best results if you choose the best format for each image. That's because the best way to *optimize* images (make them download faster over the Web) depends on how many colors appear in the image.

It's always best to edit an image in the highest resolution possible and then resize the image and reduce the resolution (as you do in the previous task) just before optimizing it for the Web.

Also note that even if a photograph is already in the JPEG format, you can almost always reduce its file size (and increase its download speed) by using the Save for Web dialog box to optimize the image, as you see in the following steps:

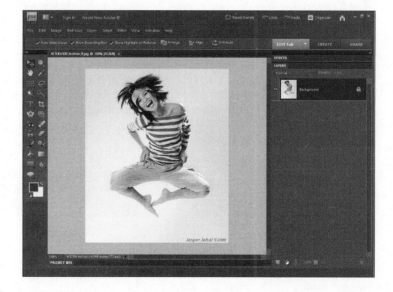

1. Create a new image or open an existing image in any format in Photoshop Elements. Because you create a copy of the image when you use the Save for Web dialog box, you don't need to worry about altering your original image.

When you're optimizing an image for the Web, it always comes down to balancing quality with file size. You want your images to download fast, but not if that means they don't look good when they arrive.

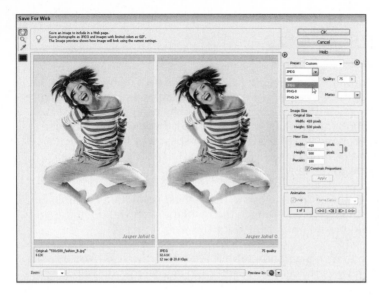

2. Choose File⇨Save for Web, and in the Save for Web dialog box, select JPEG from the Optimized File Format drop-down list. Note: The original version of the image appears on the left side of the dialog box, and the version on the right is a preview of how the image will look with the specified settings.

3. If the image, like the one shown in this example, is larger than the preview area in the Save for Web dialog box, choose the Hand tool from the upper-left corner of the dialog box. Then click the image and drag to position the most important elements in the image where you can see a better preview. You can also change the image's display by right-clicking directly over the preview image and choosing Fit on Screen or any of the magnification settings.

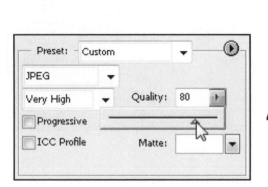

4. To reduce the size of a JPEG image, use the slider to alter the Quality setting or enter a number, up to 100. Compression is measured as a percentage: The lower the number, the higher the compression and the smaller the file size.

5. Notice in the bottom of the Save for Web dialog box that the original file size appears under the preview of the image on the left, and the optimized file size appears under the preview on the right. In this example, you can see that when the Quality field is set to 80, the image is reduced from 612K to 34.74K.

6. Alter the Quality setting until the image uses the greatest amount of compression (the greater the compression, the lower the number in the Quality field), without degrading the appearance of the image too much. In this example, I reduced the Quality setting to 60, creating a file size of 28.28K.

7. Keep a close eye on the preview screen as you adjust the Quality option. If you reduce the quality too far, you degrade the image's appearance noticeably.

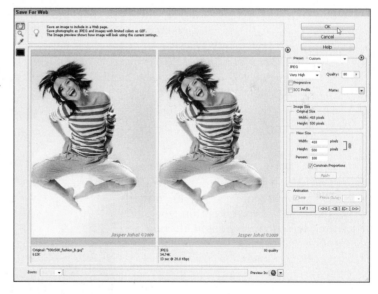

8. In this example, I decided I wanted to preserve as much quality as possible (reducing it to 60 made it look a little pixilated), so I've changed it to 80. After all the image settings are the way you want them, click OK, and in the Save dialog box, give the image a new name and specify where you want to save it on your hard drive. Then click Save to save a new version of the JPEG with the specified settings and preserve the original unchanged.

Optimizing Graphics in GIF or PNG Format

Stuff You Need to Know

Toolbox:

- ✔ Adobe Photoshop Elements (or a similar program)
- ✔ A digital image with limited colors

Time needed:
Less than half an hour

The GIF format has long been considered best for drawings, cartoons, and other images that have only a few bands of solid color, although many Web designers now prefer the PNG format. (As described in the previous section, the JPEG format is ideal for photographs and other images with millions of colors.) GIFs and PNGs are also the best format to use when you want to create images that use a transparent background, a trick that makes images appear to float on a Web page. As the Web has matured, the PNG format has gained popularity. PNGs are superior to GIFs in all ways except one: GIFs are better supported by Web browsers older than Internet Explorer 6.0, especially in the area of transparency.

If your goal is to ensure that your pages display well to *anyone* who may ever visit your site, GIF is the safer option. If you want your images to look their best with the smallest file sizes, you produce better results with the PNG format. Also, you can rest assured that very few people are still using browsers so old that they don't support PNG. In the step-by-step exercise that follows, I chose the PNG format, but the process is the same for both options. This task shows you the best way to reduce the number of colors in any image when you save it in either the PNG or GIF format using Photoshop Elements.

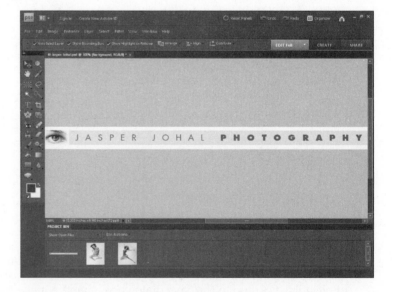

1. Create a new image or open an existing image in any format in Photoshop Elements. Because you save a copy of an image when you use the Save for Web option, you don't have to worry about altering your original image (just don't save over the original).

TIP

When you use the PNG or GIF formats, you can reduce download time by decreasing the total number of colors used in the image, which makes it ideal for graphics that need only a few colors in order to display well, such as cartoons or simple logo designs. When you reduce the number of colors in a PNG or GIF image, you're essentially removing colors you don't need. If you take away too many colors, however, the change can be drastic (and look terrible); but if you limit the image to only the number of colors that are necessary, you might not even notice the difference, and the image will download much faster.

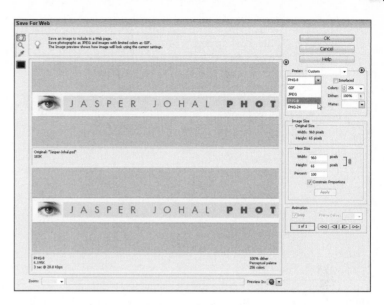

2. Choose File➪Save for Web. In the Save for Web dialog box, choose PNG-8 from the Optimized File Format drop-down list. (PNG-24 supports color and alpha transparency better, but with a much higher file size, so you're almost always better off with PNG-8.)

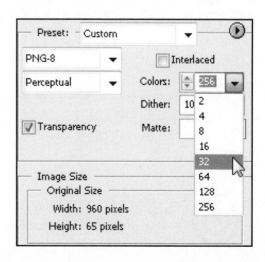

3. If you're creating an image with a transparent background, select the Transparency check box and then specify a matte color. The matte color should match the background color of the Web page where the image will be displayed. Using a matching matte color helps prevent "jaggies" from appearing around the edges of the image. To change this color, first select the eyedropper from the upper-left corner of the dialog box. Then click in the Matte field to open the color panel where you can select the Eyedropper Color option to apply the color you just sampled with the Eyedropper tool. You can also select any of the other color options in the drop-down list.

4. To reduce the size of the image, lower the number of colors by entering a number less than 256 in the Colors field or by selecting a preset number from the Colors drop-down list. In this example, the image is reduced from 256 (the maximum number of colors a GIF can have) to 32. You can change the numbers to see the results in the preview and then change them again if you're not happy with the results, as I do in the next step).

5. Notice at the bottom of the Save for Web dialog box that the original file size appears under the preview of the image on the top and the optimized file size appears under the preview on the bottom. Compare these numbers to see how much smaller the image is with the number of colors reduced from 256 to 64. In this example, you can see that by reducing the number of colors, the image has been reduced from 183K to 4.452K.

6. Reduce the number of colors further to make the file size even smaller — but don't go too far. In this example, you can see that when the image is reduced to only two colors, the text gets jagged and the detail is lost in the image of the eye. That's because even though the image appears to use only a few colors, along the edge of the letters, many variations of the main colors are used to create a clean line between the text and the background. With only two colors in the image, those color variations are lost and the smooth edge becomes jagged.

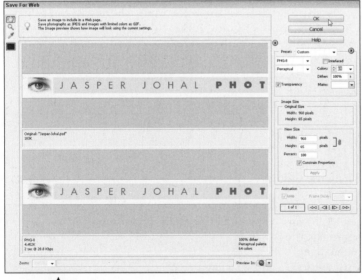

7. Adjust the number of colors and other settings until the image uses the smallest number of colors (and therefore has the smallest file size) without degrading the appearance of the image. In this example, I was able to reduce the image to 64 colors without a noticeable loss of quality.

8. After all the image settings are the way you want them, click OK. In the Save dialog box, name the image, and specify where you want to save it on your hard drive. Then click Save.

When you use the Save for Web dialog box, Elements automatically saves a copy of the image in the new format and leaves the original image unchanged.

Combining Photos and Text in a New Image

Stuff You Need to Know

Toolbox:
- Adobe Photoshop Elements (or a similar program that supports layers)
- Digital images

Time needed:
About half an hour (unless you get carried away)

Creating a new image with photos and text is almost as easy as editing an existing image, such as the banners and buttons included in the templates in this book.

In general, I find that the best method is to create a new image in Photoshop Elements and then copy any photos or other graphics into the new image file. After the images are in place, you can easily add text to pull it all together. Just follow these steps to create your own banners and buttons:

1. In Photoshop Elements, choose File⇨New⇨ Blank File to create a new image. In the New dialog box, specify the size, resolution, and background color. In this task, I'm creating an image that's 760 pixels wide by 410 pixels high with a resolution of 72 ppi, in RGB color with a white background. (For the Web, the color mode is always RGB for JPEG images.)

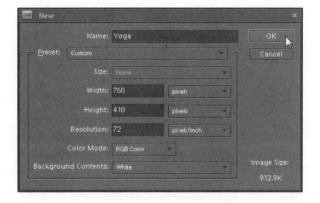

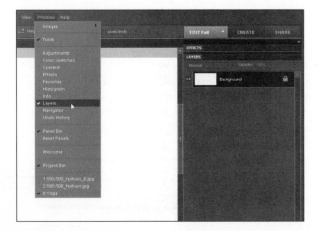

2. If the Layers panel isn't already open on the side of the workspace, choose Window⇨Layers to open the Layers panel. (It must be open if you want to keep track of the layers as they're automatically created when you copy in images or add text to the image.)

3. Open any image or images that you want to add to the new file by choosing File➪Open and selecting the image from your hard drive. You can open as many images as you want at once in Photoshop or Photoshop Elements (or as many as your computer's memory can support) in any of the many supported formats, including JPEG, GIF, TIF, and PSD.

4. When you're working with multiple images in Photoshop Elements, you may want to open the Project Bin, at the bottom of the workspace: If it isn't already open, choose Window➪ Open the Project Bin. You can select any open image by double-clicking its thumbnail image in the Project Bin.

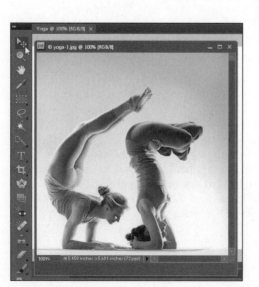

5. To copy an open image into the new file, first click to select the Move tool from the upper-left corner of the Toolbox. Then click anywhere on an open image to make it active and choose Select➪All.

6. With the image selected, choose File⇨Copy or press the key combination Ctrl+C (on Windows) or ⌘+C (on the Mac).

7. Here's the tricky part: You need to select the file where you want to add the image before you paste it. If the Project Bin is open at the bottom of the workspace, you can select the destination image there. You can also select any image that's visible in the workspace by clicking it. In both Photoshop and Photoshop Elements, you can also select any open image by choosing the name of the file from the bottom of the Window menu.

8. If any of the open images are in your way, you can minimize them, keeping them open and available in the Project Bin, but out of the workspace.

9. With your new, blank image active in the workspace, choose File⇨Paste, or use the key combinations Ctrl+V (on Windows) or ⌘+V (on the Mac), to paste the copied image into the new image.

10. To position the pasted image, click to select it and then drag it to the place where you want it to appear in the new image. For more precise images, use the arrow keys — you can adjust a selected layer pixel-by-pixel in any direction. You can resize an image with the Move tool by clicking and dragging any corner to adjust the height and width.

11. To add and position additional images, repeat Steps 6 through 10. Notice in this example that the Layers palette displays three layers — the white background layer and a separate layer for each photo pasted into the image. As I added those images, Photoshop Elements added the layers automatically.

12. To add text to an image (whether or not it already has multiple layers, like this one does), you must first select the Text tool from the Toolbox.

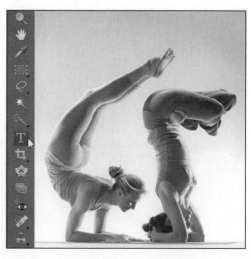

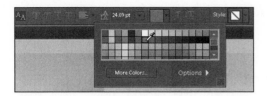

13. When you select the Text tool, a new collection of options appears at the top of the workspace. On the Options bar, you can change such text options as the color (shown in this figure), by clicking the color well to open the color selection palette and then clicking any color in the palette. Use the scroll bar, to the right of the palette window, to display more colors.

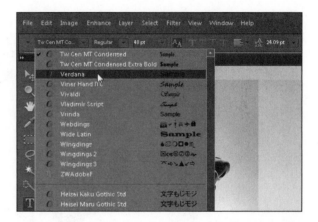

14. With the Text tool selected, you can also use the Text tool options at the top of the workspace to change the font size, face, and alignment.

15. To add text to the image, click to place your cursor where you want it and then type. You can add as much text as you want to an image and press the Enter (or Return) key to add line breaks.

16. You can also use the text options at the top of the workspace to edit the text after you type it. To do so, simply select the text you want to change, and then choose any of the formatting options to alter the color, font, size, or other settings. To edit the words, click to select the text and then delete or type to replace it.

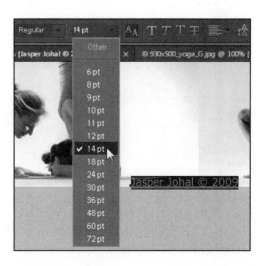

17. When you add text, Photoshop automatically places it on a new layer, which appears in the Layers palette. To move or edit a layer, you must first select the Move tool from the Toolbox. Photoshop Elements automatically selects a layer when you click it, and then you can click and drag to position it on the page. To move a layer so that it appears in front of another layer, click and drag it above the other layer in the Layers palette.

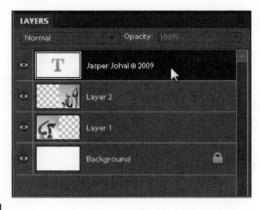

18. You can continue to add text layers and images, and edit and adjust them, forever by repeating this set of steps. One of the best ways to become comfortable with using Photoshop Elements is to take time to experiment with combining and rearranging text and images in multiple layers.

As you create more and more layers in an image, it's good practice to give your layers names as you create them so that you can better identify a layer when you want to edit it later.

Turning layers on and off or rearranging them

Sometimes when you're working on an image with many layers, it's handy to turn them on and off so that you can experiment with different combinations or clear the workspace while you work on a detail. By clicking the small eye icon to the left of any layer, you can make the layer invisible in the workspace. Don't worry — you can turn the layer back on by simply clicking in the same field again to make the eye icon reappear. That's the beauty of this feature: Now you see it, now you don't.

You can also rearrange the order of layers in the Layers panel, which is how you can control which layer is on top in the image. To change the stacking order, click to drag the layer up or down in the Layers panel. The higher the layer is in the panel, the higher its position is in the stacking order in the file.

Editing Images with Multiple Layers

One of the most confusing features in a program like Photoshop Elements is the way it divides different parts of an image into layers. In the previous task, Photoshop automatically created a new layer each time you added a new image or text to the file. Keeping each element of an image on a separate layer is a bit like keeping a bunch of sticky notes on your desk. If each photo or piece of text is on a separate layer, you can move them around independently, much like you might rearrange your priorities by changing the order of the sticky notes.

Using Layers to separate one image into multiple sections makes it possible for you to do things like edit text without changing the photo underneath it or move separate images around a photo montage until you get them just the way you want them.

Without layers, text would become stuck on a photo in a banner, like the one shown in this task, and you couldn't edit the text again after you added it to the image. The layers feature is especially useful for customizing the banners and other graphic elements included in the templates used in this book.

When you open an image that has many layers, such as the image templates included with this book, it's a good idea to open up the Layers panel by choosing Window⇨Layers (if it's not open already).

Before you can edit any text or image contained in a layer, you have to first select the appropriate tool from the Toolbox and then select the corresponding layer. That's where the Layers panel comes in, as you see in this task.

1. Open an existing image in Photoshop Elements that includes multiple layers, such as the banner shown in this task.

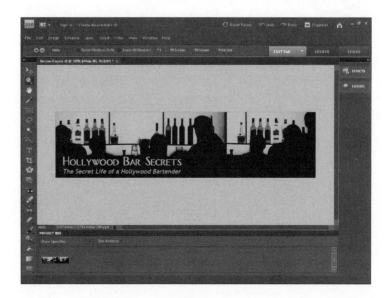

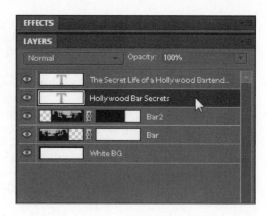

2. Choose Window➪Layers to open the Layers panel. In the Layers panel, click to select the layer you want to edit. In this example, I selected the layer that corresponds to the words `Hollywood Bar Secrets`.

3. In the Toolbox, select the tool that you need in order to edit the contents of the layer. In this example, I selected the Text tool so that I can edit the words.

4. Use the selected tool to alter the selected image. In this example, I double-clicked the name *Hollywood* to select it and then typed the name *Los Angeles* in its place.

5. To edit text in another layer, you must again select the corresponding layer in the Layers panel. In this example, I selected the layer that contains the text in the second line of the banner image. Because I had already selected the Text tool, after the layer was selected, I simply selected the text I wanted to edit and replaced it by typing new text.

6. After you make changes to the text, choose File⇨Save As and give the image a new name. This step saves the changes without altering the original image.

Enlarging and reducing image display

As you're working on images in Photoshop Elements, it's often helpful to enlarge or reduce the display size of the image so that you can view more of it on the screen or to zoom in on details you want to edit. You can use the Zoom tool to increase or decrease the size at which the image appears on your screen.

First, click to select the Zoom tool from the Toolbox; then click anywhere on the image to increase its display size. Alt+click (in Windows) or Option+click (on the Mac) to decrease the display size.

Tip: By changing the display size, you can figure out how much you may need to change the actual size of your image to make it appear the way you want on a computer screen. To do so, use the Zoom tool to size the image the way you want in your Web page, and then notice the percentage (displayed at the top of the screen, next to the filename). Then you know the number you need to enter in the Size field in the Image Size dialog box when you resize it using a percentage.

To redisplay the image in its true size on your monitor, double-click the Zoom tool.

Chapter 6

Getting Started with Dreamweaver

The high-end features in Dreamweaver make it the preferred choice for professional Web designers, but its easy-to-use graphical interface makes it popular among novices and hobbyists as well. This book is designed to help you create a Web site as quickly as possible by providing you with templates for a variety of common Web sites and instructions for how to customize those templates in Dreamweaver. If you're eager to get started, feel free to jump ahead to Chapters 7, 8, or 9, where you find instructions for using Dreamweaver to customize the ready-to-use templates that come with this book.

Before you do, though, I suggest that you at least skim through this chapter so that you have some familiarity with the most important features in Dreamweaver, how I've used Dreamweaver's advanced template features to help you create sites quickly, and how you can edit those templates with this great Web design program. This chapter is designed to introduce you to Dreamweaver and to show you how to do some the most common tasks with this popular design program, such as creating new pages, inserting images, setting links, and defining CSS styles.

 At the beginning of this chapter, you find detailed instructions for one of the most important features in Dreamweaver: the Site Definition dialog box. Defining a site in Dreamweaver is important whether you use one of the templates featured later in this book or create your own, custom design using the instructions in the rest of this chapter. Before you work on any Web site in Dreamweaver, you should start with the site-definition process.

 In my effort to keep things simple in this book, I cover only a small portion of the features in this complex program. You can read lots more about Dreamweaver in my book *Dreamweaver CS4 For Dummies* (Wiley).

Setting Up a New or Existing Site

As a general rule, when you create a Web site, you first create all the pages on your computer's hard drive, where you can preview your pages in a Web browser and test the site before it's visible on the Internet. Then, when the site is ready, you transfer the files to your *Web server,* a computer with a permanent connection to the Internet that uses special software to communicate with Web browsers, such as Internet Explorer, Safari, Chrome, and Firefox.

Because all the files you work with on your hard drive must be in the same *relative* location on the Web server, you need to store all your site's resources in one folder on your hard drive and identify that folder as the *local root* folder in Dreamweaver.

As you progress through the site-definition process in the following task, you can create a new folder on your hard drive and designate it as your local root folder, or you can identify an existing folder if you're updating or redesigning a site. The location where you save the local root folder on your hard drive doesn't matter, as long as you identify it as the main folder for your Web site in Dreamweaver. ***Note:*** If you move the local root folder, you have to go through the site setup process again so that Dreamweaver knows where to find it.

When you're ready to publish a completed site, you can transfer it to your Web server by using the Dreamweaver built-in *File Transfer Protocol* (or *FTP*) features. You find detailed instructions for testing and publishing a Web site in Chapter 10.

Throughout this book, I use Adobe Dreamweaver CS4, but most of the features I cover have not changed much in the last few versions, so even if you're using another version of Dreamweaver, such as 8 or CS3, you should be able to follow most of these instructions with few, if any, adjustments. Just be aware that some panels and other options may be in different locations in earlier versions.

Working with an existing Web site

If you're working on redesigning or editing an existing site, your first challenge is to get a copy of the site on your hard drive. Fortunately, Dreamweaver can help you download an existing site off a Web server with the same features you use to publish a site. All you need is the login information, username, and password to access the Web server.

To download an existing site, first complete the site setup process featured at the beginning of this chapter. Then create a new, blank folder where you can store all files in the Web site on your local hard drive. Follow the instructions in the section "Setting Up FTP in Dreamweaver" in Chapter 10 to connect Dreamweaver with your server. After you establish a connection, just select all the files on the server and click the Get button (also shown in Chapter 10) to download all files in the existing site.

After you have your site on your hard drive, you can edit and add pages using Dreamweaver just like you would edit any other files on your computer, even if the site was created in another Web design program. Keep in mind, however, that if you're doing a major redesign of an existing site, you might be better off to start from scratch. In that case, you can download the existing site into one folder, and then create a new site in another root folder in Dreamweaver. With both the old and new versions of a site on your hard drive, it's easy to copy the existing text, images, and other materials into the new pages as you create the new site.

Defining a Web Site in Dreamweaver

If the site-definition process seems a little confusing at first, don't worry; it's a quick, relatively painless process, and you have to do it only once for each site. Just trust me — don't skip this preliminary step.

Whether you're creating a new site or working on an existing site, the following steps walk you through the process of defining a local root folder for your Web site.

Browse icon

1. Choose Site➪New Site to open the Site Definition dialog box.

2. Click the Advanced tab. *Note:* If you prefer, you can use the basic wizard that steps you through the setup process, but I find it faster and easier to view all the options at once from the Advanced tab.

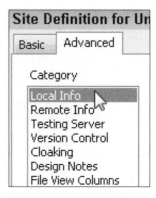

3. In the Category box on the left, make sure that the Local Info category is selected so that you can specify the location of the folder on your local hard drive. This category should be open by default when you click the Advanced tab. (You find instructions for setting up the options in the Remote category so that you can publish your site to a Web server in Chapter 10.)

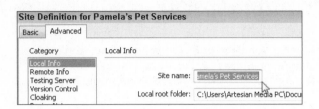

4. In the Site Name text box, type a name for your site. You can call your site whatever you like; this name is used only to help you keep track of your sites. Many people work on more than one site in Dreamweaver, and this feature enables you to keep track of them by name. The name you enter here appears in the drop-down list in the Files panel and in the Manage Sites dialog box. You use this list to select the site you want to work on when you open Dreamweaver. In this example, I named the new site Pamela's Pet Services.

5. Click the Browse icon next to the Local Root Folder text box to locate the folder on your hard drive that you want to serve as the main folder for all files in your Web site. (*Hint:* The Browse icon in Dreamweaver always looks like a small, yellow file folder and is usually located at the right side of a text field.) If you're setting up a new site, create a new folder on your hard drive, using the Create New Folder icon in the Choose Local Folder dialog, and then select that folder as the local root folder. If you're setting up an existing Web site, select the folder that contains the files for that site to designate it as the Local Root Folder.

6. Click the Browse icon next to the Default Images folder field and then select the images folder in an existing Web site. If you're creating a new site, create a new folder inside your local root folder, name it `images`, and select it. Although you don't *have* to identify an `images` folder, it has some advantages. For example, if you ever insert an image that isn't located in your local root folder, Dreamweaver copies it into the `images` folder you identify during the site setup process. If you create an `images` folder, Dreamweaver copies images into the main folder. (You can also store images in other folders within your local root folder.)

7. For the Links Relative To radio buttons, leave the Document option selected unless you know that you want your links to be set up relative to the root level of your site. This setting controls how the path is set in links. If you're working on a site with other developers and you're not sure, check with your colleagues. If you're working alone on your own site, Links Relative to Document is the simplest option and should already be selected because it's the default option in Dreamweaver.

8. In the HTTP Address text box, type the URL of your Web site. The *HTTP address* is the URL, or Web address, that your site will have when it's published on a Web server (see Chapter 2). If you don't yet know the Web address for your site or you don't plan to publish it on a Web server, you can leave this box blank. If you do fill it in, include `http://` at the beginning and `/` at the end.

9. Select the Use Case-Sensitive Link Checking check box. Unless you know for sure that you don't have to worry about the case of your filenames, selecting this box makes Dreamweaver ensure that the case matches for all your site's links (which many Web hosting services require).

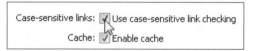

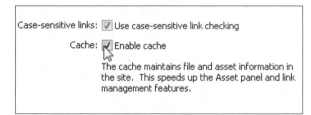

10. Select the Enable Cache option. Dreamweaver creates a local cache of your site to quickly reference the location of files in your site. The local cache speeds up many site management features of the program and takes only a few seconds to create.

11. Click OK to close the Site Definition dialog box and save your settings. If the folder you selected as your local site folder already contains files or subfolders, they're automatically cached and any files or folders in your site are displayed in the Files panel. In this example, because I'm creating a new site, only the images subfolder is displayed. If you haven't checked the Enable Cache option, a message box appears, asking whether you want to create a cache for the site. Doing so is good practice because it helps Dreamweaver work more efficiently.

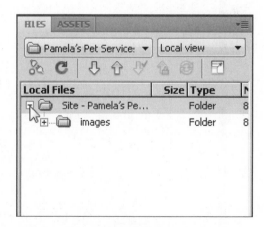

You can make changes and additions to a site by choosing Site➪Manage Sites, selecting the site name in the Manage Sites dialog box, and then clicking the Edit button. The defined site then opens in the Site Definition dialog box, where you can make changes to any setting, such as selecting a different `images` folder or local root folder. Remember that if you move the local root folder on your hard drive, you need to edit the site definition to identify the new folder location.

12. If you work on more than one site in Dreamweaver, be sure to define each site the first time you work on it. After that, you can easily switch among defined sites by selecting the one you want to work on in the Files panel. You can define as many sites as you like in Dreamweaver. To load a different site into the Files panel, click the drop-down arrow next to the site name and choose the name of the site you want to display. In this figure, you can see that I'm opening the site named Pamela's Pet Services by selecting it from a long list of defined sites.

Naming Web pages

Filenames are especially important in Web sites because they're included in the HTML code when you set links. Over the years, I have received more e-mail messages from panicked Web designers because of broken links caused by filename conflicts than almost any other issue. Because these problems usually don't occur until after a Web site is published on a server, they can be especially confusing and difficult to understand. Following a few simple pointers can help you avoid or troubleshoot filename-related problems:

✔ **When you save Web pages, images, and other files for your site, the basic rule is to not use blank spaces or special characters in a filename.** For example, don't name a Web page with an apostrophe, such as cat's page.html. If you want to separate words, you can use an underscore (_) or a hyphen (-). For example, cat-page.html is an acceptable filename. Numbers are okay in most cases, and capital letters don't generally matter, as long as the filename and the code in the link match.

The potentially misleading point is that links with spaces and special characters work just fine when you test pages on a Mac or PC, but the software used on many of the Web servers on the Internet don't accept spaces or special characters in links. Thus, links that don't follow these rules can be broken when you publish the site to a Web server.

✔ **All files in a Web site must also include an extension at the end of the filename to identify the file type (such as .html for HTML files or .jpg for JPEG images).** Dreamweaver automatically adds the .html file extension to the end of HTML files, but you may need to change your Windows settings if you want to be able to see the extension. Similarly, programs like Photoshop automatically add the extension on Windows computers; if you're using a Macintosh, you may need to add the extensions manually.

✔ **Another confusing rule, and one of the most important, is that the main page (or _front page_) of your Web site must be named index.html or default.html, depending on your Web server.** Most Web servers are set up to serve the index.html page first. To ensure that you use the correct name, check with your service provider or system administrator. (Some servers are set up to handle home.html, or default.asp for dynamic sites, but most commercial service providers serve index.html before any other page in any folder in a site.) The rest of the pages in your site can be named anything you like, as long as they don't include spaces or special characters (except for the dash or underscore).

Creating New Pages in Dreamweaver

In this task, I show you how easy it is to create a new page in Dreamweaver and add and format text. Whether you're creating a simple design or a complex one, it's almost always easier to start with one of the prestyled Cascading Style Sheet (CSS) layouts included in Dreamweaver. You can use Dreamweaver's collection of layouts to create a variety of one, two, and three-column designs using CSS, and as you see in the steps that follow, you can customize these layouts in many ways. Before you rush off to take a look at all the layouts included with Dreamweaver, let me warn you that they're not much to look at when you first open them. They're intentionally designed with a basic, gray color scheme. Fortunately, though, color styles are some of the easiest to alter in CSS.

If you're new to CSS, altering one of these layouts may seem confusing at first, but it's certainly easier than starting a page layout from scratch yourself. In this chapter, I focus on a simple, one-column design, a great way to practice the basics before you get into the steps you'll need to follow to customize the more complex layouts included in the templates later in this book. Before you begin creating new pages, make sure that you complete the site setup process covered in the preceding task in this chapter.

1. To create a new page, choose File⇨ New. In the New Document dialog box that opens, choose Blank Page from the options on the far left (as shown here). Under the Page Type column, you can now select from many different file types, including HTML, XML, and PHP. To create a simple Web page, like the one I use throughout this book, choose HTML.

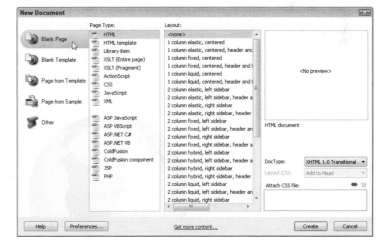

A fixed layout is generally an easier option to start with, but "liquid" designs have advantages because they're more flexible. You can find a longer description of the layout types in the Dreamweaver Help files, but essentially here are the options. *Liquid layouts* are designed to expand and contract, depending upon the size of the browser window; *fixed layouts* are centered within the browser and set to a width of 780 pixels (easy to change); *elastic layouts* use the EMs measurement to adapt to different text sizes and other variations in display; and *hybrid layouts* use a mix of options.

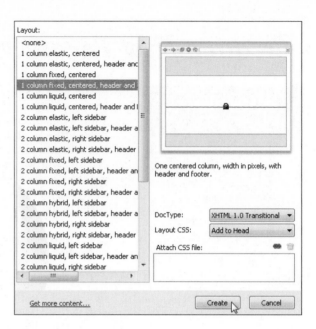

2. When HTML is selected in the New Document dialog box, a list of CSS layouts appears in the Layout Column. In the close-up view of this dialog box, shown in this figure, you can see that I selected a design that creates a one-column fixed layout with a header and footer. The rest of the options in this dialog are optional, so keep things simple and just click the Create button.

3. Get into the (excellent) habit of saving a new page as soon as it's created. Choose File⇨Save and give the file a name. Remember, don't use any spaces or special characters in the filename, and be sure to retain the `.html` extension. I named this file `index.html` because it will serve as the first page of my site. As soon as you save the file, it's also good practice to add a title right away by replacing the words *Untitled Page* with your own title at the top of the workspace, as you see in this figure.

4. Adding or editing text in a new page in Dreamweaver is relatively simple. For example, if you want to change the text at the top of the page, just select the word Header and type in the text you want to use to replace it. In this case, I entered Pamela's Pet Services. Because I selected the Header first, the font, style, and size of the text in the original layout are preserved. Replace the subheadings and main text in the page in the same way.

Inserting text from another program

Dreamweaver gives you many options for maintaining formatting when you copy and paste text from another program. You can change the default method for how Dreamweaver handles formatting when you choose Edit⇨Paste and alter the preferences in the Copy/Paste category. And, you can choose Edit⇨Paste Special to make all options available each time you paste new content. Here are your six options:

✔ **Text Only:** Dreamweaver strips any formatting and inserts plain text.

✔ **Text with Structure:** Dreamweaver includes paragraphs, lists, tables, and other structural formatting options.

✔ **Text with Structure Plus Basic Formatting:** Dreamweaver includes structural formatting as well as basic formatting, such as bold and italic.

✔ **Text with Structure Plus Full Formatting:** In addition to the previous options, Dreamweaver includes formatting created by style sheets in programs such as Microsoft Word.

✔ **Retain Line Breaks:** Selecting this check box ensures that line breaks are preserved, even if you don't keep other formatting options.

✔ **Clean Up Word Paragraph Spacing:** This option is designed to address a common problem in the way Microsoft Word paragraph spacing is converted when content is pasted into an HTML file.

5. All Dreamweaver layouts include a collection of corresponding styles. As a result, to edit many of the elements, such as the background color of the header area, you must edit the corresponding style. First, open the CSS Styles panel (if it's not already open) by choosing Window⇨CSS Styles, and then click the plus (+) sign next to `<style>` (or whatever the external style sheet is named) to open it. Dreamweaver displays all styles that correspond to the style sheet associated with this page. (*Tip:* Make sure that the All button is selected at the top of the CSS Styles panel to display all styles.)

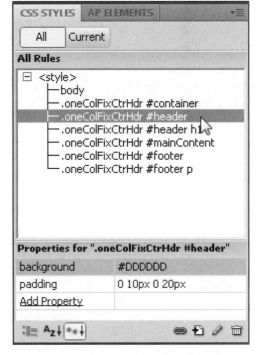

6. To change the color or other style options for the header, double-click the style named .oneColFixCtrHdr #header to open it in the CSS Rule Definition dialog box. Click to select the Background category, and use the color palette to change the background color. Choose the Type category to access font, size, and other text options. Click Apply to see how the settings look, and then click OK to save them and close the dialog box.

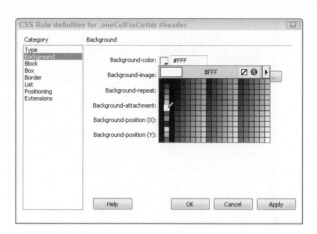

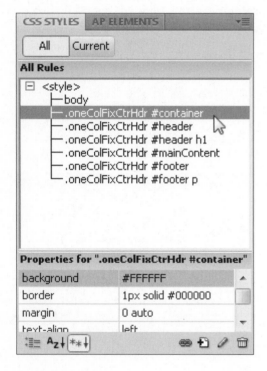

7. To change the width of the one-column layout, you need to edit the Div tag that surrounds all the content on the page. By following the common practice of using Div tags to "contain" elements on a page and styles, to describe how they should be displayed, Dreamweaver includes a Div identified as container in every layout. The container controls the overall width of the design area; to change the width of your design, you need to change the corresponding style. To do so, double-click the style named .oneColFixCtrHdr #container to open it in the CSS Rule Definition dialog box. (The Div is the foundation of the box model, which I explain in Chapter 4.)

TIP

This is an advanced tip. If you don't like the compound styles used in Dreamweaver layouts, you can simplify them. Dreamweaver includes a body class for each of these layouts and includes it in the name of each style. In this case, the body class is oneColFixCtrHdr. You can remove the body class by deleting .oneColFixCtrHdr from the front of each style name, but if you do so, you must also delete it from the body tag in the HTML code. To do so, first click the Split View button at the top of the workspace to open the HTML code, and then search for the body tag and delete class="oneColFixCtrHdr". Although removing the class style is optional, it simplifies the rest of the style names by making them all shorter, which many designers find easier when working with style sheets. To save you from having to find the body tag in the HTML code, I leave the longer style names the way Dreamweaver creates them in this task.

8. In the CSS Rule Definition dialog, choose Box from the Category list (left) and then use the width field to change the width as desired. In this case, I'm changing the width from 780 pixels to 980 by replacing the number in the Width field. Limiting the width of your page to 780 pixels is good practice if you want your page to display well in an 800 x 600 resolution monitor, but most Web designers today design for a monitor resolution of 1024 x 786 and a width of 980 is well suited to that size, leaving just enough room for scrollbars and other elements of the browser that take up space on the screen. Click Apply to preview your changes, and then click OK to save your changes and close the dialog box.

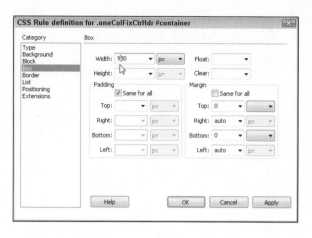

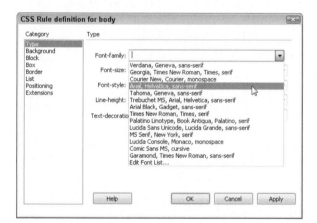

9. You can also change the font or color of any or all text on a page by changing the corresponding styles. If you aren't familiar with HTML, you may not guess that to change the font style for the entire page, you need to alter the Body style. That's because the `<body>` tag controls page-wide settings, like font face and link styles. You can use multiple fonts on a page by changing the font style for a specific section of text, but to change the default font for the entire page, double-click Body in the CSS Styles panel, choose the Type category and use the Font-family drop-down list to select a font collection.

If the body tag isn't already defined with a style, you might find it easier to use the Page Properties dialog box, described in the section, "Changing Page-Wide Settings with Page Properties," later in this chapter. For more information on font collections and using XHTML and CSS together, see Chapter 4.

Adding paragraphs and line breaks

When you create page designs for the Web, you must work within many limitations that might be confusing at first, even if they serve a purpose. How you create paragraph and line breaks is a good example.

If you're working in Design view in Dreamweaver and press Enter (Windows) or Return (Mac), Dreamweaver inserts a `<p>` (Paragraph) tag in the code, which creates a line break followed by a blank line. If you want a line break without the extra blank line, hold down the Shift key and press Enter or Return; Dreamweaver inserts the `<br />` tag into the code, to create a single line break.

If you want to add a lot of space, press Enter or Return multiple times to have Dreamweaver insert `<p> </p>`. These Open and Close paragraph tags have a nonbreaking space in the middle.

You can also add space to a page by using margins or padding settings in CSS styles. You find instructions for working with these style options in the section, "Creating New Pages in Dreamweaver," earlier in this chapter.

Note that you can add as much space as you like to HTML code without changing the page design. If you're working in Code view in Dreamweaver, you can add space within the code by pressing Enter or Return without affecting the way the page appears in a Web browser.

Inserting Images in Dreamweaver

Stuff You Need to Know

Toolbox:

- ✔ Adobe Dreamweaver CS4
- ✔ A Web site with a root folder defined in Dreamweaver
- ✔ A GIF or JPEG image (sample images are available at this book's companion Web site at www. DigitalFamily. com/diy)

Time needed:

Less than half an hour

You can add images in the JPEG, PNG, or GIF format to your pages in Dreamweaver. In Chapter 5, you discover how to optimize images for the Web. In this task, you learn how to insert image into a Web page in Dreamweaver.

1. For many designs, such as the one featured in this task for Pamela's Pet Services, you may want to use a graphic instead of text in the Header. First, simply delete the text in the Header area, and then choose Insert⇨Image to select the graphic you want to use in its place. If you insert a graphic that's not in your local root folder, Dreamweaver automatically copies it into your `images` folder. Unless you have Accessibility Attributes turned off in the Dreamweaver preferences, you're also prompted to enter alternate text. Type a description of your image in the Alternate text field in the Image Tag Accessibility Attributes dialog box. Alternatively, you can click to select any image and type a description into the Alt field in the Property Inspector.

Alternate text, which is displayed if an image isn't visible, provides a description of the image for visitors who are visually impaired and use special browsers that "read" Web pages aloud. Including key words in Alt text can also make your page more search engine friendly.

2. Although I changed the width of the layout to match the width of my banner (in the previous task), the banner didn't line up properly when I inserted it into the header. That's because the header is styled for text and includes padding to better position the text away from the sides of the layout. To make an image, such as this banner fit in the header properly, you need to remove the extra space. First, click the style named `.oneColFixCtrHdr #header` in the CSS Styles panel. Then expand the Styles panel to display the Properties for the `#header` style and delete everything in the padding field by selecting it and pressing the Delete key.

3. Even after deleting the padding, you're still likely to have extra space at the top and bottom of the banner; this space is caused by the H1 tag attributes that make the header text large and bold. If you deleted the H1 tag when you deleted the text, you won't have this problem, but it's easy to leave the H1 tag behind. Here's a good way to remove any unwanted HTML formatting. First, click to place your cursor in the Header area. (It doesn't matter whether you select the image). Then in the tag selector at the bottom of the workspace, right-click the H1 tag and choose Remove Tag.

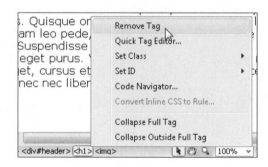

4. To insert an image in an area of the page where you have text, click to place your cursor where you want the image to appear and then choose Insert⇨Image. Find the image you want to insert on your hard drive and double-click to select it. If it's not already in your root folder, click Yes to let Dreamweaver copy it into the main folder of your site. Finally, add a text description in the Alternative text field in the Image Tag Accessibility dialog and then click OK. The image appears in the page, forcing any text down below it.

5. To align an image to the right or left and wrap the text around it, your best option is to use a CSS style. In all the templates included with this book, and in many of the CSS Layouts included with Dreamweaver, you'll find styles with the name fltrt (or float-right) for aligning images to the right, and fltlft (or float-left), for aligning images to the left. To use these styles, first click to select the image. Then, in the Property Inspector, click the Class drop-down list and choose the alignment style you want to use. In this example, I selected fltlft.

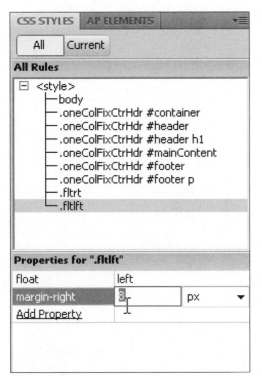

6. The alignment styles, such as float-right and float-left, include a margin setting of 8 pixels (px) to create a small margin between an image and any text that wraps around it when it's aligned to the left or right of a page. You can change the margin settings to increase or decrease this space by clicking to select the style in the CSS Styles panel, and then changing the number of pixels in the Properties pane. Alternatively, you can double-click the style name to open the CSS Rule definition dialog and change the margin settings in the Box category.

You can adjust the margins and padding around images, Div tags, and other elements to control spacing and positioning. The simplest way to understand padding and margins is to remember this statement: Padding adds space to the inside of an element, and margins add space to the outside. The same statement is true whether the element is a Div tag, an image, a table cell, or anything else. If you want more space around a photo, for example, add margin space. If you want a gap between the edge of a Div tag and its contents, add padding. Here's an advanced tip: When you add padding, you increase the overall size of the element. For example, a photo that's 200 px wide and has 10 px of padding on each side expands to fill 220 px of space in the design.

Setting Links to Other Pages in Your Site

Dreamweaver is truly a dream when it comes to setting links. The most important thing to keep in mind is that a link is essentially an address (a URL) that tells a visitor's browser which page to open when the visitor clicks the text or image containing the link.

If the page you want to link to is within your Web site, you can create a *relative* link, which includes a path describing how to get from the current page to the linked page. A relative link doesn't need to include the domain name of the site — just the instructions for a browser to move from one page within your site to another. (If you want to link to a page outside your site, see the next section, "Linking to Another Web Site.")

When you link from one page to another page in your Web site, the most important thing to remember is to save your pages in your site's root folder (as described in "Defining a Web Site in Dreamweaver," earlier in this chapter) before you start setting links. Here's how to create a link from one page to another within a Web site:

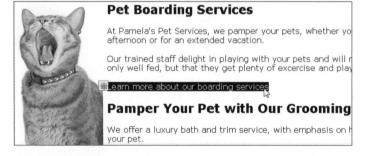

1. In Dreamweaver, open the page where you want to create a link. Select the text or image that you want to serve as the link (the text or image that a user clicks to trigger the link). Click and drag to highlight text, or click once to select an image. In this example, I select the text `Learn more about our boarding services`, and I want to link it to a page named `boarding.html` located in a folder named services. Note that all these files and folders are located inside the local root folder that I defined for this site in Dreamweaver.

2. To set the link, click the Link icon on the Common Insert panel to open the Hyperlink dialog box. (Alternatively, you can choose Insert➪Hyperlink.)

3. In the Hyperlink dialog box, click the Browse icon (the yellow file folder) to the right of the Link field. In the Select File dialog box that appears, navigate on your hard drive to the page to which you want to link your image or text. Click to select the filename of the page, and then click OK (in Windows) or Choose (on a Mac). The rest of the settings in this dialog box are optional. (See sidebar on "Targeting how links open".)

4. The link is automatically set, and the dialog box closes. If you create a link by using text, as I do in this example, the text changes to reflect the style for a link. By default, Active links appear underlined and in dark blue. To test your links, you must view the page in a Web browser. Choose File⇨Preview in Browser and then choose any browser you associated with Dreamweaver to preview the page and test the link. For more detailed instructions on previewing a page in a Web browser, see Chapter 10.

If you haven't already saved your page, a message box opens, explaining that you can create a relative link only after you save the page. Always save the page you're working on before you set links.

Targeting how links open

When you create a link in Dreamweaver, you can specify the Target options by using the Target drop-down menu in the Properties inspector, or by selecting a Target option when you set the link in the Hyperlink dialog. These are the target options and their effect:

✔ **_blank:** Opens the linked page in a new browser window.

✔ **_parent:** Opens the linked page in the parent frameset or window that contains the link.

✔ **_self:** Opens the linked page into the same frame or window as the link. This is the default, so if you don't specify a target, it should open in the same window.

✔ **_top:** Opens the linked page into a full browser window, which removes any frames if they are in use.

Linking to Another Web Site

Stuff You Need to Know

Toolbox:

- Dreamweaver CS4
- A Web site with a root folder defined in Dreamweaver
- The address of the page to which you want to link

Time needed:
Less than 15 minutes

Linking to a page on another Web site — called an *external link* — is even easier than linking to an internal link. All you need is the URL of the page to which you want to link, and you're most of the way there.

To create an external link, follow these steps:

1. In Dreamweaver, open the page from which you want to link and click to select an image, or click and drag to highlight the text that you want to act as a link. You can also click to select any image on the page to serve as the link. In this example, I selected the text `visit www.petfinder.com.`, at the bottom of the page.

2. In the Link text box in the Property Inspector, type the URL of the page you want your text or image to link to, and then press Enter (in Windows) or Return (on the Mac). You can also copy and paste a URL from the address bar in a Web browser, which is an excellent way to ensure that you don't enter the address incorrectly. You must always use the full URL, including the `http://` part, when you create an external link in HTML. Otherwise, the browser can't find the correct external site address.

3. The link is set automatically, and the text changes to indicate that it's an active link. To test a link to another Web site, you must view your page in a browser and be connected to the Internet. Choose File➪Preview in Browser and then choose any browser you've associated with Dreamweaver to preview the page and test the link. For more detailed instructions on previewing your page in a browser, see Chapter 10.

Setting a Link to an E-Mail Address

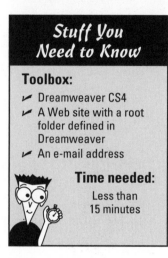

Stuff You Need to Know

Toolbox:
- ✔ Dreamweaver CS4
- ✔ A Web site with a root folder defined in Dreamweaver
- ✔ An e-mail address

Time needed:
Less than 15 minutes

Another common link option directs site visitors to an e-mail address. Visitors can send you messages easily with e-mail links. I always recommend that you invite visitors to contact you because they can point out mistakes in your site and give you valuable feedback about how you can further develop your site. Adding contact information also lends credibility to a Web site because it shows that you're accessible and open to being contacted.

Setting a link to an e-mail address is just as easy as setting a link to another Web page. All you need to know is the e-mail address you want to link to and which text or image you want to use when you set the link.

Pamper Your Pet with Our Grooming Services

We offer luxury bath, trim, and other grooming services. Keeping your pet healthy and safe is the most important part of any groomming session.

Making your pet comfortable and happy is our top priority. Dressing them in business suits is optional.

We also offer free pick up and delivery for your pet on certain days! For more information or to schedule a pickup, email us at info@pamelaspetservices.com

1. To create an e-mail link, select the text that you want to serve as the link.

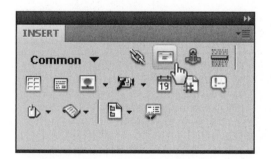

2. With the text selected, click the Email Link icon on the Common Insert panel. Alternatively, you can choose Insert➪Email Link.

When visitors to your Web site click an e-mail link, the visitor's computer system automatically launches the default e-mail program and creates a blank e-mail message to the specified e-mail address. This is a cool trick, but it can be disconcerting to users who don't expect it to happen, and it doesn't work if they don't have an e-mail program on their computer. That's why I always try to let users know when I use an e-mail link. For example, rather than just link the words *Contact Janine,* I link the words *Email Janine.* Even better, I often link the actual e-mail address.

3. In the Email Link dialog box that opens, enter the e-mail address in the E-Mail field and click OK. The dialog box closes and the text automatically changes to the style for an active link.

4. The Email Link dialog box works only with text. If you want to use an image as an e-mail link, you must select the image and then enter the e-mail address, preceded by `mailto:` in the Link field in the Property Inspector. In this example, the image is selected, and the e-mail link has been created by entering **mailto:info@pamelaspetservices.com**.

When you create an e-mail link on a Web page to be displayed on the public Internet, you open yourself to spammers, some of whom use automated programs to "lift" e-mail addresses off Web pages. That's why many sites don't include e-mail links, but instead use text such as "Send e-mail to Janine at jcwarner dot-com." You can also use a form to get around this potential problem. By setting up a form with a script that delivers the form's contents to an e-mail address, you can shield your e-mail address from spammers while still making it easy for visitors to your site to send comments. A relatively new alternative is offered by the Web site AddressMunger.com, which you can use to create a special script that shields your e-mail address from spammers. You can find more information in Chapter 15 about AddressMunger.com and other services that you can use to enhance your Web site.

Changing Page-Wide Settings with Page Properties

Stuff You Need to Know

Toolbox:
- Dreamweaver CS4
- A Web site with a root folder defined in Dreamweaver

Time needed:
Less than half an hour

You can change many individual elements on a page in the Property Inspector, but if you want to make changes that affect the entire page, such as changing the background color of the entire page or changing the way links and text are formatted, you can use the Page Properties dialog box. Although you can apply global settings, such as text size and color, in the Page Properties dialog box, you can override those settings with other formatting options in specific instances. For example, you can set all text to the Helvetica font in the page properties and then change the font for an individual headline to Verdana via the Font field in the Property Inspector. To change the font settings, background and text colors, and link colors for an entire page, follow these steps:

1. Choose Modify➪Page Properties or click the Page Properties button in the Property Inspector to open the Page Properties dialog box. Select the Appearance (CSS) category, click the Page Font drop-down list, and choose the font collection you want to serve as the main font for the text on your page. (See the earlier sidebar "Why so many fonts?" in Chapter 4.)

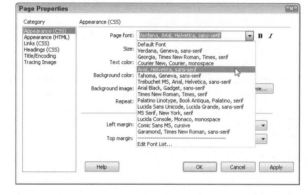

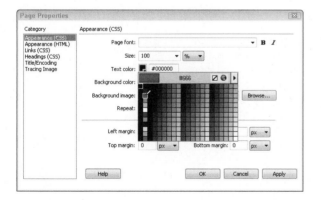

2. In the Size drop-down list, specify the font size you want for the text on your page. (In this example, I selected 100%, but you can choose from a variety of size settings.) Click the Text Color swatch box to reveal the color palette. Choose any color you want for the text color on the page. The color you select fills the color swatch box but doesn't change the text color on the page until you click Apply or OK.

TIP

When you change the background, text, or link colors, make sure that the colors look good together and that your text is still readable. As a general rule, go for high contrast pairings: light text is best displayed on a dark background, and dark text is best displayed on a light background.

3. Click the Background Color swatch box and choose a color if you want to fill the background of the page with a solid color. If you want to insert a graphic into the background of your page, as I did here, click the Browse button next to the Background Image box, and in the Select Image Source dialog box that appears, select an image and click OK to return to the Page Properties dialog box. When you insert a background image, it automatically repeats (or *tiles*) across and down the page unless you choose the no-repeat option from the Repeat drop-down list or use CSS to further define the display.

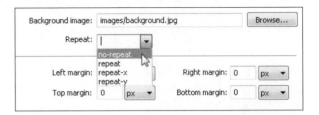

4. Use the margin options at the bottom of the dialog box to change the left, right, top, or bottom margins of your page. Entering **0** in all four fields removes the default margin settings, which automatically add margin space at the top and left side of a Web page, enabling you to create designs whose edges begin flush with the edge of a browser. Most professional designers prefer to set the margins to 0 and then use other CSS settings to control the positioning of the design within a browser window.

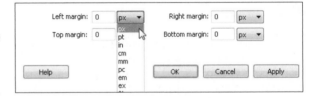

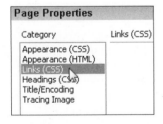

5. To alter the display of links on a page, first select the Links (CSS) category from the left side of the Page Properties dialog box. Specify the font face and size you want for the links on your page. If you don't specify a font, links appear in the same font and size that are specified for the text in your document.

Although you can vary the link styles to suit the design of your site, it's good practice to use the same link styles throughout your site so that your visitors can easily identify links.

6. To the right of the Link Font drop-down list, click the **B** or *I* icon if you want all links on your page to appear in bold or italic, respectively. Specify a color for any link option (or all link options) by clicking the color palette and selecting a color for each of the link states separately. The color you select is applied to links on your page based on the link state. All four link states can be displayed in the same or different colors:

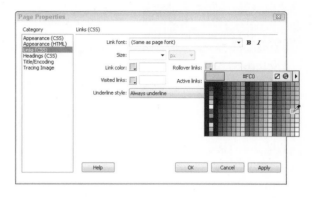

- *Link Color:* This option controls the color in which a link appears when it's first displayed on a page.

- *Visited Links:* This option controls the color of links that a visitor has already clicked, or visited.

- *Rollover Links:* A link changes to this color when a user rolls the cursor over the link (also known as *hovering*).

- *Active Links:* A link changes to this color briefly while a user is actively clicking it.

7. In the Underline Style drop-down list, specify whether you want links underlined. By default, all links on a Web page appear underlined in a browser, but many designers find the underline distracting and prefer to turn it off by selecting Never Underline. You can also choose Show Underline Only on Rollover to make the underline appear when a user moves a cursor over a link. Hide Underline on Rollover causes the underline to disappear when a user moves a cursor over a link.

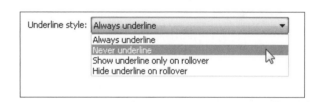

8. As you alter the different settings, you can click the Apply button to see how the changes appear on your page. After you specify all the settings, click OK to finish and close the Page Properties dialog box.

Defining New Styles in Dreamweaver

Stuff You Need to Know

Toolbox:
- Adobe Dreamweaver CS4
- A page or Web site you where you want to add a new style

Time needed:
About 15 minutes

Whether you create a new, blank page in Dreamweaver or start with one of the Dreamweaver CSS layouts, as described in an earlier task in this chapter, you can create your own styles to format text, images, and other elements in your pages.

As you move through the steps to create a new style in Dreamweaver, you might be surprised by the number of options in the numerous panels and dialog boxes available for creating CSS. As you explore the possibilities, remember that you can leave attributes unspecified if you don't want to use them and that you can always go back and edit styles after you create them.

To define a new style, either create a new document or open an existing Web page in Dreamweaver and follow these steps:

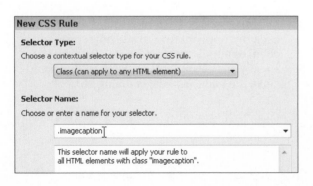

1. Choose Format⇨CSS Styles⇨New.

2. In the New CSS Rule dialog box, choose the type of CSS selector you want to create from the Selector Type drop-down menu. (If you need a refresher on the four selector options and choosing selector types, see Chapter 4.) In this example, I'm creating a class style that I will use to format the captions for my images. In the Selector Name field, type a name. Because class styles must begin with a period (.), I named this style `.imagecaption`.

3. In the Rule Definition area at the bottom of the New CSS Rule dialog box, select where you want to define your new style. Choose This Document Only from the drop-down menu to create an internal style sheet. In this example, I'm adding my new style to an external style sheet that's already attached to my page (`design.css`). To create an external style sheet, click to select the name of the style sheet, or choose New Style Sheet File to create a new style sheet file as you create the style. If you choose to create a new style sheet, enter a name in the Save Style Sheet File As dialog box and then click Save to continue. Usually, you want to add a style to an external style sheet; see Chapter 4 for details about internal versus external style sheets.

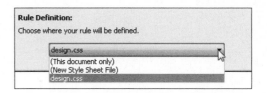

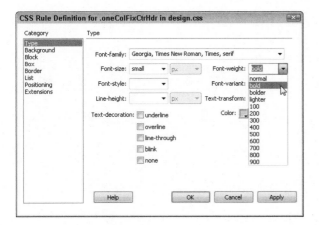

4. In the CSS Rule Definition dialog box, choose a category on the left. For this example, I chose the Type category to specify font options for this style because I want the font to be different from the main page font. As you can see in this figure, I chose the Georgia, Times New Roman, Times, serif font collection; set the Font size to Small; and set the Font weight to Bold. (See Chapter 4 for more information about font collections.) Click OK to save the style and close the dialog box.

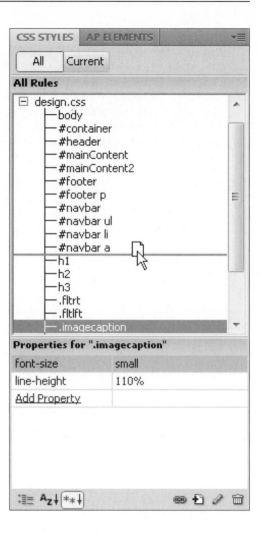

5. The new style appears at the bottom of the CSS Styles panel. You can change the order of styles by clicking to select a style name and dragging it to another position in the panel.

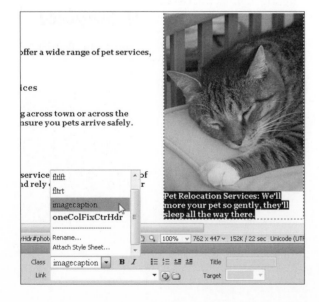

6. To apply a new class style, like the one I created in this task, select a section of text in a Web page and then use the Class drop-down list to select and apply the style. For more information on how to apply other kinds of styles, see Chapter 4.

Creating and Using Templates

After all the time you spend creating a page design in Dreamweaver, you might be pleased to know about templates. When you save a file as a Dreamweaver Web Template, it becomes available from the New File dialog box, which makes it easy to use to create new pages quickly. But the greatest time-saving benefit of Dreamweaver's Web Templates becomes evident when you want to make changes to a design after you use it to create numerous pages because you can use templates to make global updates across many pages at once.

Most of the templates included with this book use the Dreamweaver Web Template features. Reading through this task not only shows you how to create your own templates but also helps you better understand how to use and edit the templates that you can download to use with this book. To find the templates, just go to www.DigitalFamily.com/diy.

In this task, you learn how to save any page as a template, use the template to create new pages, and then edit the template to make global updates to those pages.

1. To create a new template, choose File⇨New. In the New Document dialog box that appears, choose Blank Template and then choose the Type and Layout just as you would to create a new page. (See the "Creating New Pages in Dreamweaver" task earlier in this chapter.) You also can turn any existing page in Dreamweaver into a template by using the Save As Template option. In this task, I build on a page from an earlier task by turning it into a template. To do so, open any Web page in Dreamweaver and choose File⇨Save As Template.

2. In the Save As Template dialog box, make sure that the site you're working on is displayed in the Site field. (This should happen automatically if you completed the site definition process; if you haven't, make sure to do so by following the steps in the first task in this chapter.) You can name the template anything you like *as long as you don't use spaces or punctuation*. When you're prompted by the Update Links dialog box, choose Yes to preserve any links to pages or images in the file.

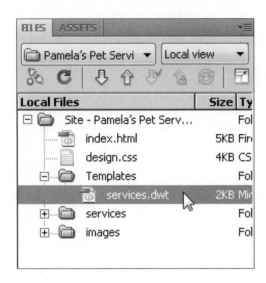

3. When you create a Web Template, Dreamweaver automatically adds the .dwt extension. In this case, my file is named services.dwt. As you can see in the Files panel shown in this figure, Dreamweaver automatically stores the new template in a folder named Templates. If you don't already have a Templates folder in your local root folder, Dreamweaver creates one for you when you save your first template. If Dreamweaver prompts you to update links as you save the page as a template, click Yes.

Although the Dreamweaver layouts are designed to display CSS and other formatting options according to contemporary standards, not all Web browsers support CSS the same way, so it's always wise to test your designs in a variety of Web browsers before you publish them. And here's a tip: Internet Explorer and Safari do not display Dreamweaver Web Templates, but Firefox does. Thus, if you're working on a template and want to preview your work as you go along, choose File➪Preview in Browser and then choose Firefox from the list of browsers. (You find more detailed instructions in Chapter 10 for previewing your pages in multiple Web browsers and for adding new browsers to the preview list in Dreamweaver.)

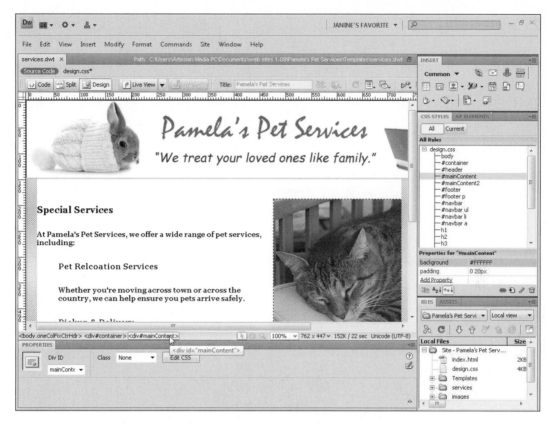

4. Before you use your template to create new pages, you need to create *editable* regions in the template: areas of the template that can be edited in new pages created from the template. You create editable regions where you want to be able to add unique content to a new page created from the template, such as the photos and stories you will want to use in the main part of each page. To create an editable region, first select a container, such as the `mainContent div`, that contains the text and image in the middle of this page. To select the `mainContent div`, I place my cursor in the content and then clicked the `mainContent` tag in the tag selector at the bottom of the page.

Any area that's not an editable region can only be edited in the template itself, and any edits you make to a part of the page that isn't designated as editable will automatically be updated on all the pages created from the page. For example, I wouldn't make the banner at the top of this page an editable region because I want to use the same banner at the top of every page in this site.

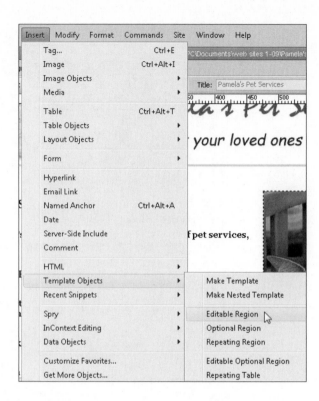

5. With a container selected, such as the `mainContent div`, choose Insert⇨Template Objects⇨Editable Region.

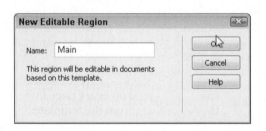

6. In the New Editable Region dialog box that opens, give the region a name (no spaces or special characters!), and then click OK. I enter the name Main in this example. If you don't have visual aids turned off, Dreamweaver will distinguish the editable region by surrounding it with a blue line and including a small tab at the top with the name you gave the region. Repeat Steps 4, 5, and 6, selecting different containers in turn to create additional editable regions.

7. After you define all editable regions, choose File⇨Save to save the template. When you're ready to create a new page from the template, choose File⇨New, just as you would do to create any new page in Dreamweaver. In the New Document dialog box, choose Page from Template from the left-hand column, choose the site you're working on from the middle column, and then choose the template you want from the right column. Notice that Dreamweaver includes a preview of the template at the far right side of the dialog box.

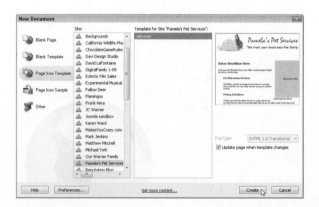

8. Always save a new page before you start editing it by choosing File⇨Save, just as you would save any other new file in Dreamweaver. You can then edit any of the editable regions in a page created from a template, adding images and text to the editable regions, such as this cat photo and text. Remember, however, that you can't alter any of the areas that aren't editable, such as the banner image at the top of the page, which can only be changed in the template.

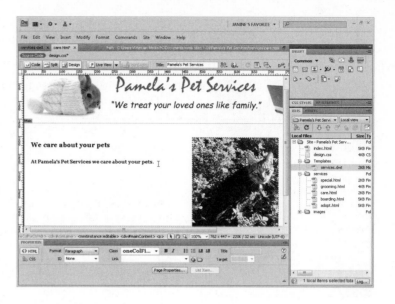

9. At any time, you can go back to the template to make changes to any area of the template that isn't an editable region, and those changes will automatically be applied to any pages created from the template. In this example, I included copyright information in the footer of the page. Because it's not an editable region, I can now change the year from 2009 to 2010, and the footer will automatically be updated on every page in the site created from the template.

10. To save your changes and update any pages created from the template at the same time, choose File⇨Save. In the Update Template Files dialog box, click Update. Dreamweaver lists all pages created from the template in this dialog box so that you can see exactly which pages will change. If you don't want to apply the changes to your pages, choose Don't Update. All new pages created from the template will include the changes you made.

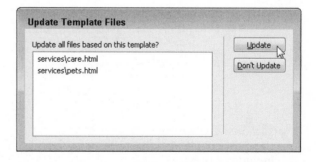

Adding Meta Tags for Search Engines

If you've heard of meta tags, you probably correctly associate them with search engines. Although meta tags are used for a variety of purposes, the most common is to provide special text that doesn't appear in the body of your page but is read by crawlers, bots, and other programs that scour the Web, reading the code behind Web pages and cataloging and ranking those pages for Bing, Google, and a long list of other search-related sites.

Some search engines read meta tags for keywords and descriptions. The keyword meta tag enables site designers to specify a list of keywords that match the content on their Web sites when someone types the same keywords into a search engine. The meta description tag is designed to let you include a written description of your Web site, and search engines often display its content as the brief description that appears in search results pages, so including a meta description in all your pages is definitely worthwhile. Follow these steps to fill in the meta description tag:

1. Open the page where you want to add a meta description. You can use meta descriptions on any page, or all pages, on your Web site. Choose Insert⇨HTML⇨Head Tags⇨Description. In the Description text box, enter the text you want for your page description. (Don't add any HTML code in this box). When you click OK, the meta description is automatically added to the HTML code behind the page.

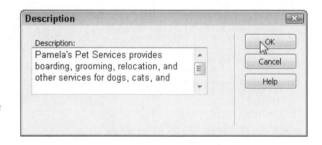

2. To view or edit the Meta description after you create it, choose either the Split or Code view option by clicking the corresponding button at the top of the workspace. In this example, I selected Split so that both Code view and Design view are visible. To edit the meta description, locate it in the HTML code, and then you can delete, change, or add text as you would in Design view. The description text you enter is inserted into the Head area at the top of the page in the HTML code. Meta content doesn't appear in the body of the page.

If you want to add keywords, repeat Steps 1 and 2 and choose Insert⇨HTML⇨Head Tags⇨Keywords in Step 1.

Inserting Code into a Web Page in Dreamweaver

Stuff You Need to Know

Toolbox:

- Adobe Dreamweaver CS4
- A Web browser, such as Internet Explorer or Firefox
- A snippet of code from a site like Google
- A Web page where you want to add the code

Time needed:
About half an hour

Many of the services featured in this book, including Google AdSense, PayPal Buttons, and Google Analytics, require that you add a snippet of HTML code or JavaScript to your Web pages.

In many cases, you need to add the same code to one or more pages in a site. In the example featured in this task, I'm adding the code needed for Google Analytics, which measures traffic to a Web site and needs to be included at the bottom of every page on a site. In this case, the most efficient way to add the code is to insert it into the template page. Adding code to a template will add the code to every page created from the template simultaneously.

When you open Dreamweaver to add your code, leave your Web browser open so that it displays the page where you copied the code, in case you want to make changes or need to copy the code again. You can easily switch between two programs on your computer by pressing Alt+Tab (Windows) or ⌘+Tab (Mac).

1. The easiest way to add code to a page in Dreamweaver is click the Split View button in the upper-left corner of the workspace to display the code behind the page in the top part of the workspace. The advantage of using Split view is that you can see Design and Code views at the same time. *Here's a tip:* When you're working on code that adds a visible element to your page, click any element in Design view, such as the Copyright information in the footer at the bottom of this page, and Dreamweaver automatically highlights the corresponding code so that you can find your place more easily.

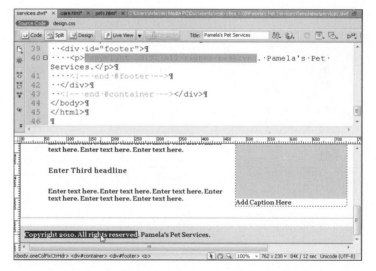

One of the most confusing aspects of adding code to your site is that sometimes you see it in the design and other times you don't. For example, when you add Google Analytics code to a page in Dreamweaver, no visible change takes place on the page in Design view because the analytics code is only used to measure traffic to the page with nothing visible to your visitors. However, some kinds of code, such as Google AdSense which displays ads in a Web page, can be viewed, but only when you preview a page in a Web browser. Another point that trips up new Web designers is that, for the code to take effect, you'll need to upload the page to a Web server so that Google can find the AdSense code and begin tracking your traffic. You find instructions for publishing your pages in Dreamweaver and more about how to use Google Analytics in Chapter 10.

```
84    ··¶
85  ⊟ <script ·type="text/javascript">¶
86    var ·gaJsHost ·= ·(("https:" ·== ·document.location.protocol) ·? ·
      "https://ssl." ·: ·"http://www.");¶
87    document.write(unescape("%3Cscript ·src='" ·+ ·gaJsHost ·+ ·
      "google-analytics.com/ga.js' ·
      type='text/javascript'%3E%3C/script%3E"));¶
88    </script>¶
89    <script ·type="text/javascript">¶
90    try ·{¶
91    var ·pageTracker ·= ·_gat._getTracker("UA-10602150-1");¶
92    pageTracker._trackPageview();¶
93  ⊟ } ·catch(err) ·{}</script>¶
94    </body>¶
95    </html>¶
96    ¶
```

2. Find the exact place where you want to add the code. Google Analytics should be added just above the `</body>` tag at the very end of a page. Click to place the cursor in the code; then choose Edit➪Paste to insert the code you copied from a Web site (like Google Analytics) into your page. Notice that the Google code is surrounded by `<script>` and `</script>` tags. If you ever want to delete or replace this code, make sure when you select the code that you include everything between and including the `<script>` tags.

The code you copy from a site like Google may include a script or other code that isn't in basic HTML. This issue shouldn't matter as long as you copy the code exactly as Google (or any other Web site) instructs you to and you paste all the code into the HTML in your Web page. For example, if the code begins with a `<script>` tag, it should include a closing `</script>` tag.

Chapter 7

Creating a Profile or Portfolio Site

Introduce yourself to the world with a profile or portfolio site. A Web site about yourself is a powerful tool that can help you land your dream job, attract high-profile clients, or even reconnect with long-lost friends and family.

Perhaps the biggest challenge to creating a profile or portfolio site is determining the best way to summarize your life experience, talents, and body of work:

✔ If you're an artist, you can photograph your paintings or sculptures to create a visual portfolio of your work to display online.

✔ If you're a consultant, you can develop a collection of case studies describing your success with previous clients or featuring your best designs.

✔ If you're a writer, you can include a collection of published articles or showcase writing that hasn't been published anywhere else — after all, a Web site enables you to become your own publisher.

No matter what you do, you probably want to create a biography about yourself. Whether your bio is serious or silly, trying to sum up your own life in a few paragraphs is likely to be one of the most challenging things you will ever write (which is why I include a few tips for writing a great biography in the sidebar "Telling your own tale.")

In this chapter, you also discover the basics of bringing your ideas to life on the Web. Working in Photoshop and Dreamweaver, you can transform the templates featured in this chapter into a Web site that best showcases your work. If you start working in this chapter and realize you still have a lot of work ahead of you to gather all the images, text, and other elements you need for your site, consider jumping to Chapter 2 and using the content check list and other resources to help you with the planning process.

Starting with Profile or Portfolio Templates

The instructions in this chapter are designed to be used with the templates and images provided on the Web site for this book (www.DigitalFamily.com/diy). You can choose a profile template or a portfolio template, depending on the type of site you want to create. To download a template, just check the Web site for this chapter number and template name listed in the Toolbox and then follow the simple instructions on the site to download the files. The step-by-step instructions in this chapter explain how to edit the template images as well as change colors, fonts, and other style options in the Web page templates.

If you're new to working with Dreamweaver, you might want to first read Chapter 6 to become familiar with the basics of working with Dreamweaver before you dive into creating a site with a template. If you know a little bit about Web design and you're ready to customize one of the templates featured in this chapter, you find everything you need in the following pages.

Introducing the profile template

If you want to showcase your personal or professional experience, the profile template is designed to make it easy to create a simple Web site that features your biography and samples of your work or hobbies in one quick and easy-to-design Web page. The first task in this chapter is the simplest of the template designs in this book. However, you can still alter the design as much or as little as you like, and you can always add more pages.

If you want to create a profile site with multiple pages, you can save copies of the page design and create links to as many pages as you need. If you know that you want to create a site with multiple sections, you may want to use the portfolio site template featured in the second half of this chapter because it's already set up for a multiple page design, with a portfolio section that already includes a collection of linked pages. (See the next section for an introduction to the portfolio template.)

These are the templates and the main pages you get when you download the Profile template folder from www.DigitalFamily.com/diy:

- ✔ index.html is for the main Web page.
- ✔ banner-graphic.jpg is for the graphic banner that appears at the top of the page.

Figure 7-1 shows an example of a design created using the first template featured in this chapter. In the section "Designing a Winning Online Profile," you find instructions for customizing the profile template text, banners, and other features. The site shown on the right, the freelance writer profile featured in this chapter, is an example of how you can customize the profile template.

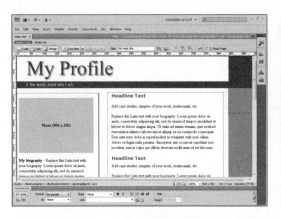

Figure 7-1: You can create your own personalized version of the profile site by altering the colors, headlines, and text in this template.

Creating a multipage portfolio site

If you're an artist, a photographer, a graphic designer, or another creative professional, the portfolio site is for you! This template is designed to showcase a portfolio with an image gallery, and thus includes six main pages: one for the front page (shown in Figure 7-2), a second for an About page (which can also be used for a biography), and finally, four pages (one each) for the four galleries. The links among the main pages have already been created in the template files, making it easy to develop your own multipage site, like the one shown in the Figure 7-2.

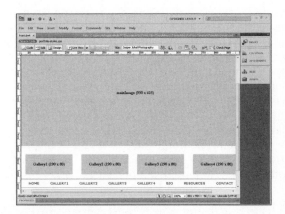

Figure 7-2: The Portfolio template is designed to showcase multiple image galleries, such as the collections of photographs in this example.

If you're a photographer with hundreds or thousands of photos that you want to share online, you might be better served by one of the many photo-sharing sites on the Web (such as Flickr) or a professional photography site (such as Advanced Photo Websites at www.ifp3.com). You find a list of photo sites in the nearby sidebar, "Many ways to share your photos."

Because the portfolio site is more complex than the profile site featured in the first part of this chapter, you find three separate tasks designed to help you fully customize this site:

- ✔ The first task, in the section "Customizing Banner Graphics," shows you how to edit the *banner graphic* (the image that appears at the top of this page design) using Photoshop Elements. However, you can edit the graphics included with the template files in any image editor that supports Layers, including Adobe Photoshop. (**Note:** If you prefer to use text for the banner, you can simply delete the placeholder graphic at the top of the page and enter text in its place.)

- ✔ The second task, in the section "Customizing the Portfolio Home Page," shows you how to use Dreamweaver to replace the text and images in these templates and how to make basic color and style changes.

- ✔ The third task, in the section "Creating and Linking Pages using the Gallery Templates," covers how to create new pages from Dynamic Web Templates in Dreamweaver, set links to new pages, and use these templates to make global changes across the pages you create.

To help you get started and to make it easy for you to build a complete site quickly, I created five template pages for your portfolio site — one for each of the gallery pages and another for the front and about page designs. You can use these templates to generate as many pages as you like for the site. Because these templates use Dreamweaver's Dynamic Web Template features, however, you will find restrictions on what can be altered in pages generated from the templates because some areas of the templates are locked, a feature that makes it possible to make global changes across all pages created from a template. You find detailed instructions on how to work with templates and locked regions in the tasks that follow.

To help you get started with this site and to ensure that the links on the navigation bars work properly, I created pages for each of the main sections from the templates. You can easily add or delete pages, change the number of galleries, and adjust the design to accommodate images of many different sizes.

These are the templates and the main pages you find in the site when you first download the template folder from `www.DigitalFamily.com/diy`:

- ✔ `index.html` is the home page of the site, which was not created with a template because it is a unique design. The home page is set up to display a banner image at the top of the page, a large main image in the middle, and four smaller images along the bottom, each linking to a different gallery.

- ✔ `about.html` is designed for a biography or other general information, but you can use it (or save copies of it) to create any page with images and text. It was created from the `main.dwt` template.

- ✔ `photo1.html` in the gallery1 folder is for the first page of the first gallery of the site and was created from the `gallery1.dwt` template. It's set up to display a banner at the top of the page, a large main image, and eight smaller images along the bottom.

- ✔ `photo1.html` in the gallery2 folder is for the first page of the second gallery of the site and was created from the `gallery2.dwt` template. It's set up like the first, but saved as a separate file so that you can alter each gallery independently.

✔ `photo1.html` in the gallery3 folder is for the first page of the third gallery of the site and was created from the `gallery3.dwt` template. Again set up like the first, but saved as a separate file so that you can alter it independently.

✔ `photo1.html` in the gallery4 folder is for the first page of the fourth gallery of the site and was created from the `gallery4.dwt` template. Again set up like the first, but saved as a separate file so that you can alter it independently.

Naming your files so that they correspond to their contents, as I have here, makes it easier to identify the pages later when you want to edit them.

Many ways to share your photos

You can find many excellent photo-sharing Web sites on the Internet, including the ones highlighted in this list:

Flickr: Flickr (`www.flickr.com`) is one the most sophisticated online photo sites, offering a wide range of services, including the ability to manage lots and lots of pictures in multiple personal albums. You also get more advanced options for adding captions and other text to your online album.

If you blog, you might appreciate the Flickr features that make it easy to add photos to a blog or online journal. You can even search through photos from other Flickr users and add their photos to your albums. (Sharing is optional: You can keep your albums private or make any or all of your images viewable by anyone who uses the site.)

Photobucket: You can manage large numbers of photos at Photobucket (`www.photobucket.com`) and also upload and share video. One feature that makes this site extremely popular is the ease with which you can add photos and videos that are hosted at Photobucket to your blog or your profile on sites like MySpace and Facebook.

Kodak EasyShare Gallery: The Kodak Gallery site (`www.kodakgallery.com`) is easy to use. You can upload photos you take using any digital camera, phone, or film; share your photos with friends, family, or whomever; and print your favorite pictures and shop for photo keepsakes and gifts, such as magnets, mugs, and coasters. Folks who look at your photos can sign a guestbook so that you know they've been there.

Apple MobileMe: If you use an Apple Macintosh computer, you won't find an easier way to share photos than iPhoto and MobileMe (`www.apple.com/mobileme`). With iPhoto, you can create photocasts to share any photo album with friends and family. When you use this free service, your photos are automatically uploaded to MobileMe, and your friends and family receive an e-mail message with a special link. When they click the link, they automatically receive your photocast. Best of all, when you update your photos, your friends and family receive updates automatically.

Shutterfly: Similar to Kodak EasyShare Gallery, Shutterfly (`www.shutterfly.com`) makes it easy to post and share photos for free, offers simple photo-editing tools, and sells printing services that you can use to create a variety of gift items and prints, including poster-size enlargements. Shutterfly has an intuitive interface, and you can use its specialized printing options to turn your pictures into greeting cards, bound photo albums, personalized calendars, coffee mugs, T-shirts, and tote bags that you can send to your friends and family.

IFP3 Advanced Photo Websites: If you're a professional photographer and want to create a Web site where you can sell photos online, consider a site like `www.ifp3.com`, designed to make it easy to upload and display photos as well as manage online sales.

Customizing Banner Graphics

You can edit the banner graphics used at both the top of the portfolio and profile templates by following the steps in this task. Change the colors and add your own text and images to make these banner graphics work best for your Web site. You can edit these graphics in any image editor that supports Layers, including Adobe Photoshop and Photoshop Elements, which is used in this task. The process is nearly the same with either program in all the most recent versions. The profile banner graphic, like all the other template images featured in this book, is designed with Layers to make it easy for you to customize the images, as you do in this task:

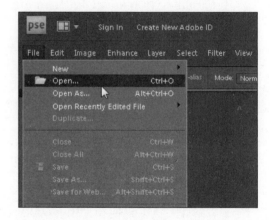

1. Launch a graphics program, such as Photoshop Elements (shown here), and choose File⇨Open to open one of the template banners.

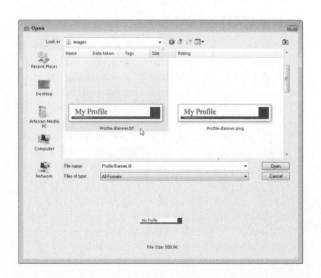

2. In this example, I'm opening the Profile-Banner.tif template image file. (You find this file in the images folder inside the Profile template folder that you download from the www.DigitalFamily.com/diy Web site.)

3. Open the Layers palette by choosing Window⇨Layers. The Layers palette displays the five layers in this banner image: one for the background, one for the text `Profile Name`, one for the smaller text that appears below the name, as well as layers that contain the colored bar and the bottom of the banner and the colored box that appears at the right. Because each section of text is on a separate layer, you can edit the text separately. For example, you can change the color of the words `Profile Name` without changing the color of the other text or affecting the background color.

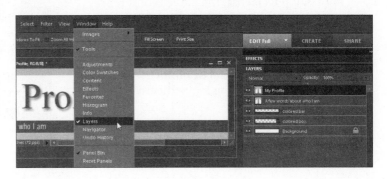

4. To edit the text in any image in Photoshop or Photoshop Elements, first select the Type tool in the Toolbox.

5. With the Type tool active, click and drag to select a section of text and then type to replace the words. Adjust the Type tool settings on the Options bar at the top of the work area to change the color, font face, size, or other options. In this figure, I'm adjusting the font for the selected text, which I changed to read `Jenny Hontz`. If you don't have the font I used in this template, Photoshop may give you a warning that the font is missing, but it's easy to fix. Just select any font available on your computer.

6. To reposition the text on the banner, click to select the Move tool from the Toolbox. (In Photoshop Elements, the Move tool is represented by the double-headed, crossed-arrow icon at the top of the Toolbox.) Then click and drag a section of text to adjust it. Note that if you click and drag a corner, you change the size of the text; if you click in the middle of a text area and drag, you move the text.

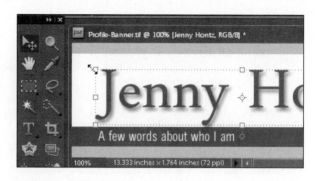

7. If you have trouble selecting text in the image, you can click to select its layer in the Layers panel to make it active in the workspace.

8. To change the background color of this image, first click to select the Move tool from the Toolbox, and then click in the Layers palette on the right side of the screen to select the Background layer. Choose Edit➪Fill to open the Fill Layer dialog box, choose Color from the Use drop-down list, and then select a new background color. To change the color of a section of an image, such as the blue bar at the bottom of this template image, first click the layer to make it active in the Layers panel. Then click to select the Marquee selection tool and use it to click and drag, selecting just the area you want to change before choosing Edit➪Fill and selecting a color.

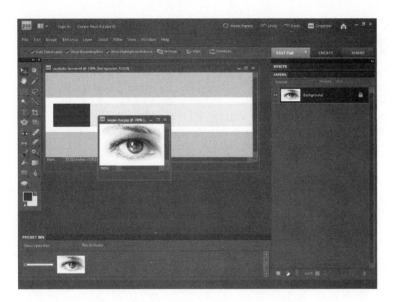

9. Each of the templates includes its own banner image, but you can mix and match them and you can add your own photos to any of them like this: First open both the photograph you want to add and the banner image from the template folder (here you see the Portfolio banner from the Portfolio template). You can open as many images at once as your computer's memory will allow by choosing File⇨Open and selecting each image in turn from your hard drive.

10. Make sure the photo you want to add to your banner is the active image in the workspace; choose Select⇨All to select the image, and choose Edit⇨Copy to copy it. Then click anywhere on the banner image to make it the active image in the workspace; if an image isn't visible in the workspace, you can make it active by clicking its thumbnail in the Project Bin at the bottom of the workspace or by choosing Window and then selecting the name of any open image listed at the bottom of the menu. With the image you want to add the photo to active, choose Edit⇨Paste to insert the photo. The photo appears on a new layer. Select the layer, and click and drag to adjust the photograph's placement on the banner.

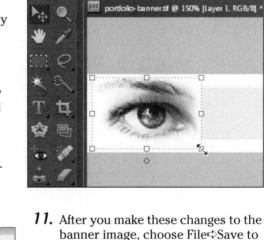

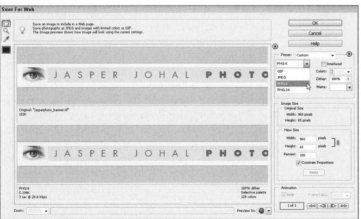

11. After you make these changes to the banner image, choose File⇨Save to save it before saving a copy that is optimized for the Web. To prepare any image for your Web pages, choose File⇨Save for Web. In the Save for Web dialog box, choose JPEG or PNG-8 from the Optimized File Format drop-down list in the upper-right corner. The JPEG format is best for images that use millions of colors, such as photographs. If this banner had a solid background and only a few colors like this one, the GIF or PNG formats are better options. (You find details about the settings in the Save for Web dialog box in Chapter 5.)

Designing a Winning Online Profile

When you have your images and content ready to go, you're ready to download the profile template from the www.DigitalFamily.com/ diy Web site and get started. If you need help writing your own biography, check out the nearby sidebar, "Telling your own tale." Follow these steps to customize the template for your profile:

1. In Dreamweaver, choose Site⇨New Site. In the Site Definition dialog box that appears, click the Advanced tab. In the Site Name text box, type a name for your site. In this example I'm creating for my journalist friend, Jenny, I entered **Jenny Hontz Web Site**. (For more detailed instructions on the site set-up process, see Chapter 6.)

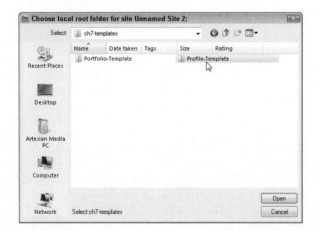

2. Click the Browse icon next to the Local Root Folder field. In the Choose Local Root Folder dialog box that appears, locate the folder on your hard drive that contains the profile template you downloaded from www.Digital Family.com/diy. (*Note:* The folder is named Profile-Template, but you can rename it, if you like.) Click Open and then click Select to select the folder and return to the Site Definition dialog box. Then click the Browse icon next to the Default Images Folder field and select the Images folder inside the profile template folder. Leave the rest of the options in this dialog box alone for now, and then click OK to close the Site Definition dialog box and save your settings. If you haven't selected the Enable Cache check box, a message box appears, asking whether you want to create a cache for the site. Click Yes to speed up some of the Dreamweaver display features.

Telling your own tale

Writing your own biography may seem like an easy task. After all, you're arguably the best expert in the world on the topic of you. But if you sit down to write your own story and find that the words don't come easily, rest assured that you're not alone. Summing up your life in a few words or paragraphs can make the most experienced writers want to procrastinate with a run to the fridge for a little snack or the inexplicable impulse to organize a desk or closet.

To help you get started, here are a few suggestions for writing your own biography:

✔ Brainstorm a list of all accomplishments or key points that you want to include without worrying about writing them well or putting them in order. Then check each one off the list as you work it into your written biography.

✔ Ask friends or colleagues how they describe you and what they consider your best skills, and then use their ideas in your biography. This strategy is also a good way to get testimonials for your Web site.

✔ Decide whether you want to create a professional biography or a personal one. Then set the tone based on that decision. Consider your goals. When visitors to your Web site read your bio, do you want them to take you seriously, or do you want them to appreciate your creative vision? Do you want to focus on achievements or use humor to bring out your personality? Chapter 1 discusses in more detail how to plan goals for a site.

✔ Professional biographies are often written in the third person ("she" rather than "you" or "I") and in a more formal style. If you're writing a professional biography, imagine that an emcee will use it to introduce you before you give a speech to an audience who has never met you.

✔ Personal biographies can be much more informal, and are more likely to be written in the first person ("I" rather than "he" or "you"). In this case, you might imagine that you're writing to a new penpal and introducing yourself for the first time.

Remember that you can combine these two approaches, using the first person with a more formal style, for example, or using the third person with a sprinkle of humor and silliness.

✔ Start your biography with your most important accomplishment, a short list of skills or titles, or a brief anecdote that captures something important about who you are. Your goal is to give readers a good sense of who you are or what you do even if they read only the first sentence or two.

When you're finished, make sure to have someone you trust review your biography to make sure it reads well and covers the most important points before you add it to your Web site.

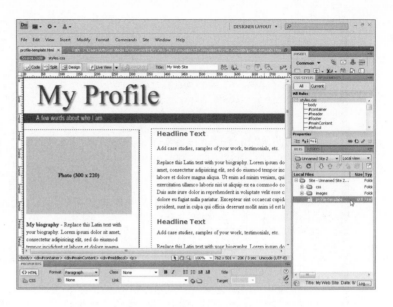

3. When you complete the site setup process, the files and folders in the profile template are displayed in the Files panel in Dreamweaver, to the side of the workspace. Double-click the `profile-template.html` file to open the profile page design in Dreamweaver.

4. Choose File➪Save As and name the page `index.html`. (See the sidebar "Creating new pages in a profile site" for details on why the main file of a site should be named `index`.) Then change the page title by replacing the text in the Title field, at the very top of the Dreamweaver work-space. (***Note:*** The page title isn't displayed in the body of the Web page; this is the text that appears on the title bar at the top of the browser window.)

5. To insert an image in the top of this design, click to select the graphic that reads `My Profile` and then click the Browse button (the yellow folder icon) for the Src field of the Property Inspector.

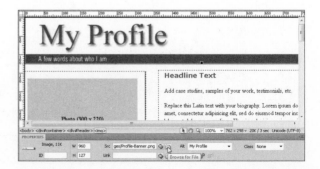

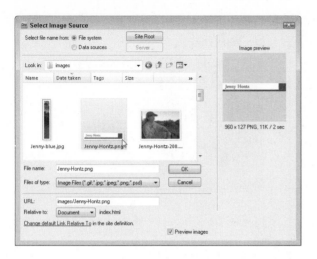

6. In the Select Image Source dialog box that appears, navigate your hard drive to find the image you want to insert and then double-click the image filename to select it. If the photo or other image you select in Step 6 isn't already located in the local root folder of your site, Dreamweaver offers to copy the file into the root folder. (You find more detailed instructions for adding images in Chapter 6.)

7. If the Image Tag Accessibility Attributes dialog box opens, type a brief description of the image in the Alternate Text box. (This text will appear on the page if the image isn't visible.) You can use the Long Description field to link to a longer description of the image in a separate file. Click OK when you're done.

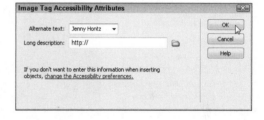

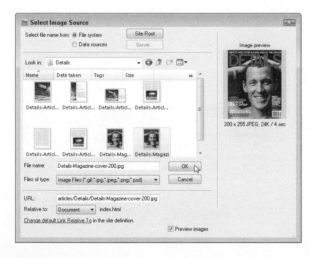

8. You can add more images by clicking to select any of the placeholder images and using the Browse button (the yellow folder icon) in the Property Inspector to replace an image. You can also add images by clicking to place your cursor where you want the image to appear, and then choosing Insert➪Image to insert any image. In this example, I'm adding a copy of the cover of a magazine from Jenny's portfolio.

9. To align an image so that text wraps around next to it, click to select the image. Then, in the Property Inspector, use the Class drop-down menu to select float-right or float-left to align the image. (*Note:* These are styles that I created when I created this template. You find similar styles with every template because aligning images and other elements to the left or right is a common option. These styles were created using the Float left and right options in CSS You find more about CSS in Chapters 4 and 6.)

Does Privacy Exist?

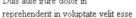

Add case studies, samples of your work, testimonials, etc.

Replace this Latin text with your biography. Lorem ipsum dolor sit amet, consectetur adipisicing elit, sed do eiusmod tempor incididunt ut labore et dolore magna aliqua. Ut enim ad minim veniam, quis nostrud exercitation ullamco laboris nisi ut aliquip ex ea commodo consequat. Duis aute irure dolor in reprehenderit in voluptate velit esse cillum dolore eu fugiat nulla pariatur. Excepteur sint occaecat cupidatat non proident, sunt in culpa qui officia deserunt mollit anim id est laborum.

Headline Text

10. To edit the text on the page, click and drag to select a headline or other section of text, and then type to replace it. Note that you can also use copy and paste to replace this text with text from another file, such as a word processing document.

11. It's good practice to use CSS styles for all your formatting, especially if you use the same styling consistently, but if you just want to add a little formatting to a few words, you can use the formatting icons in the Property Inspector (at the bottom of the work area) to add bold, italic, and other formatting options. To remove bold or italic formatting, simply highlight the formatted text and then click the Bold or Italic button.

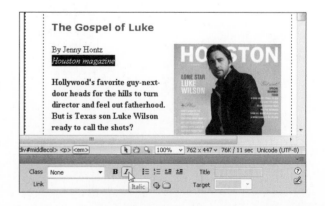

12. This template is designed with a set of heading styles. If you want to add more headings or change the formatting of a heading, click and drag to select the text you want in your heading and then choose one of the Heading styles.

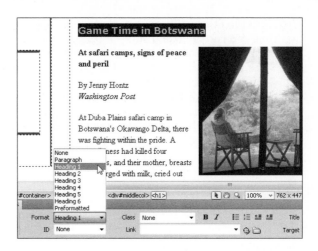

13. This template includes CSS styles that control the font, color, and size of the text when you apply Heading sizes 1, 2, and 3. To change these options, in the CSS Styles panel (choose Window⇨CSS to open it), double-click to select the h1 or h2 style. The CSS Rule Definition dialog box appears, where you can edit the style settings, such as color and font face. You find more details on editing and creating styles in Chapters 4 and 6.

14. To change the colored stripe down the right side of this template design, you need to remove or replace the background image that is set in the style called #mainContent. The advantage of creating this stripe of color with a background image the way I did in this design is that it automatically adjusts to fill the column whether you have a little text or a lot of text in the other two columns on the page. To change the background image, double-click the style named #mainContent in the CSS Styles panel and then choose the Background category in the CSS Rule Definition dialog box.

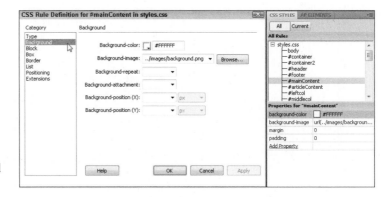

15. I included three different background images that you can choose from — `background-blue.png`, `background-red.png`, and `background-grey.png` — but you can create your own background image using any color. (*Tip:* To ensure that the background fits this design, open the file `background.tif` in Photoshop or Photoshop Elements and replace just the colored region in the image.)

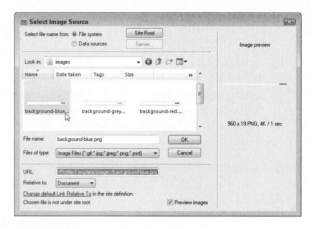

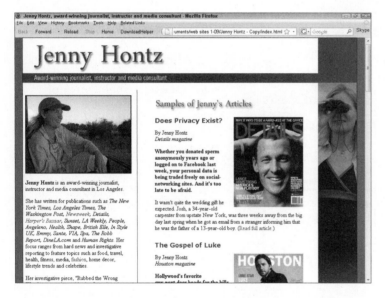

16. To view how your page will appear in a Web browser, choose File⇨Preview in Browser and select any browser you've associated with Dreamweaver. It's always good practice to test your work in a variety of Web browsers. (You find instructions for previewing in different Web browsers and adding browsers to Dreamweaver in Chapter 10.)

Creating new pages in a profile site

The main page of any Web site should be named `index.html`. (If you use a Windows server, you may need to change the name to `default.html`.) The rest of the pages can be named anything you like, as long as you don't use spaces or special characters (hyphens [-] and underscores [_] are okay), and you include the `.html` extension at the end of every page. (Dreamweaver adds the extension for you automatically when you create and save pages in Dreamweaver.)

You can create new or additional pages for your site from the profile template featured in this chapter by simply choosing File⇨Save As and giving the file a new name. (Just be sure that you don't delete the extension.)

Customizing the Portfolio Home Page

Stuff You Need to Know

Toolbox:

✔ Adobe Dreamweaver
✔ The portfolio template
   (portfolio.zip
   from www.
   DigitalFamily.
   com/diy)
✔ Your own text and
   images, to personalize
   the template banner

Time needed:
About half a day

After you edit the image that will appear at the top of your page design, you're ready to start working on the template by adding your own text and images to make the site your own. If you followed the planning steps in Chapter 1, think of this step as the one where you get to add all the content you collected at the beginning of this book. If you skipped that chapter, don't worry: You just have to do more preparation to get your own content ready before you can follow all the steps in this section.

The portfolio template created for this chapter is made up of several pages, including five template files that can be used to generate additional pages. The template files are saved in the Templates folder, which is inside the main Portfolio Template folder. These template files are special because they use the Dreamweaver Dynamic Web Template features, which is why the filenames end in .dwt rather than .html, like the other pages in this site. One of the biggest benefits of using Dynamic Web Templates (as you see in the following steps) is that when you make a change to a template file and then save it, that change is automatically applied to all pages in the Web site that were created from the template file. You find instructions for how to create and edit templates like these in Chapter 6.

In this task, you find instructions for editing the portfolio template files to add the banner image to all pages in this site, as well as how to edit the front page of the site. To set up your portfolio site in Dreamweaver and edit the home page, follow these steps:

1. In Dreamweaver, choose Site⇨ New Site. In the Site Definition dialog box that appears, click the Advanced tab. In the Site Name text box, type a name for your site. In this example, I entered **Jasper Johal Photography**.

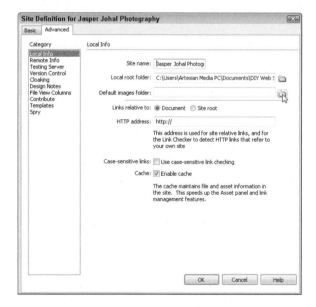

2. Click the Browse icon next to the Local Root Folder text box and locate the folder on your hard drive that contains the portfolio template files you downloaded from www.DigitalFamily.com/diy. Then click the Browse icon next to the Default Images Folder field and select the Images folder. Leave the rest of the options in this dialog box alone for now, and then click OK to close the Site Definition dialog box and save your settings. If you haven't selected the Enable Cache option, a message box appears, asking whether you want to create a cache for the site. Click Yes to speed up some of the Dreamweaver display features. (For more detailed instructions on the site setup process, see Chapter 6.)

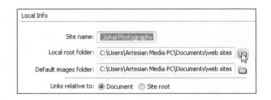

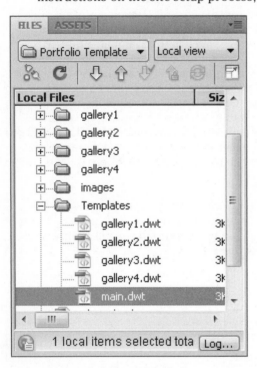

3. After you complete the site setup process, the files and folders in the template are displayed in the Files panel in Dreamweaver, to the side of the workspace. To open a folder in the Files panel and display its contents, click the plus (+) sign to the left of the folder. In this figure, you can see five templates in the Templates folder. To create the first page in this template site, choose File➪New to open the New Document dialog box.

4. In the New Document dialog box that appears, choose Page from Template from the far left. Then choose main from the list of templates. A preview of the template is displayed in the far right of the dialog box window. Click Create to create a new page using the selected template.

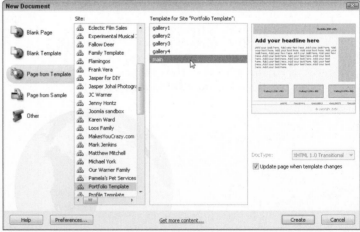

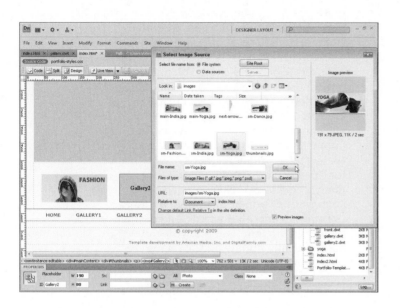

5. You can replace any of the images in this page design except the banner. Just double-click the gray box that serves as an image place-holder for the image; in the Select Image Source dialog box, click to select the image you want to use in its place. (If you use this method, be sure to then click to select the image; then, in the Property Inspector at the bottom of the page, change the text in the Alt field by deleting the word Photo and typing in a text description of your image.) For the best results, insert images that are the height and width specified in the image place-holders so that they fit within this Web page design. If you want to use larger images, you may need to change the width settings in the corresponding styles. See Chapter 5 for help resizing and optimizing images for the Web.

6. Repeat Step 5 until you replace or delete all the images except the banner. (Don't worry: You'll get to the banner soon.) If you don't want to use images in all three boxes, you can delete any of the image placeholders by first clicking to select the image and then pressing the Delete or Backspace key on your keyboard. Then simply enter any other image or text in its place. Note that when an image is selected, the options for that image appear in the Property Inspector.

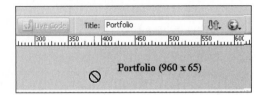

7. If you try to select the banner image at the top of any page created from a template like this, you may be frustrated that you can't edit it in a page created from the template, such as this `index.html` file. That's because it's in a locked region and can be changed only in the template file. You can tell the difference between locked and unlocked regions because when you click anything in a locked region, the cursor changes to a circle with a line through it — the universal symbol for "You can't do that." Among the many benefits of locking a region, such as this banner, in a template in Dreamweaver is that when you edit the banner in the template file, you can automatically update all the pages created from that template.

8. To change the banner image in the template, first open the template file named `main.dwt`, which is saved in the Templates folder. You can open a template file like you would open any other page in Dreamweaver, by double-clicking its name in the Files panel or by choosing File⇨Open and selecting the file.

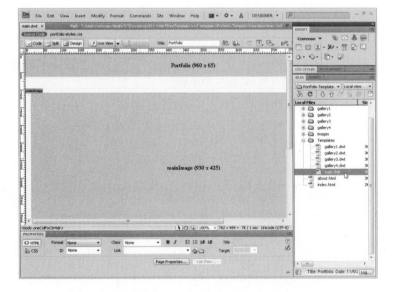

9. With the template file open, you can change the banner image at the top of the page by double-clicking the banner image and then using the Select Image Source dialog box to select the image you want to use in its place. In this case, I replaced the placeholder image with the template banner that I customized in the first task in this chapter, "Customizing the Banner Graphics." (Remember that you should click to select the image after it's inserted and then enter a text description of the image in the Alt field in the Property Inspector.)

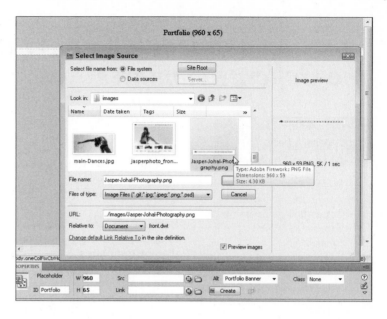

10. When you save the template file with the new banner, Dreamweaver launches the Update Template Files dialog box with a list of all files created with the open template. In this case, only the index page was created from this template, so it's the only one listed. To apply this change to the index page, click the Update button. If the template had been used to create many pages, this process would update all pages created from the template — a useful time-saver when you're working with many similar files, such as the gallery sections of this Web site.

Creating and Linking Pages using the Gallery Templates

The Portfolio template features four Dynamic Web Template files that can be used to generate additional pages. I've given you four gallery templates, and you can create as many as you need to manage as many galleries as you want to feature in your site. In this task, you create new pages from the `gallery1` template and make global changes to the pages in the first gallery by editing the `gallery1` template file.

Because the gallery pages in this Web site include many thumbnail images that are repeated on every page of the gallery, this is an ideal use for templates. I find it simplest to start by creating all the gallery pages from the `gallery1` template and inserting the big image (the only image that changes from page to page). Then I go back and insert the corresponding thumbnails and set the links in the gallery file itself because it's always easier to set a link when you already have pages created to link to. The thumbnails in these gallery pages are intentionally saved in a region that can be edited only in the template itself so that you add them all just once in the template, and they automatically update in all the pages created from the gallery. You see how this works in the following task.

Before you can complete this task, you must complete the site setup process to load this entire template folder into Dreamweaver. If you completed the preceding task, "Customizing the Portfolio Home Page," you should be ready to go; if not, you first need to complete Steps 1–3 in the previous task. (For more detailed instructions on the site set-up process, see Chapter 6.)

1. Start by creating a new page from the `gallery1.dwt` template by choosing File⇨New. In the New Document dialog box that appears, choose Page from Template from the far left. Then choose `gallery1` from the list of templates. A preview of the template is displayed in the far right of the dialog box. Note this template is designed to create a gallery with eight thumbnail images and one large image in the main area of the page, but you can alter the design by adding or removing image placeholders or by replacing them with images of different sizes. Click Create to create a new page using the selected template.

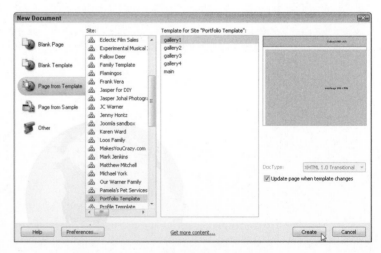

2. Keep each collection of gallery pages in a separate folder so you don't have to worry about duplicate file names. In this example, I created a new folder called gallery1 and saved the file with the name `photo1.html`. (You can create a new folder similar to how you save a file in Dreamweaver: Clicking the New folder icon in the Save As dialog box.)

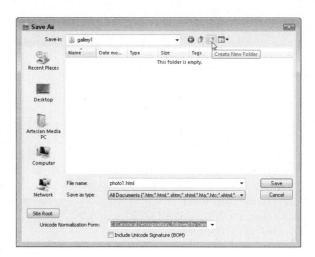

3. To replace the image placeholder in the middle of the page with a photograph, double-click to select the placeholder image. Then, in the Select Image Source dialog box, click to select a photograph to insert into the page in its place. Click to select the image after it's inserted and enter a text description of the image in the Alt field in the Property Inspector. To add a caption, click to place your cursor beneath the photo and then type to enter text. (Don't worry about the banner image at the top of the page or the thumbnail images across the bottom. You replace those images in Step 5.)

TIP

Add a unique title to the top of each page as you create it by replacing the text in the Title field at the very top of the page. Using specific titles with keywords can improve search engine results for pages in your site.

4. To create additional pages for the gallery, repeat Steps 1–3, saving all the files in each gallery with a new name, such as photo2.html, photo3.html, and so on in the same gallery1 folder. In this site for Jasper, I used eight thumbnails and eight pages in each gallery. If you use eight images the same size as the ones I used, you can use this template exactly as I created it. If you delete or add images, or if you change the sizes, you may need to make adjustments to the designs in the CSS. (You learn more about editing CSS and templates in Chapters 4 and 6.)

5. In the gallery templates, the banner graphic is in a locked region at the top of the template, and the thumbnails and copyright information are in a locked region at the bottom. To edit these images, first open the gallery1.dwt file, located in the Templates folder. Replacing the banner at the top of all these gallery pages is easy. Double-click the place-holder image at the top and select the banner image you created for your site. (Find instructions for customizing a banner image in the first task in this chapter.) After I add the banner image to the template, I choose File⇨Save to save the template, and Dreamweaver prompts me to update only the eight pages I created with this template.

6. Adding and linking all the thumbnail images at the bottom of each
gallery template will take a little
time, but it works the same
whether you're adding four thumbnail images to the home page
design or eight to each of the gallery templates. Because you're
adding the thumbnails images and
links to the template, Dreamweaver
will add them to all the pages in
your galleries automatically, saving
you having to set all those links
multiple times, and making it easy
to add or remove images to all the
pages later. To replace each thumbnail, double-click the placeholder
image in the template and select
an image sized to fit this template
design and saved in the PNG or
JPEG format. (You find instructions
for resizing and optimizing images
before you insert them into a template in Chapter 5.)

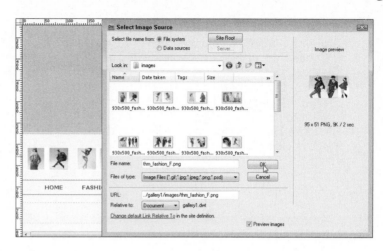

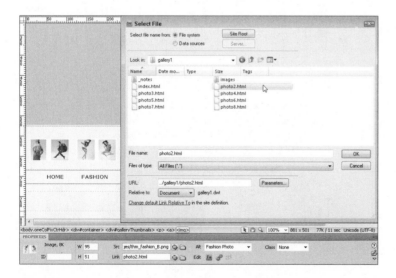

7. Link each thumbnail image to its
corresponding page by first clicking
to select the thumbnail image in
the page and then choosing
Insert⇨Hyperlink; or, click the
Browse button (the yellow folder
icon) next to the Link field in the
Property Inspector. In the Select
File dialog box that appears, click
to select the page you want to link
the thumbnail image to, and then
click OK to set the link. Repeat this
step for each thumbnail. After I add
and link all the thumbnails, I save
the page again, and again click
Update in the Update Template files
dialog box to add the thumbnails to
all the pages.

8. To test the links, double-click to open the `photo1.html` page in the gallery1 folder. Choose any of the pages you created in the gallery1 folder, click the Preview in Browser icon at the top of the workspace (it looks like a globe), and then choose the browser you want to use to test the page. You can also choose File⇨Preview in Browser and then select a browser.

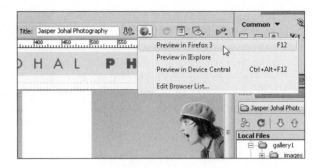

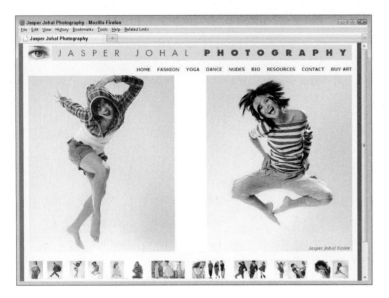

9. Click each thumbnail image in turn to make sure that you set the links properly. If you find one that doesn't link to the correct page, open the template again in Dreamweaver and correct the link in the template. When you save the template, the corrected link will be updated in all related gallery pages.

10. To test the links on each thumbnail, preview the page in a Web browser by clicking on the Browser icon at the top of the workspace or by choosing File⇨Preview in Browser and then selecting a browser. Clicking the each thumbnail in turn across the bottom of the gallery and each thumbnail should link you to the next page in the sequence. If you find that you missed one or need to fix a link, just open the file again in Dreamweaver, click the graphic, and re-create the link as you did in Step 7.

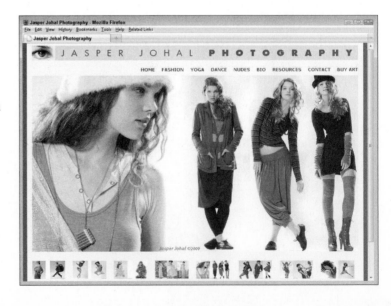

Chapter 8

Creating a Business Web Site

Tasks Performed in This Chapter

✔ Editing images for templates

✔ Putting together a business home page in Dreamweaver

✔ Creating other pages from a Web template

✔ Using background images in Web designs

O nce in a while, I still meet small-business owners who ask, "Do I really need to have a Web site?" Today, the answer is easy: "Yes." And, increasingly, the owners of even the smallest businesses have caught on to the many advantages of creating, or extending, their business online: Creating a site for a business can help sell more of its products, attract more customers, and better serve the existing customers.

Whether you're creating a site for the first time or redesigning a site, you can customize the templates featured in this book to create nearly any kind of Web site, whether you want a site for your carpentry business, law firm, photography studio, or nearly anything else you can imagine promoting online.

In this chapter, you walk through the steps of customizing templates designed to meet the needs of many small businesses.

Introducing the Business Site Templates

Although every business is different, most good business Web sites have some things in common: basic information about the business or service, photos, sample work, contact information, and so on. A testimonials page is another good idea for any business, such as the one my friend, actor Yuval David, features on his site, shown in Figure 8-1. By altering the template used in this chapter (shown in Figure 8-2), you can create a site for your own business with all these features and a design as professional-looking as Yuval's.

Figure 8-1: By simply replacing the banner image and adding a photo with a frame, I've customized this template to create this page on www.yuvaldavid.com.

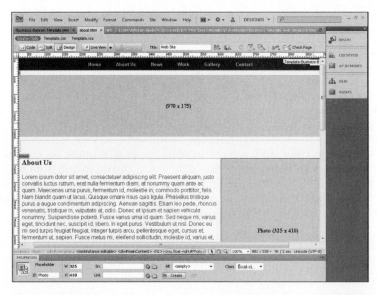

Figure 8-2: This template can be altered to create a site for many kinds of businesses or professionals.

By altering the names of the sections in this template, you can quickly create a similar Web site that fits the needs of your Web project, and you can use the template to create new pages and build a bigger Web site, like I did for my friend's acting site, which includes videos, photo galleries, and other special sections. (You can download all the templates featured in this book from the companion Web site at www.DigitalFamily.com/diy.)

The Business Template, included with this chapter, comprises the following files:

- ✔ images: All your template image files are in this folder, in TIFF format. These image files include layers, which makes it easy to edit them in a program like Photoshop or Photoshop Elements. You also find in this folder optimized JPEG files that you can use if you want to practice as you go through these tasks. (You learn more about resizing and optimizing your own images for the Web in Chapter 5.)

- ✔ index.html: The main page of any Web site should be named index. You can alter the basic template design to use multiple images or to include more text, but it's always good to include a clear description of what your site is about on the home page.

- ✔ about.html: This is a good place to include a description of your business, your biography, or other background information. A larger business can expand this into a series of pages that make up a Who We Are section for staff, executives, board of directors, and so on.

- ✔ news.html: The news or press section can feature your latest activities. You can even link to a blog. You find out how to set up a blog in Chapter 11.

- ✔ work.html: This section can include videos, case studies, articles you've written, or other samples of your work.

- ✔ gallery.html: List additional information or create a new section of your site, such as a listing of products, services, or photos.

- ✔ contact.html: Making it easy for customers to reach you is always good, but be careful about giving away too much information on your Web site. If you work at home, for example, you may want to leave off your street address and just include an e-mail address on your contact page. Figure 8-3 shows a contact page.

You also find subfolders in this Business template. The images folder contains the starter image for the banner for this site and is a good place for you to save any new images you want to add to the site. You also find the Templates folder, which is where Dreamweaver saves the Template file that goes with these page designs. (Flip to Chapter 6 for a refresher on Dreamweaver template files.)

If you want to rename any of the files or folders in this template site, be sure to do so in the Dreamweaver Files panel to ensure that Dreamweaver automatically adjusts the links that correspond to the files. You can add pages to the Business template site by following the instructions in the section "Creating and Editing Pages with a Web Template in Dreamweaver," later in this chapter.

Figure 8-3: You can change these template pages a little or a lot to create more dramatic pages, such as this contact page with a long background image.

Editing and Sizing Images for the Template

I generally start my design work in a program like Photoshop and recommend you prepare at least some of your images in a program like Photoshop or Photoshop Elements before you start working on the templates in Dreamweaver.

To help you get your images ready for this business site, I included three *starter images:* one for the banner, one that can serve as a photo frame, and one for the home page. These graphics files are composed of different layers, each containing a separate element in the design, so you can change the text, colors, and even add more photos. I've included all the starter images in the images folder so all you have to do is add your own text and photos.

In this task, I use Photoshop Elements to transform the starter images into the images for the actor site, but you can follow these same steps in whatever program you prefer (or have handy), including Photoshop, Photoshop Elements, or Fireworks. After you prepare each image, you use the Save for Web option to optimize them for the Web. (You find more about creating and optimizing images for the Web in Chapter 5.)

1. Launch a graphics program, such as Photoshop or Photoshop Elements (shown here); choose File➪Open; and open the file named `Banner-Template.tif`.

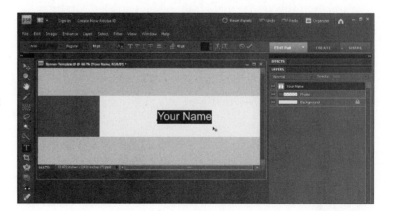

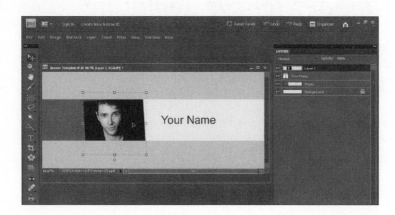

2. You can copy and paste images into this template by choosing File⇨ Open and selecting any image from your hard drive. In this example, I opened a photo of Yuval, which I want to use in the banner at the top of his page. To copy an image into the template, first choose Select⇨ All to select the image and then choose File⇨Copy to copy it. Click anywhere on the template image to make it active in the workspace. (If the template image is hidden by the new image, choose Window⇨ Banner-Template.tif to bring the template to the front of the workspace before you paste.) Choose File⇨Paste to insert the new image into the template.

3. After you paste an image, like this photo, you can click anywhere within the image and drag to adjust its placement. You can also click and drag a corner to adjust the size of the image. And here's an advanced Photoshop tip (that also works in Elements): If you hold your cursor just outside the corner of an image, the arrow becomes curved like the one in this figure, indicating that you can rotate the image, to set it off at an angle, as I've done to position this photo in its frame. You can also rotate an image by choosing Edit⇨Transform⇨Rotate.

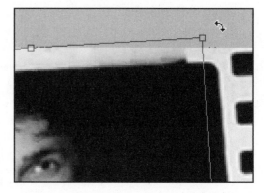

If the image you're adding to a template is significantly larger than the template file, resize the new image before you copy and paste it into the template image. The image size for each image is displayed in the template. You can change the resolution and dimensions of an image by choosing Image⇨Size and adjusting the settings. You can make minor changes to the size of an image by clicking and dragging any corner of an image after it's inserted into the template image. (You can find more detailed instructions for resizing and optimizing images in Chapter 5.)

4. To edit the text, select the Text tool from the Toolbox. Then click and drag to select the text and type to replace it. Use the options at the top of the workspace to change the font, size, and color. In this example, I clicked the color well at the top of the page to change the text color. *Tip:* To reposition text on the page, click to select the Move tool from the Toolbox. (In Photoshop, the Move tool is represented by the double-headed crossed arrow icon at the top of the Toolbox.) Then click and drag any section of text.

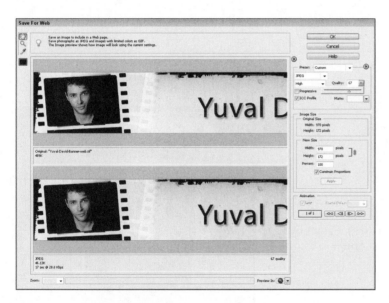

5. When you're done customizing the banner image for your Web page, choose File⇨Save for Web and use the settings to optimize the image. In this case, because the banner includes a photo, I'm saving it as a JPEG. (You find more about the options for optimizing images in Chapter 5.)

6. You can insert images of many different sizes into the templates in this business site and align them to the left or right so that text can wrap around them. To dress up your images, you can use a background as a frame. I've included a starter image called `Photo-Frame-Template.tif` in the images folder for you.

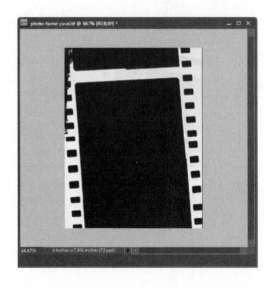

7. Because this site is for an actor, I thought it would be fun to use a frame around the photos that makes them look like they're stills in a film strip. I start by adding the filmstrip image to serve as the background.

8. When you layer images like this, make sure the right image is on top in the Layers panel, because that controls how the final image looks. In this case, I need to make sure the image with the photo is above the background image with the filmstrip.

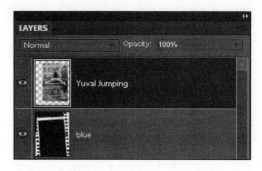

9. With a photo like this positioned above a background image, like this filmstrip, you can use the Move tool to click and drag the image into position, change the size, and adjust the alignment until you get it framed just the way you want it.

10. When you have everything set the way you want it, choose File⇨Save for Web to optimize the image as a JPEG or PNG file. (You find more about the options for optimizing images in Chapter 5.)

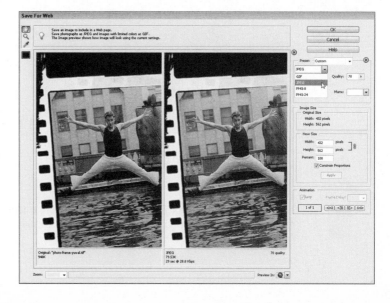

11. You can create images as large as you want. Just beware that the more you put on a Web page, the longer it takes to download. If you're going to create a page like the home page design my friend Davi Cheng created for Yuval's acting site, you need to limit what else you put on the page. If you're going to use a large image on a page, that's probably all you should put on that page. In this case, I created one, big layered image by copying in each image (and cropping out the main photo).

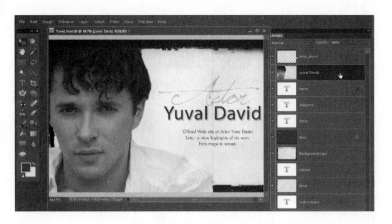

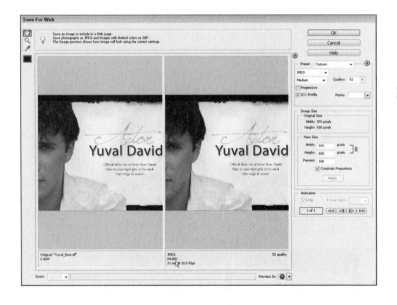

12. Even large, layered images like this one can be optimized for the Web so that they load fairly quickly. Because this is the only image I'm placing on the home page of his site, it should load quickly at only 84K in size.

When you use the Save for Web dialog box, you create a copy of the image in its new, optimized format. As a result, after you close the Save for Web dialog box, the original image remains open and unchanged in Photoshop Elements.

Putting the Pages Together in Dreamweaver

Stuff You Need to Know

Toolbox:

- ✔ Adobe Dreamweaver
- ✔ The Business template (from this book's companion site at www.DigitalFamily.com/diy)
- ✔ Text and other materials to customize the site
- ✔ Images you've resized and optimized in a program such as Photoshop Elements, covered in the previous task

Time needed:
About half a day

In this task, you set up a new Web site using the Business template and start customizing the pages.

As you work through the following steps, remember that you can alter this template a little (by simply adding your own text and images) or a lot (by changing the colors, font options, and other style settings) to make the design more your own. Also notice that by using a large photo on the home page and a smaller, banner photo on the inside pages, I can create a very different look for the home page with the same template I use for the inside pages.

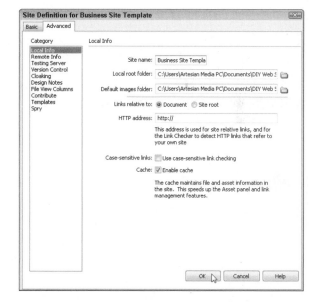

1. In Dreamweaver, choose Site➪New Site. In the Site Definition dialog box, click the Advanced tab. In the Site Name text box, type a name for your site. In this example, I entered Business Site Template. Click the Browse icon next to the Local Root Folder text box and locate on your hard drive the folder that contains the Business template files. (*Note:* You can rename the folder.) Click the Browse icon next to the Default Images folder field and select the Images folder in the Business template folder. Then click OK. If you haven't yet selected the Enable Cache option, a message box appears, asking whether you want to create a cache for the site. Click Yes to speed up some of the Dreamweaver display features. (For more detailed instructions on the site setup process, see Chapter 6.)

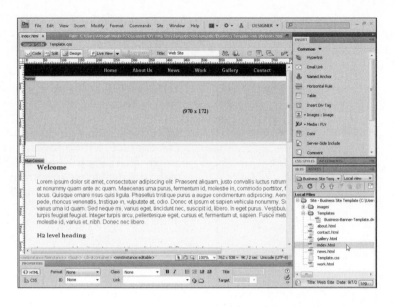

2. When you complete the site setup process, the files and folders in the template are displayed in the Files panel in Dreamweaver, at the side of the workspace. Double-click the `index.html` file in the Files panel to open the home page in Dreamweaver.

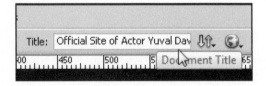

3. At the top of the home page, you can change the page title, as I'm doing here, by replacing the text in the Title field. Enter your name or business name or a brief description to identify your site, such as I did in this example, with the words *Official Site of Actor Yuval David.* The *page title* is the text that appears in the title bar at the top of the browser window when someone views a page online; this text is saved in a list of sites if someone bookmarks the page.

4. You can replace any of the image placeholders with images you prepared for your site. To insert an image, double-click any image, such as the banner at the top to open the Select Image Source dialog box. Navigate on your hard drive to find the image you want to insert and then double-click the image filename to select it. As you see in this example, I'm inserting the home page image I created and optimized in the previous task. If the image you select isn't already located in your root site, Dreamweaver offers to copy the file into the root folder after you select it.

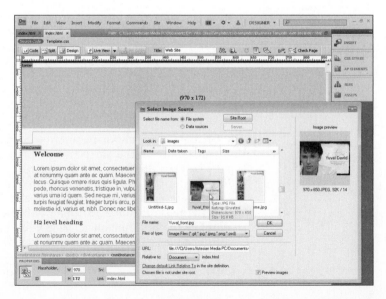

5. The way this template is made, the design expands to fit images of any height, but the width should not exceed the overall width of this design, which is set to 970 pixels wide. Because this home page is just one big image, it's one of the easiest pages to create in Dreamweaver. Simply delete any text you don't want in the template and save the page. (Remember, the home page should always be named `index.html`.)

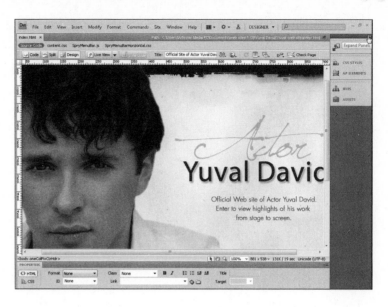

6. On the rest of the pages in this site, I use a smaller banner image at the top of the template to leave room for text and images I want to include on these pages. This template is set up to let you use a different banner on each page, which enabled me to use different photos of Yuval throughout the site, but you can use just one banner if you prefer.

The links in all the pages in this Business template can be changed only in the template file used to create these pages. That makes it possible to set the main links on all the pages at once, as you do in the next task.

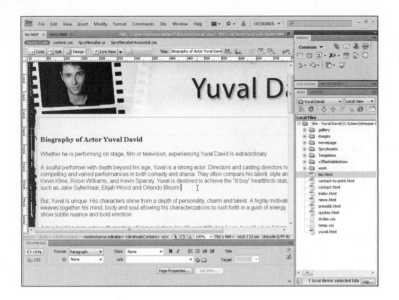

7. You can add text by typing it into any part of the page, but be careful not to delete the formatting when you delete the Latin (Lorem ipsum) text, which is included as filler in the template. If you have trouble adding text without altering the format, use Undo (Ctrl+Z on Windows, or ⌘+Z on Mac) to back up a step and try again, making sure to select just what you want to replace on the page.

8. You can insert images anywhere in the main area of the template by clicking to place your cursor where you want the image to appear and then choosing Insert⇨Image. You can align images to the left or right of a page and wrap text by using the class styles, float-left and float-right, included with this template. First click to select the image; then use the Class drop-down list in the Property Inspector to select the alignment option you want for your image.

9. To change the text size or color in these templates, you need to edit the style that controls the elements. To do so, open the CSS Styles panel (if it's not open already) by choosing Window➪ CSS Styles. In this template, to change the style of the headlines, you need to change the corresponding styles I've defined for Heading tags 1 and 2. The h1 is the largest heading style; h2 provides a second-level heading. To change the Heading 1 style, double-click the h1 option in the CSS Styles panel, and change the text settings in the CSS Rule Definition dialog box. Click OK when you're done to return to the Dreamweaver workspace.

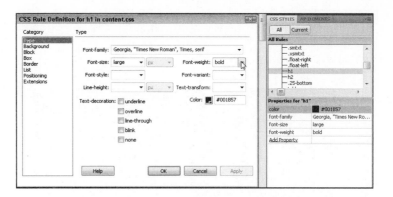

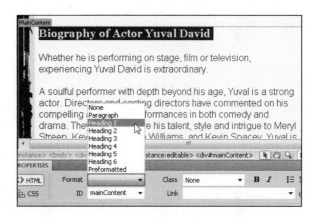

10. To apply the heading styles to text in the page, select the text and then use the Format drop-down list in the Property Inspector to choose a Heading size.

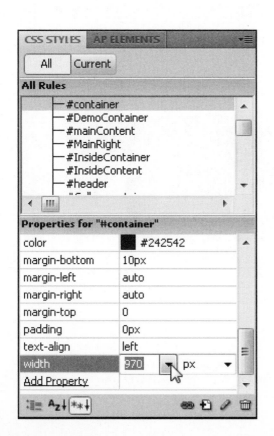

11. To change the layout of the page, you need to change other styles, such as the width of the style named #container, which controls the overall width of the page in this template. You can double-click the name of a style in the CSS Styles panel to open the style in the CSS Rule Definition dialog box and edit it there. Or make changes in the lower half of the CSS Styles panel as you see in this figure.

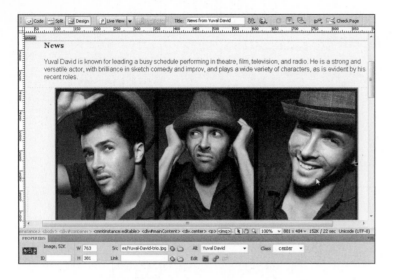

12. You can change the layout dramatically from page to page using the same template in a Web site simply by using images in different sizes and aligning them differently on the page. In this example, I'm adding a big image with three separate photos to fill most of the width of the page.

13. To test your work in a Web browser, choose File➪Preview in Browser and select any browser on your hard drive. For best results, test your work in a variety of Web browsers to ensure that your pages' designs look good for all visitors. In this figure, the page is displayed in Internet Explorer. For more instructions on working with CSS, see Chapter 6. For instructions on how to upload your site to a Web server, see Chapter 10.

You can change the width of the page, but I've designed this template to be 970 pixels wide because that size is a good width if you're designing for a screen resolution of 1024 x 768, a common resolution on 15- and 17-inch monitors, considered the most common in use on the Web today.

Creating and Editing Pages with a Web Template in Dreamweaver

As described in the previous task, you can add your own images and text to the pages of the Business template to create a variety of different looks for your site. When it comes to editing the main links and copyright information that appear on every page, however, you need to change those in the template file itself. Although this requirement may seem limiting at first, the benefit is that you edit these links in only one place to update the main navigation links on all the pages in the site.

Dreamweaver templates are designed so that some regions of the page can be edited in pages created from the template, and other regions can be edited only in the template itself. The navigation links that appear above the banner in this template and again at the bottom of the page with the copyright information can be edited only in the template.

In this task, you make global changes to pages by editing the template file, and you create new pages from a Dreamweaver Web Template. Before you can complete this task, you must complete the site setup process in Dreamweaver, covered at the beginning of the preceding task.

1. To give you a head start on this Web site design, the Business template folder has several pages that are already linked together. You can edit any of these pages, such as the work.html page, by simply double-clicking the name in the Files panel to open it. It's common practice to include a page on your Web site that showcases what you do, like you see in this figure, and it's easy to add images, text, and even video files to this page that was created from the template.

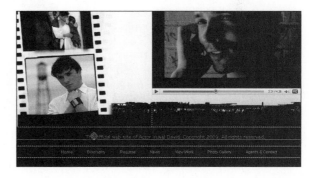

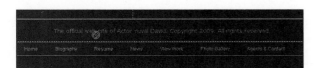

2. If you try to click the links or the copyright information on the work.html page or any of the other HTML pages that were created from this template, your cursor turns into a circle with a line through it, and you can't make any changes in the HTML file. To edit this part of the page, you need to open the template.

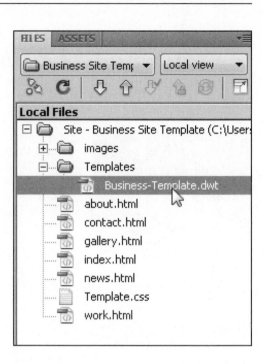

3. To edit the template itself, double-click the name in the Files panel. In this Business template site, the template is called `Business-Template.dwt` and it's in the Templates folder.

4. You can edit anything in the template file, but you should do it carefully so as not to disturb the formatting and links that surround the text. For example, to change the name of a section (at the top or bottom of the page), click to select the section of text, such as About Us, and replace it by typing the text you want to in its place. In this example, I changed About Us to Biography. As you can see in the Property Inspector at the bottom of the screen, when the text is selected, the link is displayed in the Link field. To change or reset the link, click the Browse button (it looks like a little yellow folder) next to the Link field in the Property Inspector.

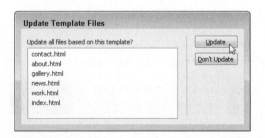

5. To apply a change in the template to all the pages created from the template, just save the template file and Dreamweaver prompts you with a dialog box that lists all the pages that will be updated. Click Update to complete the changes.

6. Changing the text links doesn't alter the file-names, but you can change those as well by clicking to select the name of a file in the Files panel and typing to replace the name. Change file or folder names only in the Files panel to ensure that Dreamweaver updates any links that go to that page. As you see here, when I changed the `about.html` page to `bio.html`, Dreamweaver prompted me with another update dialog box listing all the pages that link to the `about.html` page. *Remember:* Folder and filenames used in Web sites shouldn't include spaces or special characters except the dash (–).

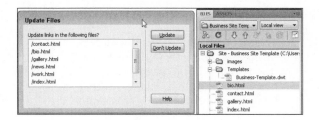

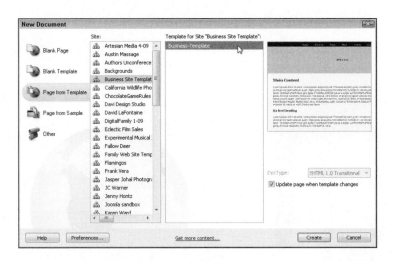

7. To add a new page to this Web site by using the template, choose File⇨New. Then, in the New Document dialog box, choose Page from Template (from the options on the left), make sure that the Web site you're working on is selected in the middle column, and choose `Business-Template` from the right column. (Notice that a pre-view of the selected template is displayed on the far right side of this dialog box.) Click Create to generate a page from the template.

8. Before you do anything else, always save the new page by choosing File⇨Save and name the page as you save it. I named this page `videos.html`. You can then change the page title (the text that appears in the title bar of a Web browser window) by click-ing to select the text at the top of the workspace and typing in any title you choose. In this case, I entered Actor Yuval David's Videos.

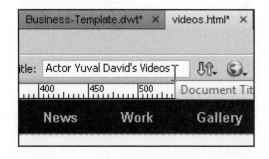

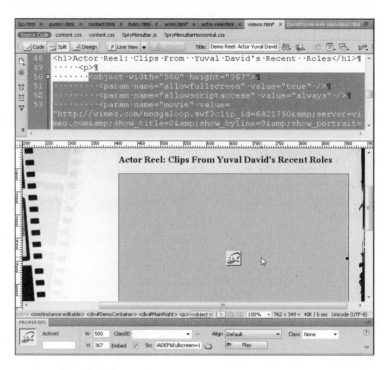

9. Like all the other pages created from this template, you can replace the text and image placeholders with your own text, images, and even multimedia files. In this example, I've added code from the Vimeo video hosting service to insert a video into this page. You find out more about how to use video services, such as YouTube and Vimeo, in Chapter 13.

10. To play multimedia, such as this video file, you need to preview your page in a Web browser by choosing File➪Preview in Browser and selecting a Web browser, such as Firefox. With a page open in a browser, you can click the links to test your work and play videos and other multimedia files.

Many Web browsers don't display Dreamweaver Web Templates well, so if you try to preview the .dwt template page, you may get an error message. To test any changes you make to a template, open one of the pages created from the template and then preview that page in a browser and test the links and other features.

Using Background Images in Page Layouts

Stuff You Need to Know

Toolbox:

✔ Adobe Dreamweaver
✔ The Background template from www.DigitalFamily.com/diy
✔ Your own text and images, to personalize the pages

Time needed:
About half a day

Whether you're working with one of the templates included in this book or you want to dress up a page you create with your own custom design, using background images can provide a great short cut to creating a distinct, professional-looking site — even if you're not a professional designer.

The best part about this trick is that you can find so much great artwork on stock image sites like www.istockphoto.com, where I got the filmstrip background image for the site. Web sites like iStockphoto.com license the rights to images, often with some restrictions. For example, for a few dollars, I bought the right to use this background image in a Web site and even feature images of that Web site in this book. If you want to use this image, or another image from iStockphoto.com, you have to buy the rights to the image for your own site. The good news is that you can choose from millions of photographs and illustrations on stock image sites and the licensing fee is a small price to pay for the professional look you get from a well-designed background. With a little creativity, you can create your own background images in a program like Photoshop or Photoshop Elements (see Chapter 5 for more on creating your own images).

1. Stock image Web sites, like www.istockphoto.com shown here, offer rights to photographs, illustrations, flash videos, and animations. You can search among many different keywords and when you find an image, you simply click to download. Most reputable sites that offer good quality images do charge for the service, but sites like iStockphoto offer images for as little as $1 each.

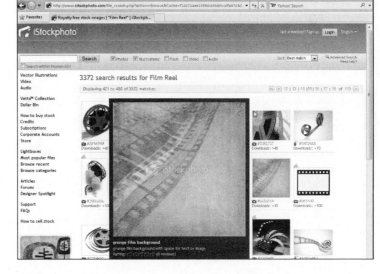

When you're designing for the Web, you don't usually need a big, high-resolution image (the higher the resolution, they more expensive it is), but you do need to make sure you get a big enough version that it will fill the entire background of your page. Because most designers are creating sites for a 1024 x 768 monitor these days, the image should be at least 1024 pixels wide. You can always reduce the size of an image, but enlarging it can lead to a loss of quality.

2. After you've created or downloaded an image to serve as the background of your Web page, you can combine it with other images and text in a program like Photoshop Elements, shown here. In this example, by placing the big image behind the text I was able to create a layered effect. You should edit and resize your background image and then use the Save for Web dialog box to save an optimized version for your Web site.

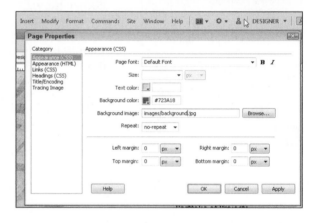

3. You can add any image to the background of the entire page by choosing Modify⇨Page Properties and using the Browse button next to the Background Image field to select the image.

4. Another way to use background images is in the background of a `<div>` tag in your page layout. In all the templates featured in this book, the designs are centered and they float on the screen so that they appear in the middle of the browser window no matter how big or small the monitor. If you use one of my templates, or create your own centered design like the one featured in this example, your best bet is to add the background image to the main div, in this case the `<div>` tag named `#container` that surrounds all the other content on this page. To do so, double-click the `#container` style in the CSS Styles panel; in the CSS Rule Definition dialog box that appears, choose the Background category and then click Browse button to the right of the Background field and select your desired background image file.

5. To view the full impact of your background image, preview your page in different Web browsers and try out the design on large and smalls screens to make sure it displays well on a variety of computers. Chapter 10 explains site testing in more detail.

6. After you've set up a background image for one page, it's easy to use the same design for any or all of the other pages in your site as well. When you add an image to the background of the page, you can add other images, text, or even multimedia files above the background to create a layered effect that can create a rich, full design effect.

Chapter 9

Creating a Family, Vacation, or Hobby Site

Tasks Performed in This Chapter

✔ Working with the templates

✔ Designing a site for your family, hobby, or vacation

✔ Editing image templates

There are many excellent reasons to create a Web site, slide show, or photo gallery. From the announcement of a new baby to sharing the latest vacation snapshots to coordinating the games for your little league team, digital designs are a great way to keep in touch with family and friends.

The best family sites include room for everyone in the clan, and as you see in the sample family site–creation tasks in this chapter, you can easily adapt this design to create sections for each member of your family, club, or organization.

Getting Started with the Family or Group Site Templates

The templates featured in this chapter are designed to showcase a lot of images and would work well for any family Web site, as well as for an art or photo collection, to illustrate business services or products, or to share vacation photos with family and friends.

For this site, you can download templates to create the pages in Dreamweaver as well as starter images designed to be used in an image editor, such as Photoshop, Photoshop Elements, or Fireworks.

All the templates featured in this book can be downloaded for free from the companion Web site that goes with this book. Just visit www.DigitalFamily.com/diy and follow the instructions to download the various graphic and Web page templates.

As you follow the instructions for creating the family site featured in this chapter, you'll see how to customize pages, as shown in Figure 9-1, and how to add or remove pages to create smaller or larger versions of this site. You also find instructions for creating interactive features in Dreamweaver, including image maps. Because customizing this site involves editing graphics as well as HTML files, you find separate tasks for each section of the site:

✔ The first task shows you how to customize the banner, text, and images by using Photoshop Elements. (I'm using Photoshop Elements 8.) You also find out how to add and position images to create the page designs for each section of the site.

✔ The second task shows you how to set up a site in Dreamweaver and how to edit the front page.

✔ The third task covers how to edit Dynamic Web Templates in Dreamweaver, make changes across many pages at once, set links to pages and remove pages from the design.

Figure 9-1: The template featured in this chapter can be altered to create a wide range of different kinds of Web sites, such as sites for small or large families.

Before you get started with these tasks, here's a quick overview of the template and files used in this chapter. You can download the family template with all these files from the companion Web site for this book at www.DigitalFamily.com/diy.

To help you get started with this site, and to ensure that the links on the navigation bars work properly, this template includes starter pages for each of the main sections of this site. Although you can add or remove pages and change links as necessary, this list describes the files and folders that get you started when you first open the Family template:

✔ index.html: This is the name of the front page of the Web site. The main page of any Web site should be named index; the rest of the pages can be named anything you like, as long as you don't use spaces or special characters.

Creating a Web site is easy with templates and step-by-step instructions

Create a professional Web site for your small business or consulting firm. Design an online portfolio to share your art, graphic design, or photography. Build a site for your favorite sports team, hobby, family, and anything else you can imagine.

I designed this book so you can easily create Web sites by customizing professionally designed Web templates. You can download these templates from the companion Web site. Just add your photos, text, and more to create a Web site that fits your style. You find everything you need in this book, from registering a domain name to preparing images for the Web to promoting your site after it's online.

This color insert highlights the templates, tasks, and examples you find throughout this book.

Edit Images for the Web: Discover how to use Adobe Photoshop (or the less-expensive Photoshop Elements) to crop, resize, edit, and optimize your images for your Web site. (Chapter 5)

Use the Right Tool: Each icon in the Photoshop Elements Tools panel serves a specific purpose, including the Move tool, which makes it easy to edit and reposition images and text. (Chapter 5)

Combine Many Images in One: Copy as many photos as you want into a new blank Photoshop (.psd) file to create a photo montage, layered designs, and other special effects. (Chapter 5)

Optimize JPEG Images: Save your photos in the JPEG format for best display on the Web. Photoshop's Save for Web dialog box enables you to easily convert and optimize images so they download quickly. (Chapter 5)

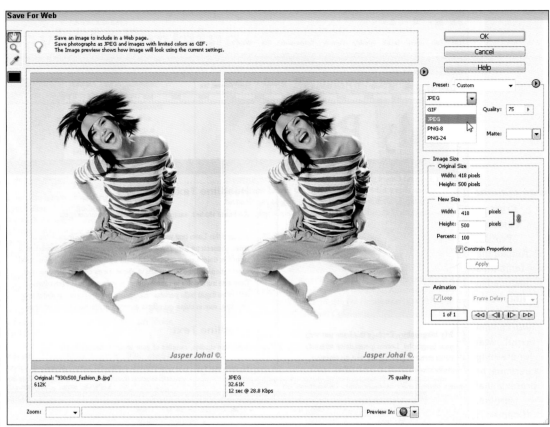

Save PNG and GIF Images: Images with limited colors are best saved in the PNG or GIF format for the Web. Discover how Photoshop's Save for Web dialog box enables you to limit the number of colors in these formats so your images download even faster. (Chapter 5)

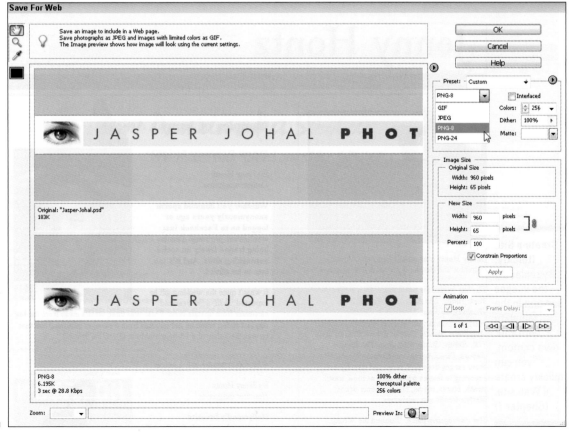

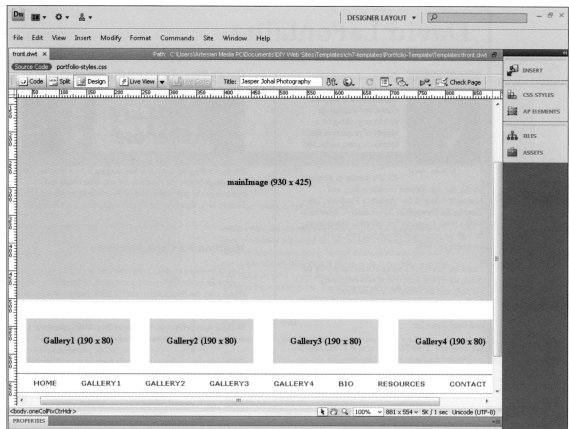

Design an Online Portfolio: The portfolio template is ideal for artists, photographers, graphic designers, and others who want to display their work in a professional and easy-to-navigate design. (Chapter 7)

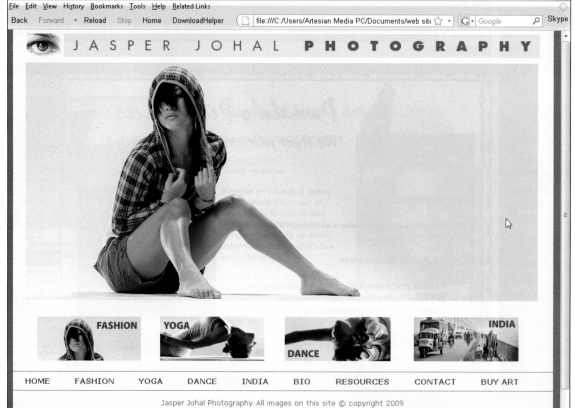

Showcase Art, Photos, and More: Add your own images to the gallery pages in this template—the links are already in place, making it easy for you to set up a complete site. (Chapter 7)

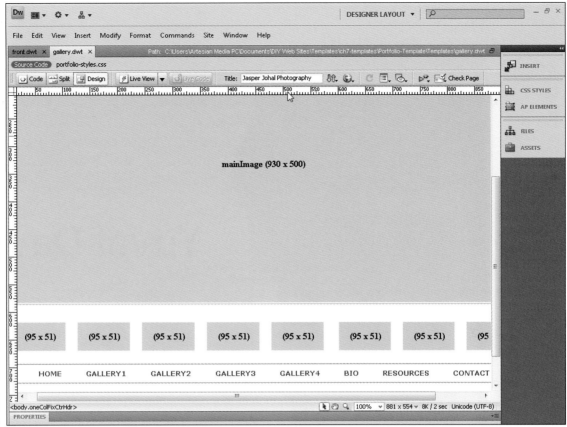

Show Off More Images: The Portfolio template is designed to make it easy to add as many images as you want to your site. (Chapter 7)

Add or Remove Images: Simply add or delete the thumbnail images in the template to change the design for your portfolio. (Chapter 7)

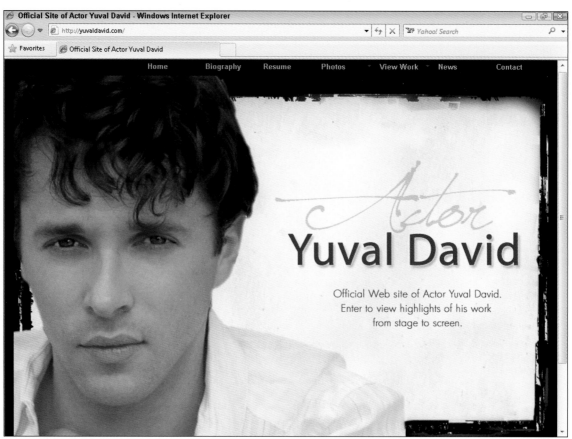

Create a Small Business Site:
Use the Business templates to create a variety of designs you can use for any small business. (Chapter 8)

Combine Images:
By varying the number and size of the images on each page, you can use the same template to create a variety of different designs. (Chapter 8)

Yuval David

Quotes from Producers, Casting Directors, Actors, and more...

"Yuval is an extraordinarily gifted young actor. He is intelligent, honest, committed and brave. He makes daring choices and executes them with total concentration and a thrilling absence of fear. He is a joy to work with and a pleasure to behold."

- Arthur Allan Seidelman
Directed Yuval in the film "The Awakening of Spring"

"Yuval was a pleasure to work with on the film and brought sensitivity and passion to his character. He is wonderful at taking direction and is committed to bringing depth and honesty to his work."

- Melora Hardin
worked with Yuval as Director/Actor on the independent feature "You"

"Yuval David consistently impresses in auditions. He's a terrifically talented actor, always prepared and deeply focused.

I knew he would be perfect for the last role I cast him in. The director, writer and producers agreed. He was great in the role and a delight to work with. He brought incredible depth and sweet vulnerability to the character.

Getting to know him, I see how passionate he is about his craft and career. He has the talent and drive to go far in the business. All who work with him come to see this too. It would be a pleasure to work with him again."

- Angela Campolla-Sanders
Casting Director

Create as Many Pages as You Need: Use the templates to create a site with 1 page or 100 by simply adding new copies of the template pages. (Chapter 8)

Frame Your Images: Add frames around your images to create more dramatic effects and personalize the templates even more. (Chapter 8)

Make Movies:
Add video,
audio,
and other
multimedia
files.
(Chapter 13)

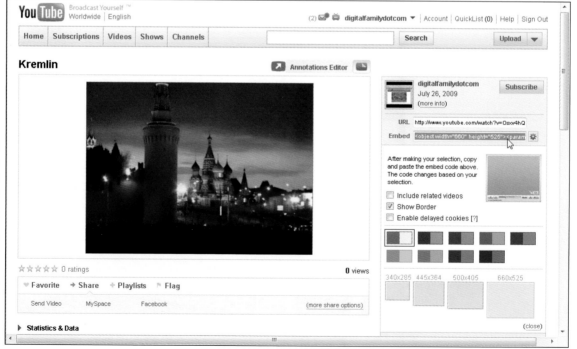

**Add YouTube
Videos:**
Adding videos
from YouTube,
Vimeo, and
other online
services to
your Web
site is as
easy as copy
and paste.
(Chapter 6)

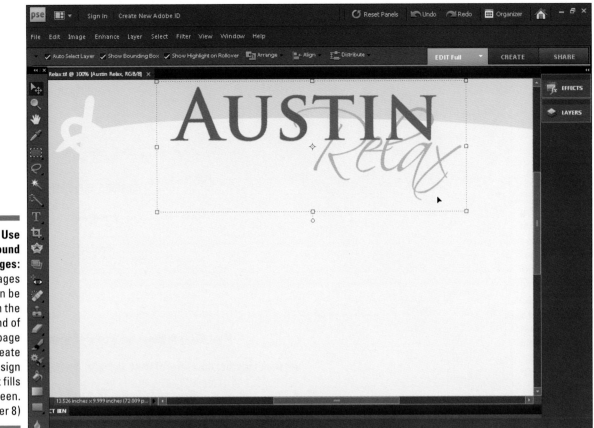

Use Background Images: Large images can be included in the background of a Web page to create a design that fills the screen. (Chapter 8)

Preview Your Site Before You Publish to the Web: After you've built a site like this one on your computer, it's easy to test and publish your pages to a Web server. (Chapter 10)

HOME
ABOUT ME
APPOINTMENTS
TREATMENTS
POLICIES
RATES
LINKS
CONTACT
CHAIR MASSAGE
NEW CLIENTS

POLICIES

Tardiness Policy:

I request that you arrive early for your appointment. Preferably 15 minutes before our session start time. Clients arriving late will receive the remainder of their scheduled massage time and will be charged the full amount of their original scheduled time. Clients arriving more than 15 minutes late may be rescheduled.

Cancellation Policy:

Our time together is important. Unless there is an emergency, it is requested that you cancel your appointment 24 hours in advance. If you cancel within less than 24 hours notice I will collect the full session fee at your next appointment.

Sickness Policy:

Austin Relax realizes that both Massage Therapist and client are susceptible to illness and asks client to reschedule their appointment when feeling sick. If the client has any of the following contagious illness the massage will be rescheduled: Diarrhea, Vomiting, Fever, Chicken Pox, Measles, Mumps, Meningitis, Hepatitis A, Conjunctivitis, Rubella, Head Lice, Impetigo, Influenza, Meningococcal Disease, Polio, Ringworm of the body, feet or scalp, Scabies, Thrush, Whooping Cough and the Common Cold. Also other illness will be evaluated at the therapist's discretion.

**Make a Big
Impression:**
Adding text
and other
elements over
a background
image, you
can create a
design that
seems to fill
the screen,
even when
you have very
little content.
(Chapter 8)

Sol Slavin

sol@solslavin.com

Portfolio of Projects

About Sol

Contact

Most of my projects were created with friends,

we work together on a level of trust and with the belief that

if we can't do it -- *it can't be done.*

**Create a
Consistent
Look:**
Use the same
background
image
throughout
a Web site
to create a
consistent
look, or
vary the
background
images to
create a
variety of
page designs.
(Chapter 8)

Sol Slavin

sol@solslavin.com

How I got started in 'the biz'

I've been working on film and video productions since 1998 when I got my first P.A. job. That feeling of spontaneous creativity and the magical possibility of making movies just flipped a switch inside of me.

I've been hooked ever since.

Skills

Grip: I have a good track record of collaborating with the D.P. and cinematographer to achieve the "look" they want without causing problems with time or continuity.

Electric: I understand the challenges when it comes to electrical work and how to rig it so the cast and crew can do their jobs without tripping on cables or getting fried.

Dolly: My goal is always to achieve smooth and seamless moves so the D.P. has a smile on his face at the end of the shot.

Camera: I learned how to operate a jib on a malfunctioning Chatman Peewee, which taught me the importance of pre-visualizing a shot so I could make it happen in my head before I had to make it happen with my body.

You can view samples of my work by visiting my Portfolio of Projects

Share Family Photos: You can use any of the templates in this book to create any type of site, but the Family template is designed to include common features, such as separate pages for each member of the family. (Chapter 9)

Resize and Optimize Photos: Each template includes image files, as well as Web pages, to make it easier for you to resize and adjust your photos to best fit the designs. (Chapter 9)

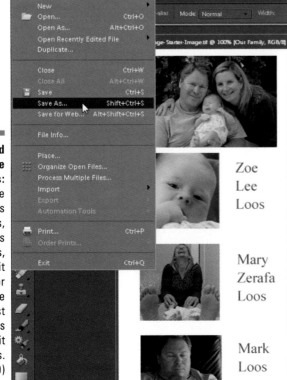

Add Your Family Photos: You can use the same template to create many different Web sites — just add your own images. (Chapter 9)

Change the Design: You can alter each template a little, or a lot, depending on the effect you want to create and how much time you want to spend on the design. (Chapter 9)

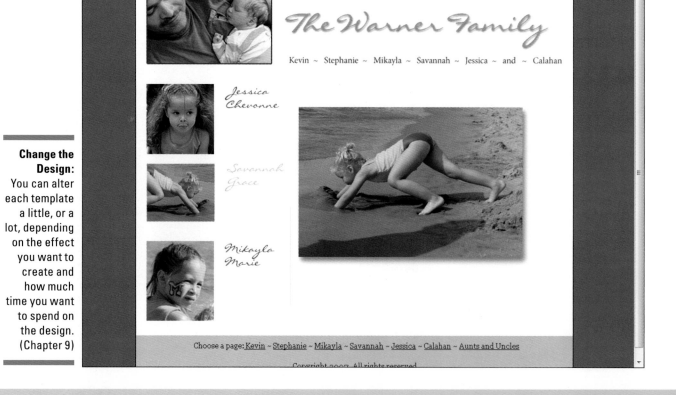

Prepare a Banner Image: Each template includes image files that can be turned into banners for the top of your Web site or blog, like the one shown here. Just add your photos, text, or other elements. (Chapter 11)

Create a Blog: In addition to templates and tips for creating Web pages, you find step-by-step instructions for creating a blog using the popular WordPress blogging program. (Chapter 11)

- **images:** You find all starter image files in TIFF format in this folder. You can create your own banner by editing the text and images in the TIFF file. You also find optimized JPEG files in the images folder that you can use as you follow along with the tasks. (You find instructions for editing the TIFF images and optimizing them in the JPEG format in the first task. You find more detailed instructions for editing images in Chapter 5.)

- **css:** You find the external style sheets that are attached to the template files in this folder.

- **Templates:** In this folder, you find the dynamic Web templates used to create the files in this site.

- **pages:** This folder stores all the pages for the individuals in your site and includes these ready-to-use pages:

    - mom.html: For a parent

    - dad.html: For a parent

    - child-1.html: For the first child

    - child-2.html: For the second child

    - child-3.html: For the third child

    - child-4.html: For the fourth child

    - other.html: For anyone else you want to add

You can rename files by using the Dreamweaver Files panel, as you see in the task "Designing a Web Page for the Entire Family." The Files panel lists all pages in a Web site; when you make changes in this panel, Dreamweaver automatically adjusts any corresponding links already set in the Web site template. If you stick to changing only filenames or folders in the Files panel, you never have to worry about breaking links.

Getting everyone working on your Web site

As you consider all the ways you can share stories and photos with family members and friends in your own family Web site, make sure to include your entire family in the planning-and-development process. Here are a few ways you can get family members of all ages involved:

- Ask older family members to write about special occasions and family traditions.

- Scan artwork from younger family members, and include those images on the site.

- Invite the family historian to help create a family tree and other historical records.

- Scan photos from old photo albums (and don't forget to sort through those boxes of old photos in your attic and closets).

- Include links to clubs, associations, and hobby sites to showcase your family's favorite activities.

- Keep the site updated with photos from everyone in the family, by sharing an online photo album at Flickr, Shutterfly, or the Kodak Gallery. It's simple and free to share photos on any of these sites, as I explain in Chapter 7.

Editing Starter Image Templates

The starter images for this template are designed to showcase images, so most of the work in creating this site is best done in an image-editing program, such as Photoshop Elements. The trick is to size and prepare all images before optimizing them for the Web and putting the pages together in Dreamweaver. In this task, you find instructions for adding your own images and text to the starter images included in the Family template.

This home page starter image has several elements — photos and text — and these files can be altered in many ways. In the following steps, I show you how to resize and add a photo and then edit the text by changing its font size, color, and spacing. After you insert and resize all images the way you want on your front page, you find instructions for using the Save for Web feature in Photoshop to optimize your images and save them as JPEGs so they're ready to insert into the template files in Dreamweaver.

1. Launch a graphics program, such as Photoshop Elements (shown in the figure), choose File⇨Open, and open the template graphic file `Home-Page-Starter-Image.tif`.

You can edit the image templates in any image editor that supports layers, including Adobe Photoshop and Fireworks. Photoshop Elements 8 is shown in this exercise. You will need to make minor adjustments if you use a different version of Photoshop Elements or you use the professional version of Photoshop, but these steps will be very similar in all recent versions of Photoshop and Elements.

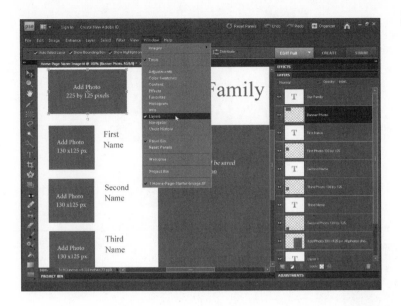

2. This starter image is made up of many layers, which makes it possible to edit each piece of text and delete or replace each image independently. You can view a list of layers by opening the Layers palette. Choose Window⇨Layers to open the Layers panel. As you see in this figure, this starter image has many layers, each named to correspond to a section of text or an image placeholder in the template. *Tip:* You can select a layer by clicking it in the Layers panel. If you select the Auto Select Layer check box (at the top of the workspace), you can also select layers by simply clicking the image placeholder or text in the starter image.

3. To edit the text in any image in Photoshop Elements, first click to select the Type tool in the Toolbox. (Look for the capital T.)

If, when you open this starter image, you see the error message `Some text layers contain fonts that are missing`, your computer's hard drive doesn't have the fonts I used in the starter image. If you choose the Text tool in Photoshop or Photoshop Elements and start to edit the text in this file, the program automatically changes the text to a font that's on your hard drive. You can then click and drag to select the text and use the options at the top of the workspace to change the font, size, and color to best suit your design. I used the Times New Roman font in this design, but you can use any font you prefer. You can purchase and download fonts from any number of sites on the Web; just search for Free Fonts in any search engine.

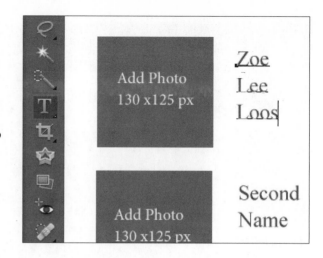

4. With the Type tool active, click and drag to select a section of text and then type to replace the words. (If you're prompted with the message `Font substitution will occur`, click OK to continue, and Photoshop automatically changes the text to a similar font on your hard drive.)

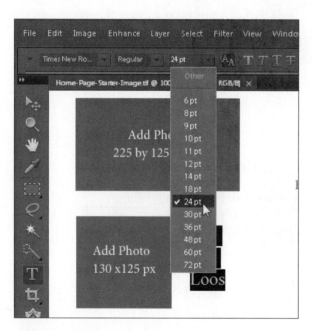

5. To change the font, color, size, or other text options, select the text you want to change and adjust the Type tool settings on the Options bar, at the top of the work area. In this figure, I'm adjusting the font size for the selected text.

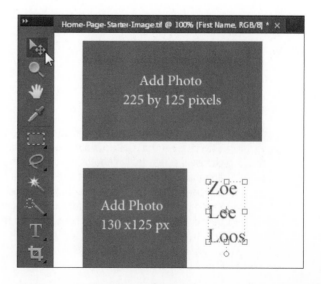

6. To reposition text or images on the page, click to select the Move tool from the Toolbox. (In Photoshop Elements, the Move tool is represented by the double-headed, crossed arrow icon at the top of the Toolbox). Then click and drag any section of text. ***Remember:*** If you click and drag a corner, you change the size of the text or image; if you click in the middle of a text area or image and drag, you move the selected item.

7. To add a photograph to a layer, you must first open the photograph as a separate file. While the starter image is still open, choose File⇨Open and select any image from your hard drive. In this example, I opened a photo of Mark, Mary, and Zoe Loos, which I want to add to the banner image at the top of the page.

8. Before you copy a photo into the starter image, it's helpful to resize it so that it will fit the design. I'm going to use this image in the banner at the top of the page, so I want to resize it to about 225 pixels wide. ***Hint:*** each placeholder image includes recommended dimensions. To resize an image, choose Image⇨Resize⇨Image Size and then change the Pixel Dimensions. (You find more detailed instructions for resizing images in Chapter 5.)

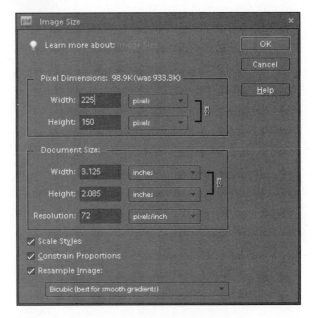

9. To copy an image into the template, first click anywhere on the image you want to copy, to make it active in the workspace. Choose Select⇨All to select the image, and then choose Edit⇨Copy to copy it. Next, click anywhere on the starter image (to make it active in the workspace) and then choose File⇨Paste to insert the new image into the template. After you paste an image, you can click anywhere within the image and drag to adjust its placement. You can also click and drag a corner to change the size of the image. (***Note:*** Make sure the Move tool is selected. See Step 6 for a refresher.)

10. As you add more images, you can adjust the layers by positioning one image in front of another, which is important when images overlap or when one image is obstructed by another. To move one layer in front of another, click and drag the layer to a higher position in the Layers panel, or right-click (Option-click on a Mac) and select an option to bring the layer forward or back. To delete an image or text, click to select it and then press the Delete key.

11. Continue to open photos you want to add to the design, resize them as necessary, and then copy and paste them into the starter image. In this design, I used three small images on the left, with larger versions in the main section of the design, but you'll need to crop a vertical image to get it to fit into the small space on the left. To cut a section off of an image that you've inserted into the design, select the Rectangular Marquee tool; then click and drag over the portion of the image you want to remove, creating a box around the part you want to delete, and press the Delete key.

You can add as many images as you like, and you can resize them and drag them around the page to change the layout. The more you alter this design in Photoshop, however, the more you need to alter it in Dreamweaver. For the purposes of this task, I show you how to edit images into these starter images just as it's designed so that you can easily reconstruct them in Dreamweaver. As you get more adept in both Photoshop and Dreamweaver, you can make more significant changes.

12. After you make all the changes you want to the starter image, be sure to save your work by choosing File➪Save. Then save the file again by choosing File➪Save As and name the new file something like `My-Family-Front-Page`. That way, you have a backup copy of the completed design before you start slicing up the image to save each piece separately, which you do in the steps that follow. ***Hint:*** If you ever want to go back to the original starter image included in the template, you can always download another copy from the Web site.

13. One of the challenges when you design a page like this one in Photoshop is deciding how to save each of the images as separate files that you can insert into your Web pages in Dreamweaver. A good place to start is the banner. Banners (including this one) typically appear at the top of every page in the site, but thanks to the magic of Dreamweaver Templates, you need only one copy of the image. To prepare the banner image for the Web, first choose the Crop tool from the Toolbox, and then click and drag to fit just the top banner area inside the cropping area.

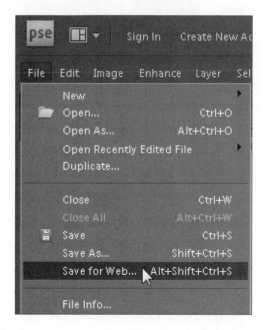

14. You can drag the corners of the crop outline to adjust how the banner will be cropped. To complete the crop, just double-click in the middle of the crop area or click the Crop tool again and click Crop in the confirmation dialog box that appears.

15. After you crop out just the banner image, choose File➪Save for Web to save the cropped portion as a new file optimized for the Web.

16. In the Save for Web dialog box that appears, choose JPEG from the Optimized File Format drop-down list. JPEG format works best for images that use millions of colors, such as photographs. Adjust other settings, such as compression, and click OK. Then, in the Save Optimized As dialog box, enter a name for the new image, make sure to save the image into the images folder in the Family Web Site template folder, and click Save. (You find more detailed instructions for optimizing images with the Save for Web dialog box in Chapter 5.)

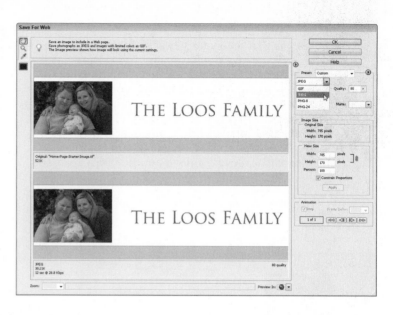

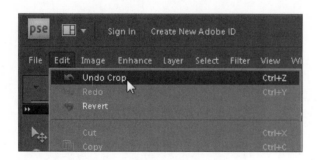

17. Now for the part that may seem tricky at first but will save you lots of time after you get the hang of it. After you save a new version of the banner optimized for the Web, you will see the original image you cropped still open in Photoshop. Choose Edit➪Undo Crop to restore the full image. Now you can crop the next part of the image you want to save for your Web site.

18. Save each cropped section of the image in turn, using the Save for Web dialog box. After you save all the pieces of your design, you're ready to move on to the next task and put them all together using Dreamweaver.

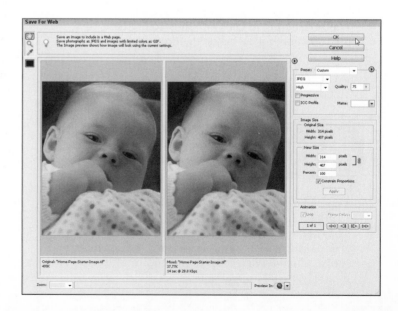

Designing a Web Site for the Entire Family

In this task, you set up a new Web site with the Family Web Site template, which can be used to create any site that features multiple people or sections. As you work through the following steps, remember that you can alter this template a little (by simply adding your own text and images) or alter the design a lot by changing the colors, font options, and other style settings to make the design more your own.

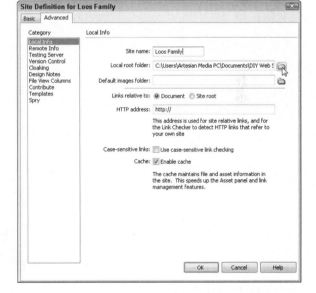

1. In Dreamweaver, choose Site⇨New Site. In the Site Definition dialog box, click the Advanced tab. In the Site Name text box, type a name for your site. In this example, I entered Loos Family. Click the Browse icon next to the Local Root Folder text box and locate on your hard drive the folder that contains the Family Web Site template.

If you want to rename the folder that contains the Family Web Site Template, do so before completing the site definition process. If you change the name of the main root folder of a Web site after you complete the site setup process, you have to repeat the setup steps to identify the renamed folder as the local root folder in Dreamweaver.

2. Click the Browse icon next to the Default Images folder field. In the Choose Local Images Folder dialog box that appears, select the Images folder in the Family template site and click Open. Back in the Site Definition dialog box, leave the rest of the options alone for now, and click OK. If you haven't selected the Enable Cache check box, a message box appears, asking whether you want to create a cache for the site. Click Yes to speed up some of the Dreamweaver display features.

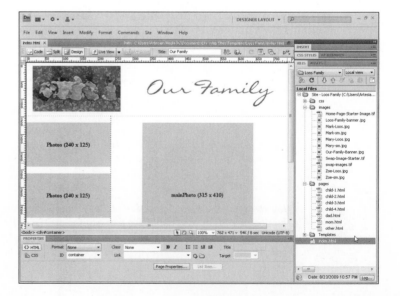

3. When you complete the site setup process, the files and folders in the Family Web Site template are displayed in the Files panel in Dreamweaver, at the side of the workspace. If the Files panel isn't visible, choose Window➪Files to open it. (For more detailed instructions on the site setup process, see Chapter 6.)

4. Double-click the index.html file in the Files panel to open the home page. The home page of this site is designed to showcase photos and text created in an image program, as you do in the previous task using Photoshop Elements. You can replace any of the image place-holders with images you've prepared for the Web.

5. At the very top of the home page, change the page title by replacing the text in the Title field. Include your name or a brief title to identify your page. (The *page title* is the text that appears at the very top of the browser window when a page is viewed online and the text that's saved when someone bookmarks your page.)

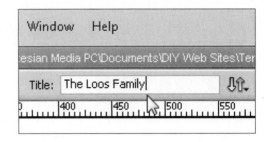

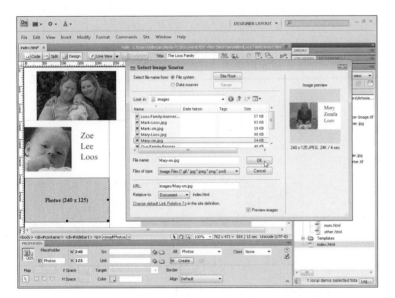

6. To insert your own images, double-click to select any image placeholder. In the Select Image Source dialog box navigate your hard drive to locate the image you want to insert, click to select the image you want to add to the page, and then click OK.

7. To add or replace other images, repeat Step 6. To delete an image or placeholder, select it and press the Delete key.

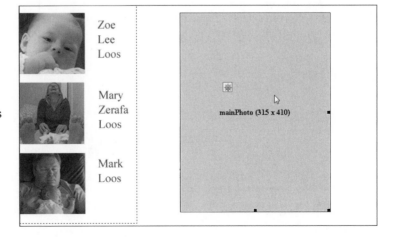

TIP

You want images on your site to download quickly and display well on-screen, so make sure that you optimize your images and save them in GIF, PNG, or JPEG format before adding them to your Web pages. You find instructions for editing the starter image for this template in the first part of this chapter and you find detailed instructions for saving images for the Web in Chapter 5.

Creating and Linking New Pages

Adding more pages to your family, business, or other Web site, is easy when you use Dreamweaver templates, like the ones I created for this book. And once you've added pages, you can use the template to automatically link the new page to all of the other pages. This family template, like all of the other templates featured in this book, includes a few pages to get you started, but you can always add more by following the instructions in this task.

In this task, you discover how to create a new page from a Dreamweaver template and link that page to all of the other pages in the site:

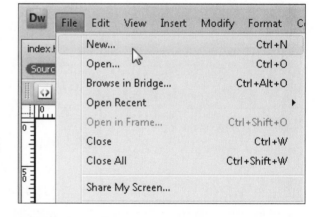

1. Before you create a new page in a site, make sure you've completed the site set up process in Dreamweaver, which is covered in the previous task. To create a new page from a template, choose File➪New.

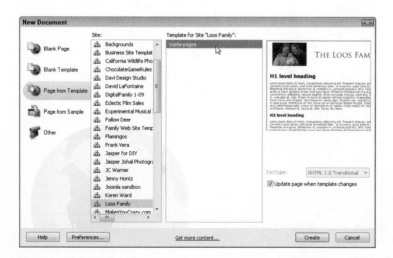

2. In the left side of New Document dialog box, choose Page from Template, in the Site section, make sure that the site you are working on is selected, and then choose the template you want to use to create your new page. A preview of the template is displayed in the right side of the dialog window. Click Create to create a new page and close the dialog box.

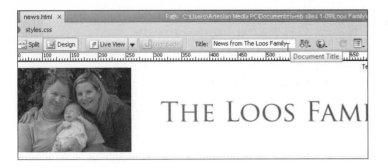

3. It's always good practice to save a new page as soon as it's created in Dreamweaver. It's also a good idea to include a brief description with a few key words specific to the content of each page in the Title field. In this example, I named the page `news.html` and I changed the title to News from The Loos Family.

4. You can edit or add text to any editable regions of the new page, which are identified with a light green box and an editable heading, such as the mainContent region shown here. Anything within the editable region is easy to change, such as the headline which I changed by selecting the text "H1 level heading" and replaced by typing in "New from the Loos Family." Remember, you can't change content in the locked regions of the page, such as the banner region at the top of the page or the links and copyright information at the bottom. Those areas can be changed only in the template. If you roll your cursor over a locked region, the cursor arrow changes to a circle with a line through it, indicating it can be edited only in the template itself.

5. To add images to an editable
region of a page, simply click to
place your cursor where you want
to add a new image and choose
Insert⇨Image. In the Select Image
Source dialog window, navigate
your hard drive to find the image
you want to add and then double-
click the image name to select it,
close the dialog, and insert it into
the page. After you insert an image
into a page, click to select the
image and you can use the
Property Inspector at the bottom
of the workspace to make additional changes, such as aligning
the image to the right or left,
which you can do by choosing
float-right or float-left from the
Class drop-down list.

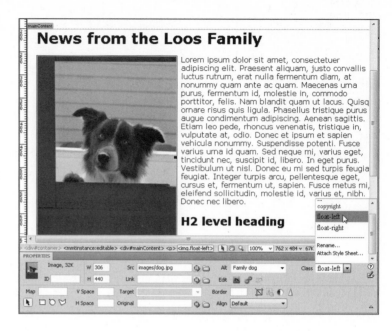

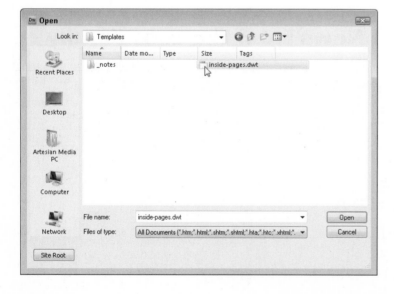

6. If you want to make changes to all
the pages created from a template,
such as adding a link to your new
page, you must first open the
Dreamweaver template itself by
choosing File⇨Open and then
opening the .dwt template file,
which is stored in the Templates
folder in the main root folder of
your Web site. In the family template, the Dreamweaver template
file is called inside-pages.dwt.

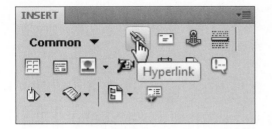

7. You can add a link to the bottom of this template by simply typing in the text you want to serve as the link. To make the text a link, click and drag to select the text and then click the link icon in the Common Insert menu (or choose Insert⇨Hyperlink).

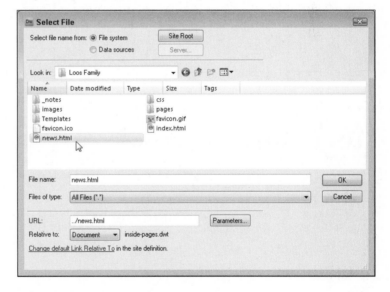

8. In the Select File dialog box, navigate to find the file to which you want to link. In this example, I selected the news.html page, which I created in the first part of this task. Click to select the file and then click OK to create the link and close the dialog box.

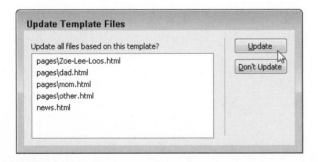

9. When you save the template file, Dreamweaver automatically opens the Update Template Files dialog box and lists all the pages created from the template. Click Update to add the new link to all the pages.

10. To test your links, preview the page in a Web browser by choosing File➪Preview in Browser and then selecting any browser you have associated with Dreamweaver. When you view the pages in a browser, even on your local computer, you can easily follow the links by clicking them just as you would on a Web page that has been published on the Internet. You learn more about previewing your Web pages and publishing your site to a Web server in Chapter 10.

You can find many more tips and tutorials for working with Dreamweaver, including advanced techniques like creating rollover images with Dreamweaver, at www.DigitalFamily.com/dreamweaver.

Chapter 10

Testing and Publishing a Web Site

Tasks Performed in This Chapter

✔ Testing Web pages in different browsers

✔ Using the Dreamweaver link-testing features

✔ Publishing a site with a Web server

✔ Using the Dreamweaver FTP features

It's a shocking scenario: You create a page design that looks just perfect in your favorite Web browser on your own computer. You publish it on the Internet and tell all your friends. And the next thing you know, your cousin in Iowa and your friends in Brazil are telling you that it looks terrible, the text is unreadable, and your Flash files don't play at all.

Don't let this happen to you. Take time to test your work before you publish the site for the entire world to see so you can make sure that it will work well in all the different Web browsers, operating systems, and monitor sizes that your visitors are likely to use.

Before you "go live" with your site, preview your pages in as many Web browsers as possible to make sure that your site looks the way you intend in the many different browsers in use on the Internet. If you don't have that many browsers on your own computer, don't worry. You can find many tips in this chapter to help you, including a collection of online services where you can test how your site will display in dozens of Web browsers on four different operating systems.

And, as you'll discover in the tasks in this chapter, it's a relatively simple step to use the many Dreamweaver testing features to ensure that all your links work properly, and to check for common compatibility problems that can lead to differences in browser display.

In the first part of this chapter, you find detailed instructions for previewing pages and using the Dreamweaver testing tools. In the second part of the chapter, you find out how to use the built-in Dreamweaver File Transfer Protocol (FTP) features to copy your Web site from your hard drive to a Web server on the Internet. And finally, you find instructions for adding Google Analytics (and other traffic-tracking services) to your site so you can see how many people visit your pages, where they come from, and how they get there — all of which play an important part of gauging the effectiveness of your site.

If you haven't been there already, check out Chapter 3 for recommendations and tips for choosing the best Web hosting and registering a domain name.

Understanding How Web Pages Look on Different Computers

One of the more confusing and frustrating aspects of Web design is that you can create a page that looks great in Dreamweaver and test it in a browser to confirm that it looks fine only to discover later that it looks terrible in a different browser or on a different computer system. Web pages can look different from one system to another for many reasons, but the following issues are the most common culprits:

- **Browser differences:** Today, dozens of browsers are in use on the Web, not counting the different versions of each browser. For example, at the time of this writing, Internet Explorer (IE) 8 is the newest release from Microsoft, but a significant percentage of Web users haven't upgraded yet and are still using IE6 or even earlier versions. (More on browser differences in the next section.)

- **Hardware differences:** Another challenge comes from the differences between Macintosh and Windows computers. For example, most fonts appear smaller on a Macintosh than on a PC (Times 12 on a PC looks like Times 10 on a Mac). Image colors can also vary from one computer to another.

- **Individual resolution settings:** In addition, the same Web page may look very different on a 21" monitor than it does on a 15" monitor. And even on the same monitor, different resolution settings can alter the way a page looks. On a PC, a common resolution is 1024 x 768; on a Mac, the resolution is generally set much higher, making the design look much smaller, even if the monitor sizes are the same.

As a result of all these differences, the same Web page can look very different to the many people who visit a Web site. For example, Figure 10-1 shows a Web page in Internet Explorer on a PC, and Figure 10-2 shows the same page in Safari on a Macintosh. Notice that the text displays in a larger font size on the PC, changing how the text wraps around the photo in the left column.

This challenging aspect of the Web is at the root of many of the limitations and complications of creating good Web designs. With patience, testing, and an understanding of the tags and styles that are most problematic, you can create great Web sites that look good to most, if not all, of the people who visit your Web site.

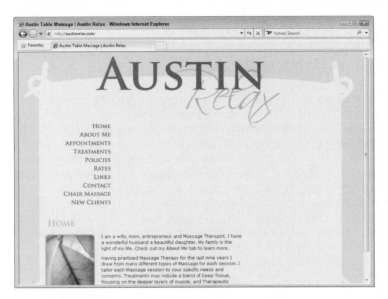

Figure 10-1: A Web page displayed in IE 6 on a PC with the monitor set to 1024 x 768 resolution. Note that the right column has been bumped down below the left column, a common problem in IE6.

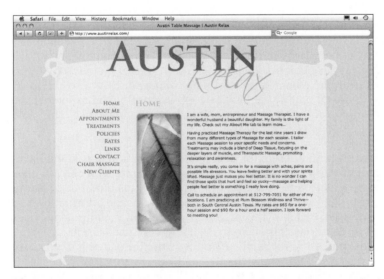

Figure 10-2: The same Web page displayed in Safari 3 on a Mac with the monitor set to 1280 x 800. This is how the designer expected the site to look.

Understanding How Browsers Affect a Site's Appearance

Of the many reasons why Web pages can look different from one browser to another, it boils down to this: Web browsers have evolved over the years to support new technologies on the Web. Thus, many older browsers still in use have trouble displaying some of the advanced features you can use on your Web pages today. Compounding this problem, the companies that make Web browsers — including Microsoft, Google, and Apple — don't all agree or follow the same rules (although most are getting better at complying with the same set of standards in their latest browser versions). Dozens of browsers are now in use on the Web, not counting the different versions of each browser. For example, as I mention earlier, IE8 is the newest release from Microsoft (at the time of this writing), but a significant percentage of Web users haven't yet upgraded and are still using IE7 or even IE6, which is notoriously bad at displaying CSS (Cascading Style Sheets) and other modern Web features.

The result is that the same Web page can look significantly different to the many people who visit a Web site. The differences can become even more pronounced in older browsers or in monitors of different sizes.

This challenging aspect of Web design is at the root of many of the limitations and complications of creating Web sites that look good to everyone who may visit your pages. HTML was designed to help ensure that Web pages look good on every computer on the planet, and as a result, some of the rules of Web design may seem strange or limiting at first. Despite these efforts, and a growing movement toward more standardized Web development, getting your pages to look exactly the same on every computer on the planet is difficult if not impossible. As a result, most designers strive to create pages that look as good as possible on as many browsers as they consider important, even if the same pages don't look *exactly* the same on all browsers.

Which browsers you should design for depends on your audience. If you have the luxury of having accurate reports on the visitors to your site, you can see a list of all browsers used by visitors to your site. (At the end of this chapter is information about using Web-statistic services that include browser usage information.) For example, your Web statistics may reveal that 27 percent of your audience uses IE7, 18 percent uses IE6, 25 percent uses Firefox 3, 23 percent uses Firefox 2, 5 percent uses Chrome, and 2 percent uses Safari. With those numbers in mind, you may decide that your pages should look attractive in IE and Firefox, but you'll settle for them not looking quite as good in Safari and Chrome, which at this point have lesser percent of your audience and display some features quite differently.

Entire books and Web sites are dedicated to the differences among browsers, and how to best design for everyone on the Web. To help keep things simple for you, I include templates in this book that are designed to look best in the most recent and most commonly used browsers on the Web, including IE8 and IE7, and Firefox 3 and 2. However, you should note that making significant changes to these designs may result in unpredictable results, which is another important reason to test your work thoroughly before you publish your site.

Previewing Web Pages in Multiple Browsers

Previewing your Web pages in a variety of Web browsers is the simplest way to make sure that they look suitable to at least most of your visitors. The following task walks you through the process of adding browsers to Dreamweaver for easy previewing and for viewing the same Web page in multiple browsers.

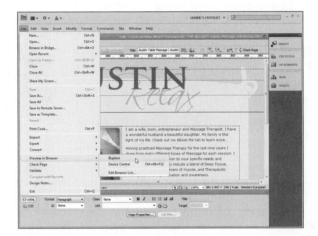

1. Open a Web page that you want to preview in Dreamweaver, choose File⇨Preview in Browser, and choose a Web browser from the list of browser options. (You find out how to add more browsers to this list in Steps 3 and 6.)

2. Study the page carefully, testing all the links, rollovers, and any other special effects to make sure that the page appears how you want in this browser.

3. Return to Dreamweaver to make any changes you want to the page. Then test the same page in other Web browsers. To add browsers to the preview list, choose File⇨Preview in Browser and then choose Edit Browser List.

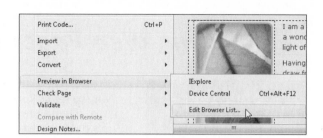

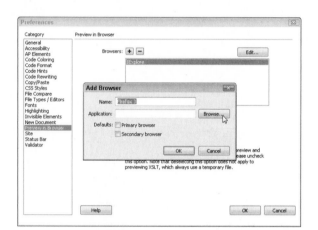

4. After the Preferences dialog box opens to the Preview in Browser settings, click the plus (+) sign at the top of the dialog box to open the Add Browser dialog box. Enter a name for the browser. (I like to include the version number as well as the name, as I have here, with Firefox 3.) Then click the Browse button.

5. Find the browser you want to add on your hard drive, click to select it, and then click Open to add it to the browser list in Dreamweaver. *Note:* You can add only those browsers to Dreamweaver that are on your hard drive. (See the nearby sidebar "Downloading new browsers" to find out more about finding and downloading new browsers for testing.) Look for the browser's executable file (with an .exe extension) rather than a shortcut on your desktop that you may use to launch the browser.

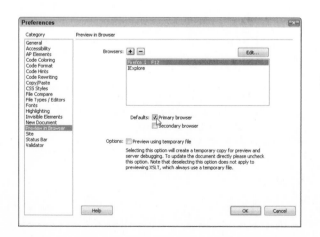

6. Repeat Steps 3–5 to add more browsers to the list. You can then designate which browser you want as your *primary* browser: the browser that's launched when the F12 key is first pressed. You can also designate a *secondary* browser, which appears second on the list and will launch and display the same Web page if you press Ctrl+F12 on Windows or ⌘+F12 on a Mac.

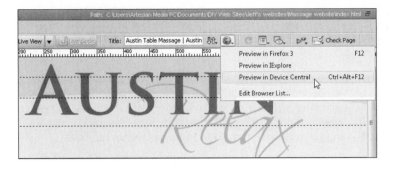

7. You can also preview a page in a browser by clicking the Preview/ Debug in Browser icon (it looks like a globe), at the top of the workspace, and selecting any browser from the list.

8. Adobe Device Central is available in Dreamweaver versions CS3 and CS4. (You don't have this option if you'reusing an older version of Dreamweaver.) Device Central is designed to help you create and test Web sites for mobile devices, such as cell phones. Using Device Central, you can preview your Web pages in many different cell phone models by first clicking the plus sign next to the device type and then any of the devices listed within each group.

Downloading new browsers

So how do you put new browsers on your hard drive so that you can preview your pages with them? The simplest way to get the latest versions is to visit the Web sites of the companies that create the most popular browsers:

✔ Microsoft Internet Explorer: www.microsoft.com/ie

✔ Mozilla Firefox: www.firefox.com

✔ Apple Safari (Mac only): www.apple.com/safari

✔ Google Chrome: www.google.com/chrome

Testing Sites with Online Browser Emulators

Unless you own a dozen computers with different operating systems and a vast collection of Web browsers, you can't fully test your Web site on your own. Fortunately, a growing number of online services are available to help you preview your pages on many different operating systems and browsers, without having to manage multiple computers and browsers yourself.

Here are some of the best places to test your Web site online:

Xenocode Browser Sandbox (`www.xenocode.com/Browsers`). The Xenocode browser sandbox makes it easy for you to test a site using any of the eight most popular browsers without having to install them all on your system. You simply download and install a plug-in from the Xenocode site and then click the browser you want to use. After the selected browser launches, you can surf the Web as if the browser were installed on your computer. The service is free (at the time of this writing). And because you can surf through the browsers, you can interact with Web sites, testing all your pages, as well as JavaScript, AJAX, and other interactive features.

Adobe Browser Labs (`https://browserlab.adobe.com`). Adobe Browser Labs makes it possible for you to test any Web page on the Internet in the most common browsers. At the time of this writing, that includes IE versions 6 and 7, Mozilla Firefox versions 2 and 3, and Apple Safari version 3. You can also test pages on different operating systems, such as Windows XP and Mac OS X. When you use this service, the result is a screenshot with a preview of the page, which offers a quick and easy way to test pages' display. Small downside: You can't test interactive features, and you can test in only two browsers at a time.

Cross Browser Testing (`www.crossbrowsertesting.com`). The Cross Browser Testing site takes Web site–testing to another level. Instead of simply providing screenshots of a Web page in different browsers, or letting you launch a few browsers to test pages in, this site lets you take over other computers connected to the Internet so that you can test interactive features using a variety of browsers and operating systems. For example, if you use a computer that runs Windows Vista and you want to see what your site will look like on a Mac, you can choose to use a computer with the Mac OS and then view your site in any of a dozen browsers on the Mac system. The advantage is that you get more than snapshots, and you also can test interactive features, such as JavaScript, AJAX, forms, and more. This service requires that you purchase a monthly subscription.

Browsershots (`www.browsershots.org`). Browsershots is a popular online testing tool. You simply enter a page's URL and choose the options you want to use for testing. Browsershots then tests the page you submitted on each computer system selected with the specified browser and takes a screenshot. Although you can't test interactive features with this service, it's one of the easiest options and provides the largest collection of browsers to choose from. (You find instructions for using Browsershots in this task.) The basic service is free, but it can take a few minutes or a few hours to complete testing. If you don't like waiting, you can upgrade to "priority processing" for a fee.

1. At www.browsershots.org, enter the URL of the page you want to test in the Enter URL Here field. (***Note:*** You can test only those pages that are published on a Web server, but you can test any of those pages. For example, I can test www.californiawildlife photography.com (as I'm doing here), and I can also test www.californiawildlife photography.com/gallery to (test the gallery page separately). Browsershots can test only one page at a time.

2. Browsershots offers an exhaustive array of browser options (more than 92 different Web browsers and versions to choose from), and you can choose to test any browser available on any or all of the major operating systems, including Linux, Windows, Mac OS, and BSD. You can't, however, select specific versions of these operating systems. Place a check mark next to each browser you want to test, but keep in mind that the more options you choose, the longer it will take.

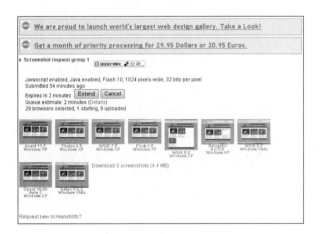

3. The result is a collection of thumbnail screenshots that give you a literal snapshot of how your page looks across many different browsers and systems. It can take a few minutes or a few hours to complete testing, depending on how busy the service is and how many options you choose.

4. Click any of the thumbnail images to see a slightly larger version. If you find that a page doesn't display properly in a browser, such as the one shown here in IE6, you can then use Dreamweaver to make adjustments to the page layout and test it again to see whether the display improves.

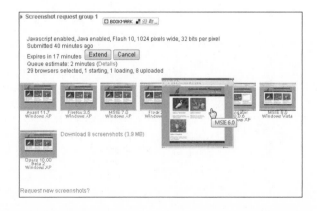

Designing for mobile devices

With the rising popularity of Internet-enabled mobile devices, a new audience of Web page visitors has emerged. Some high-end mobile devices (think iPhone and BlackBerry Storm) are capable of loading Web pages and do so reasonably well. However, the screen is much smaller, and the interactions with the Web browser is much different — specifically, navigating by touch. Lower-end regular mobile devices that make up the vast majority of the market often have small screens, reduced color display, and allow only minimal interaction.

To best manage the dramatic differences on mobile devices, my best recommendation is that you create a second version of your Web site designed to best serve the limited display options of mobile devices and link to the alternate design from your main site. If you have experience writing server scripts (or can hire someone to do it for you), you can create an auto-detect script that can determine whether a visitor to your site is using a mobile phone or a computer and direct them to the best version of your site automatically.

Here are a few important tips to consider when designing for mobile devices:

- Because download times are much slower on mobile devices, adjust the number of features you offer to mobile devices, and keep the number of images and style minimal.

- Use CSS for the design and layout of the Web page. Outdated HTML styling and layout options (such as frames) may not display at all on mobile devices.

- Screen size on a mobile device is extremely limited, with less width and more height than traditional computer monitors. (The view is more rectangular than square.) Optimize your content and design accordingly.

- There is no mouse on the mobile phone — only up and down arrows, and at best a touch screen. Adjust your design to require as little scrolling and user movement as possible.

- Always validate your Web page code (numerous validation services are online, such as the one at `http://validator.w3.org`). Mobile browsers are even less forgiving than traditional Web site browsers about errors in your code.

- Very few mobile devices support JavaScript, so don't use it in the mobile version of a Web site.

- Not all mobile devices support Flash or other multimedia formats. Use multimedia sparingly and make sure to include links to alternative content for visitors who may not be able to view these features.

- Test with mobile phone emulators, such as Dreamweaver's Device Central (featured in the first task in this chapter), and the online emulators available at `http://ready.mobi` and `http://mtld.mobi/emulator.php`.

- Test interactive features on a variety of mobile phones. If you can't afford to buy several phones (and who can?), ask your friends and coworkers to test your site on their phones.

- Visit stores that sell mobile phones and ask for a demo of the phone's Web browser capabilities; then make sure to view your own site while you're testing the phone. Although it can take some time to run around town visiting mobile phone stores and doing demos, it's a cheap way to test in a variety of modern devices, and you might even find your new favorite phone.

To read more about designing for mobile devices, check out my book *Mobile Web Design For Dummies* (Wiley).

Using the Dreamweaver Link-Testing Features

Stuff You Need to Know

Toolbox:
- ✔ Adobe Dreamweaver
- ✔ A Web site with linked pages

Time needed:
About half an hour

Test, test, and test some more. To help you ensure that all the bells and whistles on your Web site ring and ding the way they should, a variety of Dreamweaver features make it easy to test your pages for broken links and other potential problems. In the task that follows, you find instructions for using some of these high-powered testing tools on a completed Web page.

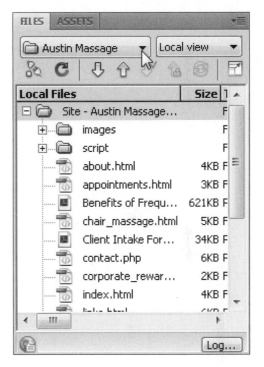

1. Make sure that the site you want to test is selected and active in the Files panel. (To open the Files panel, choose Window⇨Files.) If you haven't yet completed the site setup process, see Chapter 6 to take care of this important initial step.

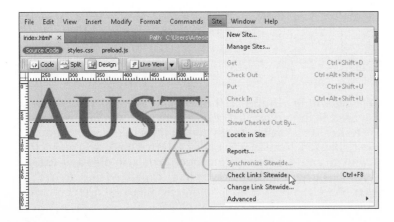

2. To test the links in a Web site, choose Site⇨Check Links Sitewide.

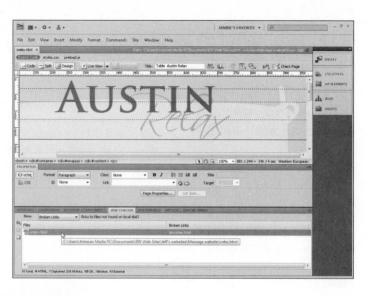

3. The report from the Check Links feature is displayed at the bottom of the workspace. If Dreamweaver reports a broken link, like the one shown here (to the `about me.html` file), double-click the filename. Dreamweaver highlights the corresponding text or image with the broken link so that you can easily see where you need to fix the link.

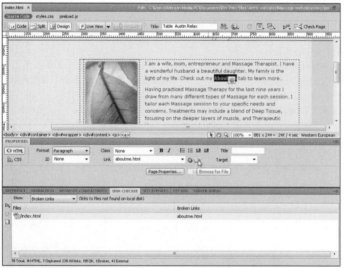

4. You can fix broken links in a number of ways; the simplest is to reset the link by following the same steps you find in Chapter 6 for creating links. As in the example shown here, where I'm fixing a link from one page in a Web site to another page in the same site, start by making sure that the linked text is selected. Then click the Browse button (the yellow file folder icon next to the Link field) in the Property Inspector to locate the correct filename. (For more detailed instructions on creating links, see Chapter 6.)

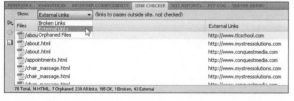

5. In addition to identifying broken links to pages within a Web site, the Dreamweaver link report lists other kinds of links. For example, you can use the drop-down list shown here to view all the external links, or links in a site that go to other Web sites. This makes it easy to test links to other sites to make sure that the Web site address hasn't changed. Note that to check external links, you must preview a page in a browser on a computer with an active Internet connection. You also display a list of unused files in a site by choosing Orphaned files from the drop-down menu. *Orphaned* files are HTML pages that aren't linked to any other pages, as well as images and multimedia files that aren't inserted into any pages in your site.

Setting Up FTP in Dreamweaver

Stuff You Need to Know

Toolbox:

- Adobe Dreamweaver
- A Web site ready to be published
- A Web server or hosting service

Time needed:
About half an hour

Okay, you created a Web site and tested it, and you're ready to upload it to the Web. It's time to put the Dreamweaver publishing tools to work. If you're using a commercial service provider, you most likely need the Dreamweaver FTP features, covered in detail in this task and the remaining tasks in this chapter.

Note that you must complete the site setup process, covered in the beginning of Chapter 6, before you can configure the site for uploading. You also need the following information from your Web hosting service (find tips for choosing a Web host in Chapter 3):

- The FTP host name
- The path to the Web directory (optional but useful, and should look similar to this: /web/htdocs/jcwarner)
- An FTP login or user name
- An FTP password

After you gather all your FTP information and complete the site setup, you're ready to access the Dreamweaver publishing tools and prepare the program to upload your Web site. In this task, you set up Dreamweaver to connect to your server via FTP, a process you need to do only once for each site you work on. In the next task, you use Dreamweaver to upload pages to your server by using the connection you establish in this task. Follow these steps:

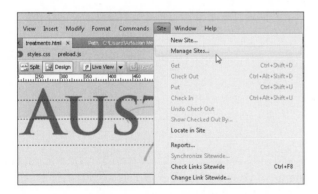

1. Choose Site⇨Manage Sites to open the Manage Sites dialog box. Alternatively, you can choose Manage Sites from the Site drop-down list in the Files panel.

2. In the list of defined sites, select the site you want to publish. Then click the Edit button.

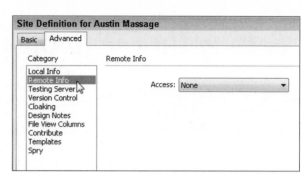

3. Select the Advanced tab at the top of the Site Definition dialog box, and then select the Remote Info category from the left side.

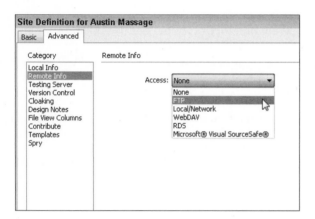

4. Click the arrow for the Access drop-down list box, and then choose the publishing option best suited to your Web server and development environment. If you're using a commercial Web host (the most common option for small do-it-yourself sites), choose FTP. If you're working at a university, a large company, or an organization that has its own Web servers, refer to the nearby sidebar, "The multiple Dreamweaver publishing options," to understand your choices here, and check with your system administrator to find out which option is best for your system.

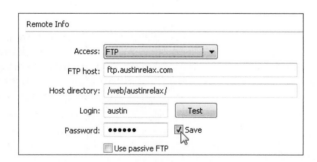

5. In the FTP Host text box, type the host name of your Web server. In my example, I used `ftp.austinrelax.com`. In the Host Directory text box, type the directory on the remote site in which documents visible to the public are stored. In my example, I used `/web/austinrelax/`. The information you enter in this field depends on your server. In some cases, you can leave the field blank if you log in directly to your site; in other cases, you use a different path, such as `users/mysite/domain`. Check with your service provider or site administrator to find out how your server is set up.

6. Enter your login name and password. Web services require a username and password to gain access to your Web server to ensure that you're the only person who can make changes to your Web site. If you select the Save check box, Dreamweaver stores the information on your local computer and you don't have to retype it every time you log in to your Web server. Click the Test button to make sure that you entered everything correctly. If there are no problems, Dreamweaver responds with the message `Adobe Dreamweaver CS4 connected to your Web server successfully`.

7. Select the Use Passive FTP option or the Use Firewall option only if your service provider or site administrator instructs you to do so. If you use a commercial Web hosting service, you shouldn't need to select any remaining options in this section of the dialog box. Select the use Secure FTP check box if you have a secure Web server, but be aware that not all hosts support secure FTP. If you select this option and see an error message when you press the Test button, deselect the option and test again.

The multiple Dreamweaver publishing options

In the Remote Info category of the Site Definition dialog box, you find the following options when you click the Access drop-down list. The following list briefly describes when you should select each choice. (If you're using a commercial Web hosting service, the FTP option should be your best choice.)

✔ **None:** When you aren't uploading your site to a server or when you aren't yet ready to fill in these settings.

✔ **FTP:** When you're using the built-in Dreamweaver File Transfer Protocol features, which are covered in detail in the following section. You're most likely to need these settings if you're using a commercial Web hosting service.

✔ **Local/Network:** When you're using a Web server on a local network, such as your company or university server. For specific settings and requirements, check with your system administrator.

✔ **WebDAV (Web-based Distributed Authoring and Versioning):** When you're using a server with the WebDAV protocol, such as Microsoft IIS.

✔ **RDS (Remote Development Services):** When you're using ColdFusion on a remote server.

✔ **Microsoft Visual SourceSafe:** When you're using Microsoft Visual SourceSafe. (This option is available only in Windows.)

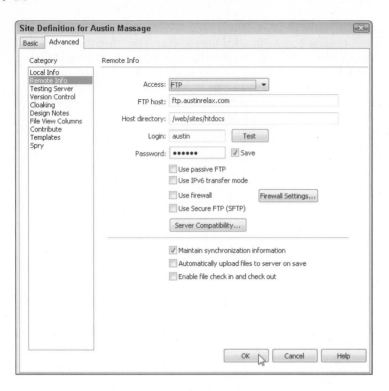

8. Select the Maintain Synchronization Information check box; Dreamweaver then automatically keeps track of any changes you make to pages on your local computer that haven't been uploaded to the server. *Note:* I never recommend that you select the Automatically Upload Files to Server on Save check box because I think that you should test your pages on your local computer before you publish them to the local site. Leaving this box deselected prevents the possibility of accidentally uploading errors automatically every time you save a page on your local computer. The Enable File Check In and Check Out option opens an advanced feature that can be used to track files when multiple people are working on a Web site. You can find more information on this and other site management features in my book *Dreamweaver CS4 For Dummies* (Wiley).

9. Click OK to save your Web server information settings and close the Site Definition dialog box. You're ready to start using the Dreamweaver FTP features, covered in the next section.

If you try to connect to your server and see the message An FTP error occurred, it usually means that you entered characters incorrectly. Be very careful as you type your username, password, and other information because most servers are case sensitive and require that these fields be filled in with the exact host, directory, login, and password information. If you still have trouble, contact your service provider or site administrator to ensure that you have all the correct information for connecting to your server. Setting up all this information correctly the first time can be tricky, and each service provider is different.

Uploading Files with the Dreamweaver FTP Features

Stuff You Need to Know

Toolbox:
- ✔ Adobe Dreamweaver
- ✔ A Web site with linked pages
- ✔ Access to a Web server

Time needed:
About half an hour

After you enter all your Web server and login information into Dreamweaver (as you do in the previous task), you can upload files to your server and retrieve them at any time by using the built-in FTP capabilities of Dreamweaver.

To transfer files between your hard drive and a remote server, follow these steps:

1. Make sure that the site you want to upload is selected and visible in the Files panel and that you entered all the FTP settings described in the previous section. Then, in the upper-left corner of the Files panel, click the Connects to Remote Host icon. (It looks like a plug and an outlet.)

If you're not already connected to the Internet, the Connects to Remote Host icon attempts to start your dialup connection. If you have trouble connecting this way, try establishing your Internet connection as usual to check e-mail or surf the Web, and then return to Dreamweaver and click the Connects to Remote Host icon after establishing your Internet connection. When your computer is online, Dreamweaver should have no trouble automatically establishing an FTP connection with your host server.

2. When the connection is established, the blue Connects to Remote Host icon changes to look like the plugs are connected (or, dare I say, plugged in). After the connection is established, you can view the files and folders on your Web server by choosing Remote View from the drop-down list in the upper-right corner. (It's shown open in this figure.) Using the drop-down arrow, you can easily switch between Local view (displays the files and folders in the root site folder on your local hard drive) and Remote view by selecting each one in turn.

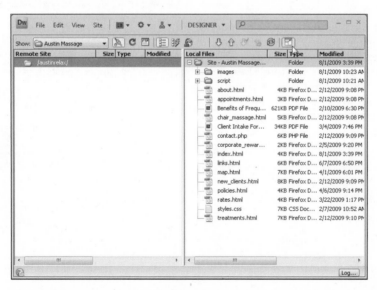

3. To see both Local and Remote views simultaneously, expand the Files panel by clicking the Expand icon, in the upper-right corner of the Files panel. With the panel expanded, you can upload and download files by dragging them from one pane to the other. To minimize the Files panel, click the same icon again. In this figure, the Files panel is expanded and the cursor is hovering over the icon, which is labeled Collapse when the Files panel is expanded.

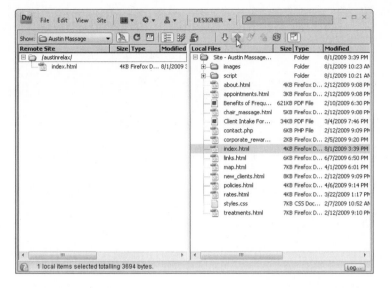

4. To *upload* a file (transfer a file from your hard drive to your Web server), select the file from the Local View panel (which displays the files on your hard drive) and click the Put Files icon (the up arrow) in the Files panel. If a dialog box appears with the message `Put dependent files`, choose No to upload only the selected file. Choose Yes, and Dreamweaver uploads the selected file, plus any files that appear within that file, such as images or multimedia files that are inserted into a page.

5. Files are copied to your server when you transfer them, leaving the file on the local computer untouched. You can select multiple files or folders to be transferred simultaneously.

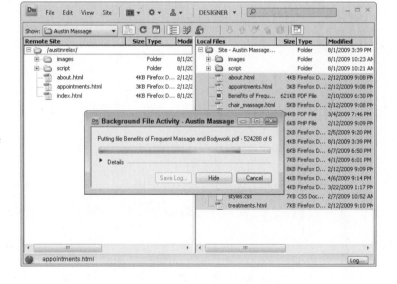

When you copy files to or from your server, the files you're transferring overwrite the files already at the destination. Dreamweaver notifies you about the overwriting if it notices that you're replacing a newer version of a file with an old one, but it's always a good idea to double-check before you overwrite a file.

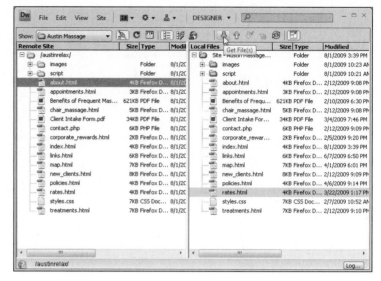

6. To *download* files or folders (transfer files or folders from your Web server to your hard drive), select the files or folders from the Remote Site panel (which displays the files on your server) and click the Get Files button (the down arrow) in the Files panel. The files are automatically copied to your hard drive when you transfer them.

After you upload files to your server, test your work by using a Web browser to view the pages online. Sometimes, things that look and work fine on your computer don't work on the server, so you should always test the pages on the server right away.

Using dedicated FTP programs

If you prefer to use a dedicated FTP program rather than the built-in Dreamweaver features, you can download one of these popular FTP programs for the Mac or PC:

- ✔ **FireFTP:** A Firefox add-on that you can download for free from `http://fireftp.mozdev.org`.

- ✔ **WS_FTP:** On a PC, you can find this program with the unusual name at `www.ipswitch.com`.

- ✔ **CuteFTP:** Download this Windows program from `www.cuteftp.com`.

- ✔ **Fetch:** If you use a Macintosh computer, check out this program, available at `www.fetchsoftworks.com`.

- ✔ **Transmit:** You can download this program, also for the Mac, at `www.panic.com/transmit`.

- ✔ **FileZilla:** This is a great open-source FTP program available for PC, Linux, or Mac at `http://filezilla-project.org`.

Adding Google Analytics to your Site

Stuff You Need to Know

Toolbox:
- ✔ A web site where you want to track traffic.
- ✔ A Web browser, such as IE, Safari, Chrome, or Firefox.

Time needed:
About half an hour

One of the greatest advantages of publishing information on the Web is that you can track how people use that information, how they find it, where they come from, and more. There are many ways to gather data about visitors to your Web site. Most Web hosting services provide access to some kind of server logs that include basic information, such as how many people visit your site every day, week, month, or year.

If you want more information, consider using one of the third-party statistic services, such as Google Analytics, covered in the next task, or any of the similar services included in the sidebar, "Using online Web-traffic services." Google Analytics is the most popular Web traffic–reporting software available on the Web today. And it's no surprise. Google Analytics is powerful, comprehensive, remarkably easy to use — and free!

Follow these steps to add Google Analytics to your site.

1. Sign up for an account at Google Analytics (`www.google.com/analytics`). If you already have a Google account, such as one you use for Gmail, just click the big blue Access Analytics button, and you can use your existing account as you sign up for Analytics. If you're new to Google, click the Sign Up Now link and create a new account when you sign up for Analytics.

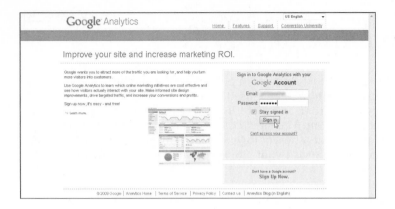

2. After you set up an account, just enter your user name and password to access your account. When you log into Google Analytics, if you already have sites set up with tracking, you'll see them listed on the Overview page. To set up a new site, click the Add Website Profile link at the bottom of the Overview page.

3. On the Create New Website Profile page that appears, select Add a Profile for a New Domain if you're setting tracking for the first time, or select Add a Profile for an Existing Domain if you want to track a domain with a second profile. Enter the URL of the site you want to track, select the country and time zone from the drop-down lists, and then click the Finish button at the bottom of the page.

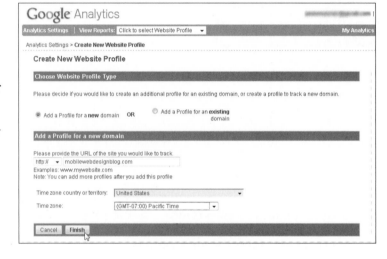

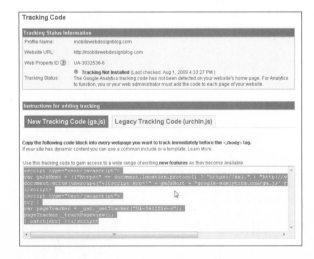

4. Google Analytics provides you with two options: New Tracking Code (`ga.js`) or Legacy Tracking Code (`urchin.js`). I recommend using the new tracking code so you have access to the latest and greatest new features that aren't available via the legacy code. Select the entire code block in the input box and copy it. Then click the Finish button at the bottom of the page to return to the Overview.

5. To add the code to a page in Dreamweaver, click the Code button at the top left of the workspace, and then scroll down to the bottom of the Web page where you want to add the code. With the cursor or mouse, select the line immediately before the `</body>` tag and then press Enter on your keyboard. Choose Edit⇨Paste, and the previously copied tracking code from Google Analytics is added to your Web page. Save your changes.

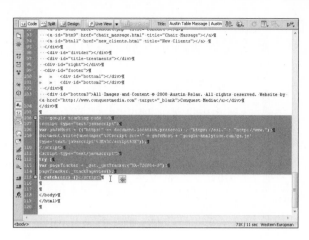

6. To add Google Analytics code to a WordPress blog, log into the Administrative tools for your blog (as if you're going to add a new post) and then choose Appearance from the left side of the Dashboard. Under Appearance, choose Editor; then, on the right side of the page, under Templates, choose Footer (`footer.php`). Scroll down to the bottom of the page code; just above the close body tag `</body>`, paste the code from Google Analytics. Click Update File, and all the pages in your blog will be tracked automatically.

If you use Dreamweaver's `.dwt` template feature in your Web site, add your Google Analytics to the template in an uneditable region, and it will automatically be added to all the pages created from the template. See Chapter 6 for more information on templates and adding code to your pages in Dreamweaver.

Using online Web-traffic services

Although Google Analytics is the most popular online traffic service, there are several alternatives, including:

Clicky (www.getclicky.com). Clicky is a hosted, real-time Web analytics service that provides statistics as they occur (unlike most other Web site statistics services). Clicky focuses more on current trends as opposed to historical data, which is also available. Clicky offers both free and paid services, and most noticeably offers a developer API, Twitter analytics, and dedicated mobile and iPhone versions. Clicky also works on browsers without JavaScript enabled. None of these services are offered by Google Analytics.

Yahoo! Web Analytics (http://web. analytics.yahoo.com). Yahoo! Web Analytics was created by IndexTools, a leading provider of Web analytics software that was acquired by Yahoo!. Data is collected in "near" real-time, which means most data is available within minutes or seconds of a Web site visit. Yahoo! Web Analytics is free, offers customizable dashboards, segmentation tools for data analysis, and campaign management features similar to Google Analytics.

AWStats (http://awstats.sourceforge. net). AWStats is a free, open source program that you can install on your Web server. If you prefer to keep all your stats on your own server, you may prefer this option over Google Analytics and other online services. This program generates advanced Web, streaming, FTP, or mail server statistics with great graphics. Setting up AWStats is a bit more complicated than using a service like Google Analytics because you need access to the Web server log files and specific scripts on your Web server. AWStats offers data similar to Google Analytics, but the presentation isn't as nice.

Piwik (www.piwik.org). Piwik is a PHP/MySQL software program that you download and install on your own Web server. Piwik positions itself as the open source alternative to Google Analytics. Piwik takes about five minutes to install, and then you copy and paste JavaScript code on Web pages you want to track, much like you do with Google Analytics. The graphs, presentation, and navigation of Piwik are more polished than AWStats, but still not as advanced as those at Google Analytics.

Part III
Going Web 2.0

Chapter 11

Designing a Blog

Tasks Performed in This Chapter

✔ Starting a blog with WordPress.com

✔ Customizing your blog template to match your content

✔ Writing and styling posts with panache

It was only a few years ago that blogs (short for *Web log*) were considered the wild and crazy new kid on the block. Next thing, it seemed like everyone had a blog. And most people didn't seem to know why they had a blog — they just knew that everyone was saying that you had to have one.

After a few introductory posts to play with this new toy, statistics from the blog search engine Technorati show that about 95 percent of people abandoned them. And that's a shame because blogging tools can be used for so much more than some lonely 14-year-old's gushing paean to sparkly vampires or a basement-dwelling conspiracy theorist warning about alien mind-control rays. Savvy technology shoppers read blogs like Gizmodo (`http://gizmodo.com`) and Engadget (`www.engagdget.com`) to figure out if the newest techno-toy lives up to the hype. Dooce (`http://dooce.com`) and Suburban Turmoil (`http://suburban turmoil.blogspot.com`) write about motherhood and child-rearing issues in a laugh-out-loud voice. Deadspin (`http://deadspin.com`) and Total Pro Sports (`www.totalprosports.com/blog`) cover the stories behind the stories on the sports page.

At its heart, blogging software allows you to post information to the Web in a quick and easy way. After you have the blog set up, all you really have to do is type (into the right boxes) what you want the world to read, click to select multimedia assets (photos, videos, audio files), and click the Publish button. The blog displays the content in reverse chronological order, sorted by category or date, and allows readers to leave comments or trackback links to add to the discussion with the writer or other readers. The format of the site, after it's set, doesn't change. That is, you don't have to choose how many columns of information you want, what the background color is, what the fonts are, or any of the other variables to designing a Web page.

In this chapter, I'll demonstrate how to use WordPress, which is a sophisticated blogging tool that can grow with you as you get more comfortable with the blogosphere. WordPress is free to use, and comes in two "flavors." You can get free hosting at WordPress.com, or you can download the software package from WordPress.org and install it on your own server. Each approach has advantages and disadvantages. I start with the simplest approach of having someone else host it for you, and then take a look at how to take total control of things yourself.

Starting a Blog at WordPress.com

Stuff You Need to Know

Toolbox:
- An updated Web browser, such as Internet Explorer 8.0 or Firefox 3.5
- An e-mail address

Time needed:
Less than half an hour

Your blogging software options are as numerous as the function keys at the top of your keyboard, so how do you choose one service over another — or know what they do in the first place? Although I can't help you with your function keys, blogging software is another matter: One of the quickest and most flexible services is available at WordPress.com. WordPress has practically become the industry standard blogging tool in the last couple of years because the open-source community has dedicated itself to developing thousands of themes and plug-ins to allow blog owners to customize and extend the basic blog concept in almost infinite ways.

If you aren't sure that you want to blog or you're thinking of using other software down the road (or you're just curious), WordPress.com is an excellent place to become familiar with how blogging software works, while offering you almost endless possibilities to expand beyond simple blogging to running a sophisticated e-commerce site or database-driven video-hosting service.

In this step-by-step task, you can see how easy it is to sign up for a blog and get started:

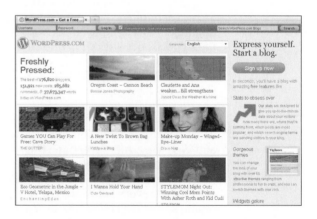

1. Open your Web browser, point it to www.wordpress.com, and click the Sign Up Now button.

Get your own WordPress.com account in seconds

Fill out this one-step form and you'll be blogging seconds later!

Username: HollywoodBartender
(Must be at least 4 characters, letters and numbers only.)

Password: ●●●●●●●●●

Confirm: ●●●●●●●●●
Use upper and lower case characters, numbers and symbols like !"£$%^& in your password
Password Strength: **Good**

2. In the sign-up page, type the name you want to use in the Username field. This can be your name, an online identity (*handle*), or the name you would like for the blog. In this case, I used HollywoodBartender. Next, type a password. WordPress advises users to choose a password that mixes uppercase and lowercase characters as well as numbers and symbols. An example of this kind of mixture would be P@ssW0rd789. Retype the password in the Confirm box.

3. In the next box down, type in your e-mail address. Like the online warning says, triple-check that you have the spelling correct. If you ever forget your password, a new one will be e-mailed to this address. You can use your existing e-mail account; or, if you want to establish an entirely new identity just to deal with your blog, you can create a new e-mail identity at a free e-mail site. Make sure that the I Have Read and Agree to the Fascinating Terms of Service check box is selected. (Please click the link and do read the terms of service before agreeing to them.) Select the Gimme a Blog! radio button, and then click Next.

4. This next page is where you pick your domain name and the title of your blog. You will need to think carefully and maybe try a number of options in this next step. Type in the domain name you want for your blog. This isn't necessarily going to be the name of your blog, but it should be as close to it as you can get. If your name is already in use by another blogger, you'll be prompted to try another domain name. The default name here is the same as your Username. Try to keep this name short and sweet so that your readers can type it as easily as possible. In this instance, I chose to keep it the same as the Username, so the resulting URL for the blog is `http://www.hollywoodbartender.wordpress.com`. *Remember:* Like the site says, after you choose this Web address, it can't be changed. You can, however, start all over later if you come up with a genius idea for a domain name.

You have to remember your password, so don't get too exotic with your made-up combinations just to please the strength bar. (The Password strength bar beneath the password entry box shows how your password suggestion ranks in terms of un-guess-ability.) A password that rates as Good is probably enough for anything other than a banking/financial information site or a Department of Defense nuclear secrets site.

5. In the next box down, give your blog a name in the Blog Title field. Most people try to come up with something memorable. Unlike the URL, you can change and tweak the blog title later. In this case, I wanted to build on the words Hollywood Bartender that appear in the URL, so the blog title is "The Secret Life of a Hollywood Bartender."

6. Choose the language you will be blogging in. This list will set the default character set available for your text. That is, if you're going to blog in Hindu or Farsi, choose that language so the characters show up how they're supposed to (rather than appearing as blank spaces and random punctuation).

7. Leave the Privacy check box selected if you want your blog to show up in search engines. (Um, clear the check box if you don't want to be listed in search engines or WordPress.) However, clearing this check box doesn't mean that your blog will be totally invisible and private — just that you're not going out of your way to publicize it and try to drive traffic to it. Click the Signup button when you're satisfied with your choices.
Remember: After you click this button, you cannot change the URL: You can only start over and pick a new URL.

8. WordPress sends a message to the e-mail account you entered. Go to your e-mail inbox and check for the message. You must click the link in the message (or cut and paste it into the browser navigation bar) to activate your blog. It may take up to 30 minutes for the confirmation message to arrive, so be patient if it doesn't show up immediately. However, you must confirm this activation e-mail within two days, or WordPress will assume that you entered an incorrect e-mail address and then delete your blog.

Howdy,

Thank you for signing up with WordPress.com. You are one step away from blogging at hollywoodbartender.wordpress.com. Please click this link to activate your blog:

http://wordpress.com/activate/d65801ae792149ac

--The WordPress.com Team

(If clicking the link in this message does not work, copy and paste it into the address bar of your browser.)

9. If you haven't received your confirmation e-mail yet, scroll down to see some other options. You can click Contact Support, or re-enter your e-mail address. When you do click the link that you receive in your e-mail, you are taken to a page that says Your Account is Now Active! Your username and password should already appear in the blanks on that page.

Your account is now active!

Username:	Password:
hollywoodbartender	*********

Your account is now active. View your site or Login

10. You are prompted to update your profile. You can do this now, or get back to it later. If you want to do it now, enter your first and last name, and write a short description about yourself and why you are blogging. Click the Save Profile button after you're done. Don't worry — you can go back and change it if you later don't like it. You will be taken to the Login screen.

Update Your Profile!
If you haven't got your activation email why not update your profile while you wait?

First Name:	**Hollywood**
Last Name:	**Bartender**
About Yourself:	I serve frothy cocktails to the rich, famous and barely clothed. It's a glamorous job -- and an absurd one.	

Save Profile ›

TIP

If you have not received your e-mail verification message, be sure to check your spam filters.

11. If the fields in the Login screen aren't filled in, enter your username and password; then click the Log In button. You can select the Remember Me check box if you're on your own computer and want to have it fill in the blanks for you.

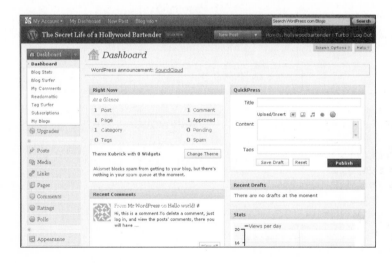

12. When you login, you will be taken to the Dashboard. This is where you have an overview of all the controls you can use on your blog. Start by customizing your template, which is the focus of the next task.

Blogging software options

I talk extensively about WordPress in this chapter, but it is by no means the only blogging solution out there. If a blog is an important part of your Web plans, spend time researching the available solutions to find the one that fits both your plans and your pocketbook.

Here are two other hosted solutions you can take a look at:

TypePad, at www.typepad.com, has three pricing levels, depending on the level of functionality you want. TypePad is proving to be the platform of choice for busy professionals who want the convenience of a hosted service with more support and a larger feature set.

Blogger is Google's blogging software. If you already have a Gmail account, you can use Blogger. Like WordPress, it's free. Although it's quite easy to use, it doesn't have as many plug-ins and features as WordPress offers. Sign up for Blogger at www.blogger.com.

If you want to install software on your own Web server, here's a description of the major players:

Movable Type is the granddaddy of blogging software, the gold standard to which all others are compared. It has tons of helpful features, and if you develop the proper skills, you can make this software jump through hoops for you. Check it out at www.movabletype.com.

Joomla! is an extremely powerful and extensible content management system (CMS). This program offers far more than just blogging tools and is great for online magazines and other complex sites. Joomla! is also increasingly used by many power bloggers. They point out that you can't beat the features it offers for the price: it's free. This software is open source, so many plug-ins, extensions, and themes are available. If you plan to build a blog that can hold up under heavy traffic, or that can be customized to do things beyond what a normal blog can handle, this excellent choice is available at www.joomla.org.

ExpressionEngine, at www.expressionengine.com, has its roots in blogging software but is evolving into a fully featured CMS with excellent blogging tools. Throw in extras like photo galleries, shopping cart modules, forums, polls, and great customer support, and you can use this product to run your blog *and* some of the biggest and most complex Web sites on the Internet.

I mention only these blogging options here, but you can check out dozens, including many on social networking sites like MySpace or Facebook. Carefully consider your needs, as well as what you might like to do in the future as you make your decision to find just the right set of features for your situation.

Customizing Your Blog Template

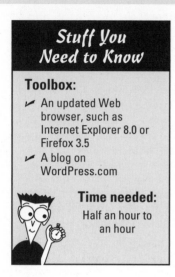

Stuff You Need to Know

Toolbox:

- ✔ An updated Web browser, such as Internet Explorer 8.0 or Firefox 3.5
- ✔ A blog on WordPress.com

Time needed:

Half an hour to an hour

One of the greatest strengths of WordPress is the stunning number and variety of templates available. A template sets the look and feel of your blog: the size and position of the banner, the typefaces and font sizes, how many columns appear, what the comment system looks like, and much more. The templates help you show off photos, videos, music, and almost anything else you can upload to the Internet. You can create your own template with Web design tools, but to start, it might be best to play around with the free themes to get a feel for what the various design and blogging choices mean.

For example, a blog with only one big column works great for photographers wanting to show off their shots in the biggest possible format for maximum visual impact. A blog with multiple narrow columns works for an organization trying to present multiple threads of complex information: say, a school that offers parents a way to see a calendar of events, the school lunch menu, and a recap of the last PTA meeting.

You can spend hours browsing through all the possibilities available for free on WordPress.com. Also hundreds of designers are willing and eager to sell you customized templates that use Flash, Silverlight, and other multimedia technologies to make your blog stand out from the crowd.

1. Log in to your WordPress account. On the Dashboard page, scroll down until you see the Appearance drop-down list. Click the Appearance button to open up that menu.

2. Under Appearance, click Themes to navigate to the directory of free themes available through WordPress. You can scroll through multiple pages to find one that suits you. Click the thumbnails to open a window showing a mock-up of what your blog would look like. When you find a design you like, click Install to make that your template. ***Note:*** You can always change your template later.

3. I'm using a theme called MistyLook as an example here because it offers a couple of easy-to-control features and allows me to show off interesting widgets. After the theme is installed, it appears on top of your Manage Themes page.

4. Start the customization by working in the Header Image first. Click the Custom Header link. I prepared an image to replace the picture of the trees and bridge over the pond. You can use any photo-editing program to make a similar Header Image, as long as it fits in with the size requirements. In this case, you can crop an image to fit; or if you have one that's 760 x 190 pixels, you can use it as is. Click the Browse button to navigate to where your image is stored. When you find it, click to select it and then click Open. Then click the Upload button.

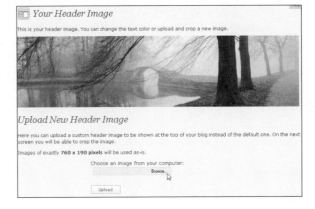

You should settle on the general look and feel of your blog within the first week or so. Making too radical of a change after you create many blog posts can be problematic because of differing photo widths, font colors, and other elements that work great under one blog theme but can "break the page" when applied to another theme. For example, say your photo blog shows off some of your breathtaking landscape shots 800 pixels wide on a white background. Then you decide to switch to a 4-column blog where each column is only 200 pixels wide to show off more photos at a time, against a black background. Unless you re-size all the photos you've uploaded, your photos will either overlap and cover up your other content, or worse yet, the conflicting standards will cause your blog to refuse to load and visitors will see only an error message. And if you've specified that some of your text appear in black, it will be invisible against the black background unless once again – you guessed it – you go back into every blog post you've ever done and laboriously track down and adjust the custom text color.

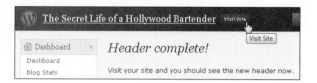

5. You see a message that reads Header complete! Click the Visit Site button to see what your new blog header looks like.

6. Check out your new blog header. You can go back and edit the source picture if you're not happy with the way it looks (using a photo-editing program like Photoshop). Click My Dashboard (top of the window) to go back to the control panel to customize a couple other things about your blog's appearance.

7. Under the Settings panel, click General. These settings control the title of your blog, the tagline, time zone, e-mail address, and other basic data.

8. Because I customized the image to include the title of the blog, I'd like to get rid of the redundant words that appear above the banner. I clicked here and deleted the words that were in the Blog Title and Tagline text boxes. You can also use this page to change the title and tagline, if you want. Click in the text boxes to make your changes; then click Save Changes at the bottom of the page to make the changes take effect on your blog. Click Visit Site (up at the top of the page, next to the title of your blog) to see what the changes you have made look like. Your tagline can be a longer explanation of what your blog is about, a favorite quotation, a joke or you can go without one.

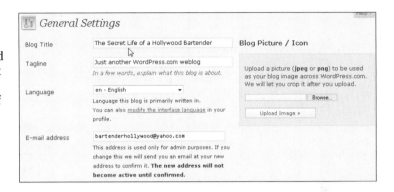

9. As you can see in the figure, I removed the distracting words above my nice new banner. Now it's time to customize what appears in your sidebar(s). (You likely noticed by now those boxes running down the side columns, depending on your layout and the features that come with your template.)

10. Click on the Dashboard button in the top left corner of the page to return to your Dashboard page, and scroll down to the Appearance panel. Click to open the Appearance panel if it's not already open and then click Widgets.

Widgets are little pieces of code that make things happen on your blog, such as making your calendar appear, showing how many spam comments have been blocked, displaying photos that you have posted on other places around the Web, like Flickr.com, or letting your readers see your most recent Twitter updates.

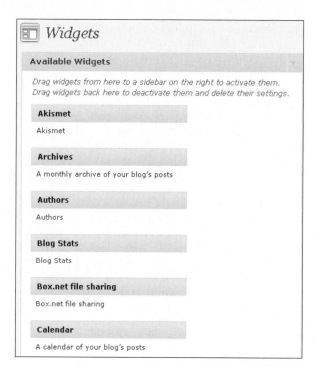

11. You navigate to the Widgets control panel. Click a widget that you like and drag it to one of your sidebars. *Hint:* If you have multiple columns in your blog layout, you will have multiple sidebars to choose from.

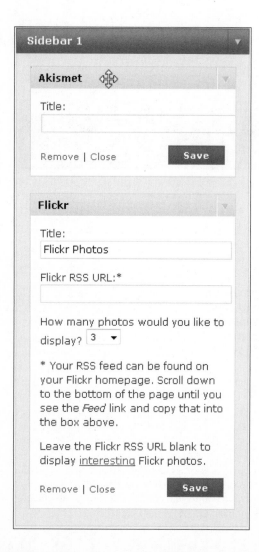

12. A four-pointed icon appears over the title bar to the widgets that you're dragging. This means that you can drag the widget to your sidebar, or drag it out of your sidebar, if you don't like how it looks or acts. You can also reorder the widgets by dragging them up or down in the sidebar. Some widgets will have boxes for you to fill in with information, such as the title you'd like to appear above your most recent posts, or the URL to a Flickr account. When you're done making entries and you want to see how the new sidebar looks, click Visit Site at the top of the page.

13. You see the new widgets as they appear in the sidebar on your page. If you don't like how they look, navigate back to the widget page and either adjust them or drag them out of your sidebar.

14. In the Appearance box, click on Themes to navigate to the Manage Themes page. The last, and most complicated option for customizing your theme, is Edit CSS. This is most definitely not for beginners. You will need to purchase a Custom CSS upgrade, which will cost you about $15 per year per blog that you want to totally customize. With this option, though, you can control the fonts, colors, sizes, arrangements, line thickness — basically everything in your layout. You can make one change here without having to pay: setting the maximum width for media files in your blog so that pictures or videos don't overflow your columns and mess up the look of your blog. If you are going to embed videos on your page, your columns should be at least 360 pixels wide. Most basic videos are 320 pixels wide. If you want to display higher-quality videos, they are 640 pixels wide, so your layout should be at least 680 pixels wide, to allow some breathing room. The total width of your blog is up to you; but most Web designers try to keep their pages under 970 pixels wide so they display well on monitors set to a 1024x768 resolution.

Posting to Your Blog

Stuff You Need to Know

Toolbox:

✔ An updated Web browser, such as Internet Explorer 8.0 or Firefox 3.5

✔ A blog on WordPress. com

Time needed:

Less than half an hour (unless you're a slow writer!)

Updates to your blog are called *posts,* or *entries.* Blog posts are generally short (although they don't have to be) and can be composed directly in the blogging software or written in more traditional word processing software and then pasted into the composition window. (For advice on creating a readable, interesting blog post, read the following sidebar, "Writing for your blog.")

Nearly all blogging software works similarly to word processing software, or even e-mail software. After typing an entry, you can use handy formatting icons in the publishing interface to create text styles. Blog software also has icons you can click to accomplish simple HTML tasks, such as inserting links, photos, or videos.

Creating a new post is easy to do. In fact, if you can write an e-mail message, you can write a blog post! Follow these steps:

1. Log in to your blog at www.wordpress.com. Scroll down to the Posts button and click it to open its drop-down list.

2. Click Add New to open the Add New Post page.

3. The Add New Post Page looks complicated, but after you work with it a few times, the basic functions are pretty intuitive. First, write a snappy headline for your post. Click in the text field at the top of the page and type in a short description of what you want to say. Then press Enter (Windows)/ Return (Mac).

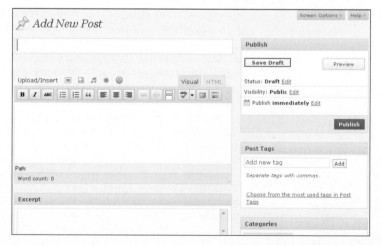

4. A URL and a couple of buttons appear below the headline text box. The URL, or *Permalink,* is the address where your post will appear when you finally publish it. You will see the Web address of your blog, followed by the date and the word(s) in your headline. You can click Edit to change the words in the Permalink if you want to make them different from your headline. Or, if you're planning on sharing your post via e-mail, or social network sites like Facebook and Twitter, click Get Shortlink, and WordPress will automatically compress the post's URL to a combination of letters and numbers.

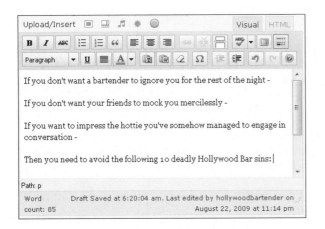

5. In the Upload/Insert area, type the text of your blog post, using the formatting icons to choose fonts, create lists and links, and customize other layout styles. ***Hint:*** To apply formatting to the text, select the text you want to affect, and then click the icon for the style you want to apply. You can choose font options, bold, italics, text color, text alignment, bulleted or numbered lists, special characters, and more. If you don't see all these options, click the Show/Hide Kitchen Sink button on the far right or press Alt+Shift+Z (Windows)/ (Mac) to open what WordPress calls "The Kitchen Sink." This is the second row of buttons that includes such functions as pasting from Microsoft Word (a handy feature that allows you to avoid contaminating your blog post with Word's formatting), or designating something with the various Heading, Paragraph or Address tags.

6. The five buttons at the top of the Upload/Insert area allow you to insert some very special content. From left to right, they allow you to add an image, insert video, add audio/music, add media (kind of a catch-all), or add a poll. Clicking each button opens a window that prompts you to choose files on your local hard drive, or that are at a URL on the Internet. WordPress does enforce some space limitations (3GB of content comes free, but you can upgrade to up to 25GB of storage) although it does offer upgrades where you can buy additional storage and bandwidth.

All kinds of considerations make writing a good headline for your post one of the most important things you do on a blog. Search engines pay special attention to the words in headlines, and a well-written description can help drive traffic to your blog. (Do a little research on search engine optimization as a primer.) Readers are also attracted to funny, shocking, or strange headlines — and Top 10 lists.

7. To insert an image into your blog entry, click the Add Image icon (looks like a rectangle inside another rectangle). (To find out how to prepare images for use on the Web, read Chapter 5.) The Add an Image window appears, where you can choose from a handful of methods: Choose an image on your computer and upload it, provide the Web address (URL) for an image on another Web site, or add an image from your Media Library. Just click the tab you want at the top and follow the directions that appear on screen.

8. To add a link, first select the text that you want readers to click to find the link. Then simply click the Link icon (the link of chain) or press Alt+Shift+A. When the URL window opens, copy and paste the Web address for the link into the window. *Note:* You need to use the full URL, including the `http://` part, to create a working link.

9. You can also add tags to your blog post. *Tags* are keywords that describe the blog post, and search engines pay special attention to tags so that they can better sort your content into search result listings. To add a tag, simply type it in the Add New Tag text box, just to the right of where you entered your post. Click the link below this box to choose from a list of tags that you frequently use so that you don't have to spend time typing in the same old words over and over again. Click each tag, and it will appear under the Add New Tag box. Click on the gray "X" next to the tag if you made a mistake, and want to delete it.

The Media Library option is particularly handy if you want to add a company logo or other image to every post; you don't have to keep uploading the same thing because WordPress allows you to navigate through your uploads and pick the one you want.

10. Click the Check Spelling icon (looks like a check mark on top of the letters ABC) to have spelling errors underlined in red in your blog post. Click any error to select from a list of corrections. You can choose the language you want the spellcheck to work in by clicking on the triangle next to the ABC checkmark button to open up the drop-down menu. You can then click on the language that you want spellcheck to operate in when checking the spelling in your post. Spellcheck will then underline words that are misspelled in that language. If you compose a post that uses words from a couple of languages and you're not sure about the spelling, this feature can come in handy because you can spellcheck in one language and then do it again in another language.

11. Before you post your entry, click the Preview button, in the upper-right corner of the Add New Post page, to see how your chosen styles look. This opens another browser window with your post in it as it will look when it is published. You can return to Editing mode by closing this window. If you decide (after previewing) to remove formatting, simply highlight any element with a style you want to remove and click the Remove Formatting icon. (It looks like an eraser.)

12. Click the Edit link next to Publish Immediately to see options for setting the date and time of your post. Click Edit next to Visibility: Public to control how the post is seen. You can choose to make this post always appear on the front page of your blog, password-protect it so that only people you authorize see it, or make it private so that only you can see the contents. Click Edit next to Status: Draft to make this blog entry either a draft; or mark it as Pending Review if you are collaborating with others and are waiting for them to look it over. You can leave all the options expanded, as shown in the figure, but you need to click OK in each area for the settings to take effect.

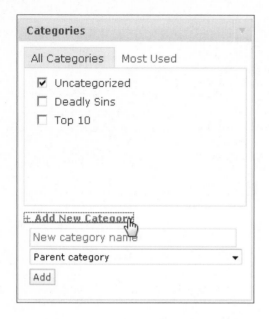

13. Click Add New Category in the Categories section. A text box opens where you can type in new categories, or select check boxes next to existing categories. This is a simple but powerful tool that allows your users to sort your blog posts based on categories that they are interested in, without them having to search through all your pages in chronological order to find the topics they are interested in. For example, a user who wants to see all the posts you've written that are Top 10 lists would click Top 10 under the Categories section of your blog to make your blog generate a page containing only posts that you have categorized as being Top 10 lists – or related to Top 10 lists.

14. The Excerpt area allows you to choose what sentences or paragraphs will appear in the RSS feed of your subscribers, or that will be weighted more heavily by search engines. You can either pick your best and most descriptive writing, or you can sum up what you have to say.

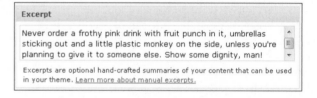

15. When everything looks right, click the Publish button. The system then confirms that your post has been published. After you publish your post, click the Visit Site link at the top of the page, or View Post, to ensure that your post was published successfully and looks the way you want.

You can assign multiple categories to your posts. If you are writing about a piano-playing cat, for example, you can assign the post into the categories "cat," "piano," and "funny." Then, when users come to your blog and want to see only posts that are cat-related, they can click on the "cat" category to zero in on only content that falls in that category. Another user wanting to read about pianos might click on the piano category, and your same post would appear in that list – along with posts about pianos that don't include cats.

If you've read other chapters in this book, chances are you learned quite a bit of HTML. If you feel comfortable using HTML, you can actually use it right in the blog post window of WordPress. (As with regular text, you can write HTML directly in the window, or create your code in another application and copy and paste it into the blog post window.) If you want to use code, click the HTML tab of the composition window to switch from Visual mode.

After your blog is up and running, you can make updates by using e-mail. Updating in this way requires you to set up a special e-mail address that you are urged to keep secret. From the WordPress Dashboard, click the MyBlogs link and then click the Enable button under the Post-by-Email column. A special e-mail address will pop up in that column. Click the drop-down menu, choose Enable Post by Email, and then click Apply. Copy the e-mail address and save it in a secure location (such as a document on your computer's hard drive). When setup is complete, simply cut and paste the e-mail address you just set up, choose a title by typing it in the Subject field, and then create a blog post in the body of your message. When you click Send, the message wings its way to WordPress and onto your blog.

Writing for your blog

Blog style is generally conversational and informal in tone and style. You should address the reader directly to play up this aspect of blogging, almost as though you're talking to a good friend on the phone or writing an e-mail message.

I don't mean that you have to throw out the rules of grammar and spelling although many bloggers do so. You'll find that many readers appreciate carefully crafted sentences when they read blogs as much as they do when they read books. Why make yourself hard to understand?

Many writing coaches say that being rigorous about spelling and grammar is a good way to sharpen your thinking. And, of course, it's true — the more attention you pay to writing well, the better your results, even if you're just blogging about the terrific play you saw last night, or the way your friends always seem to call just when you get in the shower.

Don't forget that blogging doesn't have to mean all writing, all the time. Many terrific blogs are devoted to displaying a photograph every day, or to video blogging. Numerous others combine text, photos, audio, and video, which keeps them fun and interesting for readers — and for the blogger.

Promoting your blog

Many bloggers subscribe to the idea that, "If I publish it, they will come." Let me be the first (or not) to burst that bubble: Blogs need to be promoted as much as any other Web site if you're trying to appeal to an audience that doesn't already know and love you. (Is it considered promotion when you e-mail everyone in your family to tell them about your blog?)

The good news is that at a very technical level, the setup of blogs helps them show up well in search engine results. And, of course, search engines love sites with fresh content, so a frequently updated blog truly has an edge over one that sees new content once in a blue moon.

Here's a quick batch of things you should do to make the most of your new blog:

Ensure that your blog has an RSS or Atom feed. A *feed* is essentially a syndication mechanism for your blog: a coded presentation of your updates that can be picked up and read by newsreaders, feed aggregators, and blog search engines, which in turn pass whatever they receive from the feed to humans visiting other Web sites. The result: eyeballs on your content and links to your blog. Most blog software can generate automatic feeds, but you should ensure that the feature is turned on and functioning. (WordPress automatically generates an RSS feed.)

Turn on trackbacks and pings. Trackbacks are a little hard to describe, but I'll try: Essentially, a *trackback* is a way for blog software to communicate in the background and build links to other blogs. It goes like this: Blogger A posts interesting material on his blog. Blogger B reads that post, and has more to say about the same topic on her blog. Using the trackback URL on Blogger A's post, Blogger B's blog software notifies Blogger A's software about the new

post. Blogger A's software then automatically builds, in the original post, a link to the new post. At the end of this (alphabet soup) process, Blogger A's readers see the link to Blogger B's post and visit her site to read it.

Pings work similarly but are basically a "heads-up" notification service sent to some of the bigger blog search engines and indexers. When you let these Web sites know that your blog has been updated, your listings are included in the results that are displayed the next time someone performs a search, and again, more readers are directed to your site.

Many blog software packages offer both trackbacks and pings, and by simply turning on these settings, you receive the benefit with little to no work each time you post to your blog.

Remember that your blog posts are an important part of promoting yourself. Keep the material you write interesting and topical. For example, if you choose to blog about a subject that's in the news headlines, you can attract readers who might never have visited your blog otherwise. Keep track of what's going on in the world, and think about how you can relate your topic to the broader context of discussion in the blogosphere.

Use social media to alert friends and colleagues. One of the best ways to keep people coming back to your blog is to remind people who already know you on Facebook, MySpace, Twitter, hi5, Beebo and other sites, that you have produced something new and interesting. This is where the shortened URLs often come in handy. You can also integrate material that you or your friends post on these sites into your blog, via the handy RSS feeds that every social networking site maintains.

Chapter 12

Podcasting Your Own Show

Tasks Performed in This Chapter

✔ Preparing a podcast

✔ Recording a podcast

✔ Editing an audio file

✔ Publishing a podcast

If you haven't been hiding in a cave on Mars, you've probably already heard the term *podcasting*. It's one of the hotter Internet buzzwords of recent years, and many people have scrambled like mad to incorporate podcasts onto Web sites.

The techie explanation is that a *podcast* is any audio file stored on the Internet that can be downloaded and played later on either a computer or a portable device. In real terms, a podcast is a radio show that you can take anywhere on a portable device, such as an iPod, or play on any computer that's connected to the Internet. Podcasts are better than radio programs because you can start, stop, and rewind whenever you want. You can play them any time, anywhere. Podcasts enable you to connect with your site visitors or community through music or talk or both, enriching the experience or content your site has to offer. You find examples of how sites put podcasting to use in the nearby sidebar "Who's podcasting?"

A good podcast can consist of a live interview that's available to listeners for as long as a Web site hosts it, a lecture by a Nobel prize-winning professor that students can use to help them study, or the wail of a newborn infant taking her first breaths. A podcast can be a long-winded blogger's rant that will be heard only by a close circle of fans, or a stirring national address that will be cherished by an entire nation.

Podcasting is limited only by your imagination. As with so many other topics, a library of books could be filled with the bottomless depths of technical specifications that can be involved in recording, editing, and posting a podcast. Fortunately, you don't need to know all that to get started. In this chapter, you find the most basic, cost-effective way to produce a professional-quality podcast, using free and easily available tools and programs.

Who's podcasting?

This list briefly describes some of the groups of people who are podcasting nowadays:

Musicians who want to connect with fans and promote their bands: Some forward-thinking bands use podcasts to share excerpts from live shows, hype concert tours, and reward fan club members with exclusive content.

Families who want to remain connected across distances: Recordings of a baby's first words, grandpa's story time, or a raucous family reunion aren't proper substitutes for being there, but they can at least allow people to get a flavor for what they missed.

Amateur DJs and novice broadcasters who want to show off their skills: A tight, well-produced podcast can be an invaluable calling card to a beginner hoping to take the next step up the career ladder.

Companies that provide training and management updates, especially to employees in far-flung offices: One of the fastest-growing usages of multimedia is corporate communications. CEOs use podcasts to reach out to customers and reassure them in tumultuous times, and HR managers find spoken-word explanations of the latest change in corporate strategy that show up in employees' e-mail inboxes helps maintain consistent corporate culture, and adds the kind of "human touch" that relaxes and reassures employees.

Churches that make their weekly sermons available: Congregation members who are ill or traveling or who otherwise can't physically attend church can still hear the weekly services.

Bloggers who want to augment their content: Audio clips from interviews are increasingly popular, as are stream-of-consciousness rants that provoke controversy and build up page traffic.

Radio producers and other professionals: Many excellent radio programs that are now available online as podcasts ensure that you never miss your favorite show. Listening to professional podcasts is one of the best ways to get new ideas for how best to create your own.

Preparing a Podcast

Be sure to take the time before you record your podcast to plan what you want to say and how you want to say it. Even trained on-air personalities rarely try to make live, improvisational recordings. After a few minutes, an interviewer who doesn't have at least an outline or some good questions for a guest runs out of things to say, and the session can turn into a nightmare of "um" and "uh."

You don't have to strictly follow a script, however, and stick to every little comma and pause. One thing that makes listeners respond and come back for more is the feeling that you're talking *to* them rather than *at* them (like a late-night infomercial). And, one of the most difficult challenges I can imagine is to make yourself sound natural and relaxed while giving a monologue.

A good place to start as you plan a podcast is to think about creating a distinct beginning, middle, and end. A good show usually starts with some kind of introduction of the host and any guests, moves on to the main topic, and then concludes with a tease to the next show you plan to produce. This outline for a music podcast gives you some ideas for what you might include — make your outline as detailed as you like:

1. Play an introductory music clip.

2. Greet the audience, introduce yourself, and state the number or date of the podcast.

3. Briefly explain the theme or topic of the podcast.

4. Mention any guests or special announcements.

5. Play new songs.

6. Provide any necessary additional explanation of the theme or topic.

7. Play more new songs.

8. Sum up the theme or topic.

9. Say goodbye, and "tease" the topic of the next podcast.

Although a podcast can theoretically last for hours, in practice, large audio files become unwieldy very quickly. Listener patience isn't infinite, either, so unless you have an absolutely fanatical audience, limit your podcasts to a half-hour or less. Some of my favorite podcasts are only two to five minutes long, and they're designed so that you can listen to as many in a row as you like. If you have a ton of material, breaking it up into smaller chunks is definitely the way to go.

The many ways to record sound

An increasing number of portable devices have audio-recording capabilities. Most smartphones record audio, laptops have built-in microphones, and MP3 players either record or use after-market add-ons. Professional radio reporters have long used minidisc recorders to capture high-quality audio, whereas some old-school podcasters just use cables to hook tape recorder headphone output into their computers' microphone input.

Podcasters are increasingly conducting interviews or round-table discussions using Internet telephone services like Skype or Vonage. These Voice over Internet Protocol (VoIP) services allow users to digitally record conversations without having to resort to recording conversations over plain old telephone lines (and entangling themselves in wires and iffy legal ground).

However, because VoIP conversations are monaural and most listeners are used to high-quality stereo, podcasters are using workaround methods to conduct interviews over the phone. For example, each party to a conversation simultaneously records it into a high-quality stereo microphone. Then, at the end of the interview, both parties edit and clean up the audio, e-mail their audio file to each other, and then stitch together the files to get both (or more) sides of the conversation.

Even if you can't get high-quality recordings of both ends of a conversation, the host should record into a microphone even while the rest of the conversation is recorded over a phone line or VoIP connection.

Recording a Podcast

Recording an audio file can be as simple as speaking into the microphone on a computer headset or as complicated as setting up a dozen high-end microphones and a mixing board to get clean sound from every instrument in a chamber orchestra. Either way, the basic principles I cover in this chapter are the same.

Many audio professionals believe that the most important link in the chain is this first one: that using a bad or inappropriate microphone taints the audio from the get-go. The old computer industry axiom "Garbage in, garbage out" applies here as well. The good news is that quality microphones are more affordable than ever, and a microphone that costs less than $100 online or in a basic electronics store fulfills all but the most demanding needs. The bottom line: You can use your computer's built-in microphone, but a good external mic provides better sound quality.

A simple option is to record directly into your computer, which is easy enough because most newer computers sport a microphone port. (It's usually red or pink and located next to the green port where you plug in headphones.) An even simpler option is to use a USB microphone. Although USB microphones aren't ideal for recording music, they are a snap to use and configure, and often come integrated into headphones, making it easy to record while also monitoring sound. Whatever you choose, just plug in a mic and then follow these steps to start recording.

1. Launch a sound-recording program, such as Audacity, as shown here. You find a list of some of the more popular software choices in the sidebar at the end of this step list. I chose Audacity for this chapter because it has enough features to empower beginners to produce decent-sounding podcasts, it works on both Macintosh and Windows computers, and it's free. (You can download it at `http://audacity.sourceforge.net` and use it to follow along with this task. If your copy of Audacity is a different version, you might see minor screen differences.)

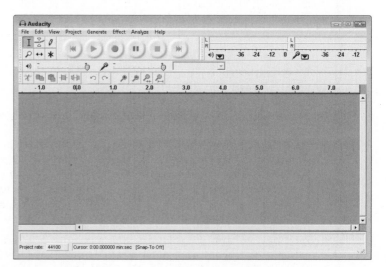

Before you begin recording, make sure that neither the computer nor the microphone is muted. This advice sounds simple, but even seasoned professionals can tell stories about apparently recording beautiful sounds, only to find (too late!) that their files contained silence.

2. Don't be overwhelmed by the mass of buttons, bars, menus, icons, and level meters that make up this program. In the upper-left area of the workspace, under the menu bar, are some familiar buttons: left to right, you've got Skip to Start, Play, Record, Pause, Stop, and Fast Skip to End. If your microphone is ready to record, just click the red Record button (the one with the big red circle) and say something into the microphone. (Sing a song, recite a poem, or act like you're creating your first radio show!)

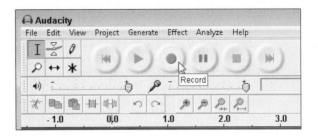

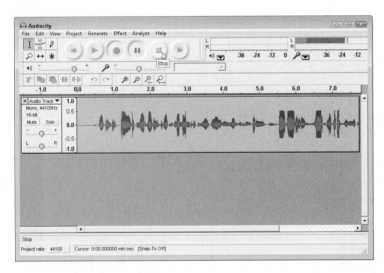

3. As you record, you see the sound represented as a spectrum across an audio track. Notice the two volume meters in the top-right corner of the workspace: The one on the left (the little speaker icon) shows the playback volume; the one on the right (the microphone icon) shows the volume of the microphone you're using to record. Under the volume controls, the drop-down menu enables you to pick from a list of sources, including microphone, line-in, aux(iliary), CD player, or stereo mix. Click the Stop button to stop recording, or click the Pause button to pause. (Be aware that Audacity will automatically rearrange the position of the various buttons and control panels, depending on how you size the window. So if your screen shows the buttons in one row, two rows or whatever, click and drag on the handle in the lower right corner of the screen to make your window match the screenshots here.)

Many beginners erroneously assume that louder is better when recording. Like a teenager with a new car stereo, they want to crank the noise to 11 on a scale of 10. If you record with the volume set to its highest level, you get distortion — or worse, listeners unsubscribing from your podcast feed.

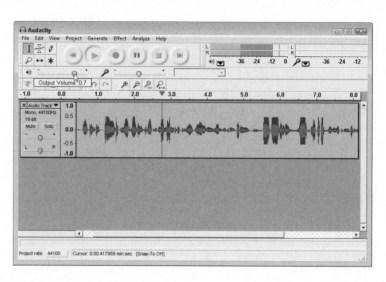

4. When you're done recording, click the Stop button. Then click the Play button to play back what you recorded. Use the volume controls to adjust the playback sound. *Remember:* Make sure you click the Stop button and not just the Pause button. With the recording set to Pause, you won't be able to play it back or to save it.

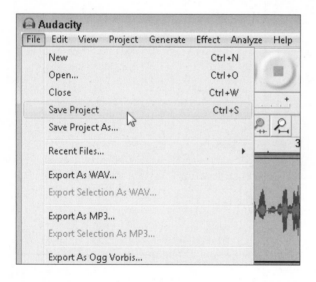

5. To save the recording, choose File⇨Save Project and then name your file. This step saves your sound file in an Audacity format (.aup) and preserves your recording in the best format for editing in Audacity. To create a new file in Audacity, choose File⇨New, and you're ready to start recording again in a new window.

6. When you're ready to publish your recording to the Web, use Audacity's export features. To export an Audacity file, choose File and then choose from any of the export options: WAV, MP3, or Ogg Vorbis. If you plan to publish your recording on the Web, your best option is MP3. Choose File⇨Export As MP3 and name your file. Congratulations! You just took the first step toward having your own podcast. In the next task, you find instructions for editing a podcast.

Audio recording programs

The programs you can use to record and edit sound files range from free to quite expensive, depending on the level of control you want and whether you want to be able to compose original music. This list describes some of the most popular programs among podcasters and audio editors:

- **Audacity:** This popular audio-editing program has more than enough features to produce a great-sounding podcast, and it's available for Mac, Windows, and Linux systems (which is why it's featured in this book). Audacity is free.

- **GarageBand:** Included on new Macintosh computers (OS X only), GarageBand is used by many podcasters who are looking for a quick and automated solution that's easily integrated with iTunes. GarageBand is free.

- **Adobe Soundbooth:** A more powerful and professional editing tool, Soundbooth comes bundled with other media programs in the Adobe CS4 suite. Soundbooth is aimed at people who want to be able to control a few aspects of their sounds but want menus with simple, easy-to-understand choices. Solo, the program costs $199 and has a free 30-day trial period.

- **Adobe Audition:** You can use this tool, intended for full-fledged audio engineers, to compose music and adjust and filter voices using complex and exacting processes. It costs $399 and has a free 30-day trial period.

- **Propaganda:** Propaganda is designed to help record and distribute podcasts. Although it has simplified sound-editing tools, you can preview your recording on your iPod or mobile device, and it writes the RSS code for you. Propaganda costs $49 and has a free 30-day trial period.

- **SnapKast:** SnapKast ($79) bills itself as a "one-click" podcasting solution that not only records and edits sounds but also creates RSS and handles the uploading and syndication chores.

- **MyPodcast Recorder:** Offered as a free download from MyPodcast.com, this simple recorder offers one-click installation and a very stripped-down interface. The drawback is that you have to put up with its ads on the site as well as the ads that are inserted into your final podcast.

If you're prompted to install the file `lame_enc.dll` to complete MP3 encoding, just return to the `http://audacity.sourceforge.net` site and search for **"lame_enc.dll"** to find the necessary file and simple instructions for downloading and selecting it in Audacity.

Editing a Recording

Stuff You Need to Know

Toolbox:

✔ Audacity

✔ A recording that can be opened in Audacity

Time needed:

A couple of hours

In this task, you perform basic sound editing to clean up a recording. You don't have to use editing tools. In fact, some podcasters wear their rough-and-scratchy recordings as badges of honor as proof that they're part of an insurgent media that rejects (what they perceive as) smooth, polished, and fake corporate style. If this is your ethos, then by all means, don't edit your sound files.

Most people, however, prefer to listen to recordings that don't sound like they were made in a gravel-sorting machine. And, if you ever venture into the field to do interviews or record your child's solo in the school play, you'll probably need to fix the volume or noise level or the big, scratchy thud of Aunt Edna's elbow knocking the microphone off the table.

Here are some basic sound-editing tips to help you reduce noise in your recordings, cut and paste segments, and *normalize* your recordings (make the too-soft parts louder and the too-loud parts softer). I encourage you to explore beyond these simple steps.

1. If your sound-recording program (such as Audacity, shown here) isn't open already, launch it and then create a recording or open an existing one.

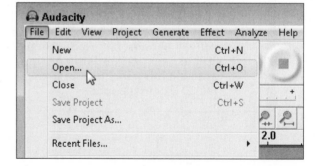

Most audio programs have tutorials and Help files to explain what all the arcane jargon means (although if you can explain to me under which circumstances I would want to use a Hilbert transformer rather than a Dyson compressor and a transient mangler, I'm all ears).

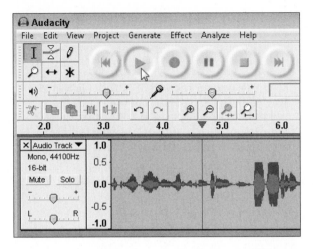

2. To listen to the entire recording, click the Play button at the top of the workspace. You should hear your voice (or whatever you just recorded) playing back. Notice that every time you hear noise in the recording, you see a corresponding spike on the graph in the Audio track.

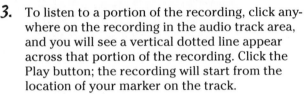

3. To listen to a portion of the recording, click anywhere on the recording in the audio track area, and you will see a vertical dotted line appear across that portion of the recording. Click the Play button; the recording will start from the location of your marker on the track.

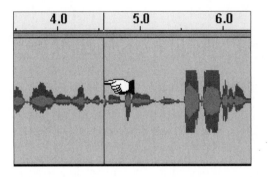

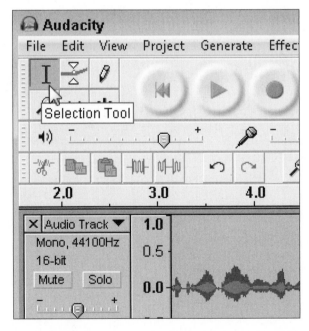

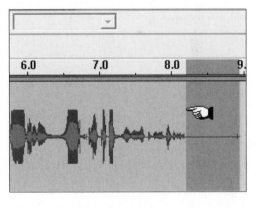

4. You can rearrange or delete sections of sound to make a better or shorter recording. Each of the following steps begins with selecting part of the sound file. Look in the small toolbox at the top of the workspace. (The toolbox has six tools, including Zoom and Time Shift.) Click the Selection Tool (which looks like an I-beam) to make it active before the next step.

5. To delete a noise (such as a sneeze), click and drag to select that section, and then press the Delete key. Or you can choose Edit➪Delete, or press Ctrl+K (Windows)/Option+K (Mac). You can also delete "non-noise," like a pause. Read more about this in the sidebar, "Getting rid of 'dead air.'" You can easily recognize silence in the audio track by its flat line in the sound spectrum graph. To adjust the selection, click and drag on either side of the selected area to enlarge or reduce the selection.

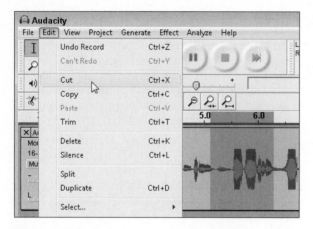

6. To cut or copy a section of sound, click and drag to select the section in the audio track, and then choose Edit➪Cut (or Copy). Click and drag on either side of the selected area to enlarge or reduce the selection.

7. To move the cut or copied sound to another part of the recording, click to place the cursor where you want to add the sound in the audio track, and then choose Edit➪Paste. The word or phrase is pasted into that point in the recording.

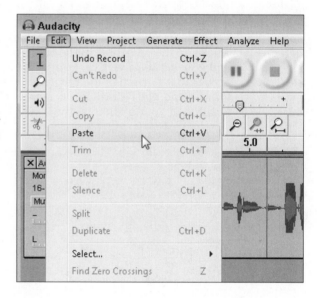

8. To hear the results of your editing, click to place the cursor where you want to begin playback, and then click the Play button.

To listen to only a particular section of the recording, click and drag to select the section and then click Play. You can then adjust the selection in the recording until you have just the part you want to cut, copy, or delete.

9. Audacity includes many effects to improve or alter your sound recordings. To apply an effect, you must first select the part of the recording you want to apply it to. Click and drag to select a portion of the recording, or choose Edit➪Select➪All to select the entire open recording.

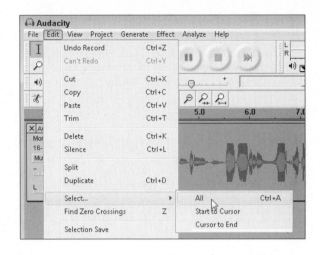

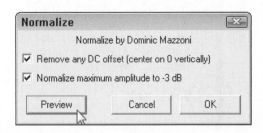

10. One of the more commonly used options on the Effect menu is Normalize. When you *normalize* a recording, you balance out the highs and lows, to make the overall volume more consistent. To apply the Normalize effect, select the part of the recording you want to apply it to and then choose Effect➪Normalize.

11. In the Normalize dialog box, mark both check boxes for default normalization. Click Preview to test how the effect will alter the sound of your recording. If you're happy with the result, click OK to apply the effect.

12. Experiment with the effects, and remember that you can apply them to any selected part or all of the recording. Click Play to test your work, and if you don't like the results of an effect, just choose Edit⇨Undo to remove it.

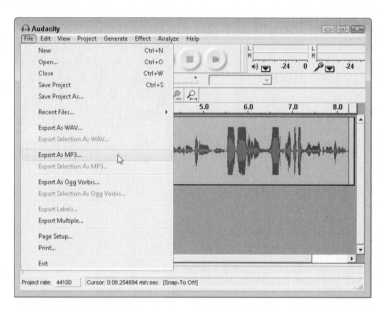

13. When you're done, choose File⇨Save Project to save the recording in Audacity format. Then choose File⇨Export to save the recording in a suitable format, such as MP3, before you publish your podcast to the Web.

Getting rid of "dead air"

Even with only the most basic understanding of audio editing, you can move a song from the beginning of your podcast to the end, or move the response to an interview question to the beginning, to use as a "teaser."

Your goal should be to interest listeners immediately and then keep them interested. One of the best ways to do that is to delete all "dead air," such as pauses and other quiet spots. This skill is essential for producing a tight, efficient podcast. Remember that listeners have lives too, and if you ask them to wait around for a couple of minutes while you fumble, they will become frustrated.

Some podcasters who are obsessed with deleting all the dead air between words review their recordings repeatedly, to shorten the spaces between words as much as possible. Although it's sometimes helpful to remove the extra breaths and any instances of "um" and "uh" between sentences, if you go too far, your recording sounds like you drank too much coffee and are babbling like a tobacco auctioneer.

Try to strike a balance. You want your recordings to sound natural, like a conversation you're having with your listeners (with all the boring parts cut out). Experience will gradually teach you the sweet spot.

Publishing a Podcast

Stuff You Need to Know

Toolbox:

- ✔ A recording saved in a Web format, such as MP3
- ✔ An Internet connection
- ✔ An account with a blog, Web site, or podcasting hosting service

Time needed:

About an hour

How you publish your podcast depends mostly on where you plan to publish it.

In the early days of podcasting, sites offering to host your files for free were springing up all over. Unfortunately, some of the sites were used to facilitate music piracy. Multimillion-dollar lawsuits filed by the recording industry have caused many sites that hosted podcasts to drastically restrict their offerings, or go completely out of business. Gcast (www.gcast.com) is an intriguing site that's still standing, offering not only free hosting for your podcast but also integrated access to podcast-safe music (that is, music you can use without getting into copyright trouble) at its sister site, www.garageband.com.

If you have a blog on one of the popular blogging sites, such as TypePad or Blogger, you find instructions and features designed to help you add a podcast almost as easily as you add a post.

Find out more about creating and publishing podcasts at these online services and other resources:

- ✔ **Apple iTunes:** (www.itunes.com) One of the most popular podcasting sites on the Web, iTunes makes it easy to download and play podcasts from a broad range of sources. And, you can use iTunes with a PC; you don't have to use a Macintosh or an iPod.

- ✔ **The Podcast Network:** (www.thepodcastnetwork.com) This site features an international collection of podcasters, useful tutorials, and helpful tips and tricks about podcasting. However, they are asking their audience to contribute $20 per month just to listen to podcasts, and require that you already have an audience of at least 500+ listeners before they will consider hosting your podcast.

- ✔ **Podcasting Tools:** (www.podcasting-tools.com) Filled with tutorials and links to audio, editing, and other types of tools, you can find many excellent resources on this site.

- ✔ **Podcast Alley:** (www.podcastalley.com) Find a wide variety of podcasts, podcast software, and instructions for creating and publishing podcasts at Podcast Alley.

- ✔ **SolidCasts:** (www.solidcasts.com) Here you can find free hosting for your podcasts although only about 100MB of space. Because even a low-quality, half-hour podcast can run about 15MB, this is a good place to start, but if you're serious about podcasting, you will quickly either run out of room or have to start shelling out money to upgrade to more storage space and bandwidth.

Mixing in music

You don't have to be a wannabe DJ to include music in your podcast. Even if you're participating in hard-hitting investigative reporting or archiving your dad's favorite fishing story, music can spice up the recording and make it seem more professional.

You can also add funny sound effects or snippets of dialogue from TV shows or old movies. Just make sure that you have the legal right to use any music or other type of recording. Type **free music** into any search engine to find places where you can download sound files. Be careful, however, because many of the sites that used to be free have started charging for the music, and don't hit you with the fees until you try to download.

Here are a few sites where you can still find free music (or at least low-cost royalty-free music): `Musicalley.com`, `GarageBand.com`, `Netlabelindex.com`, `Magnatune.com`, `CCmixter.org`, `SoundClick.com`, and `Freemusicarchive.org`.

You can add a music track to a sound file in a program like Audacity by using the Import feature, listed on the Project menu. Adding a basic audio track isn't difficult, but managing all the format options, permissions, and settings can become complicated, and is well beyond the scope of this book. However, you'll find many great books and online resources if you want to become more proficient in podcasting. One place to start is *Expert Podcasting Practices For Dummies,* by Tee Morris and Evo Terra (Wiley).

Chapter 13

Multimedia: Adding Flash, Audio, and Video

Tasks Performed in This Chapter

- ✔ Adding a Flash animation
- ✔ Inserting Flash video
- ✔ Comparing audio and video formats
- ✔ Uploading videos to YouTube
- ✔ Inserting a YouTube video into a Web page

Make your Web pages sing and dance by adding audio, video, and other multimedia to your pages. If you want to provide a richer experience for your users, to *show* rather than just to *tell*, or to entertain as well as inform, add animation or video. Not only does multimedia help tell stories more vividly, it can also make you look more professional.

And adding animation or video isn't as hard as you might think. One simple way to add video to a Web page is to upload a video file to YouTube (or search for video already on YouTube) and then insert it into your page. You find detailed instructions in this chapter for using video on YouTube, Vimeo, and other video hosting and social networking sites. You also find step-by-step instructions for using Dreamweaver to insert Flash animations and videos in into your Web pages.

Perhaps the most complicated aspect of multimedia on the Web is choosing the best format for your audience, which is why this chapter starts with a primer on audio and video formats and how multimedia works on the Web today.

Playing Animation and Video on the Web

When you add video or any other kind of multimedia to a Web site, your visitors may need a special player to play your files. A *player* is a small program that works alone or with a Web browser to add support for functions such as playing audio, video, or animation files. Among the best-known multimedia players are Adobe Flash Player, Windows Media Player, and Apple QuickTime.

The challenge is that not everyone on the Web uses the same player, and your site visitors must have the correct player to view your multimedia files. If your visitors don't have the right player, your video or animation file won't be displayed at all. If your multimedia file can't be displayed, you can include information on where to download most players for free, but many visitors find these messages confusing or irritating. As a result, many Web developers help out by doing one or more of the following:

- ✔ **Use Flash:** By far the most widely used multimedia player, Flash supports video, audio, and animation.

- ✔ **Offer audio and video in two or three formats:** For example, you can insert a video in the Flash format and then include links to the video in Windows Media Video and Quicktime so that visitors can choose the format that best fits the player they already have.

- ✔ **The same multimedia files in different file sizes:** Including multiple versions of the same video in different sizes enables visitors with slower connection speeds to get the video file faster, while still providing a higher quality version for visitors who do have high-bandwidth connections.

- ✔ **Information about where to find the necessary player:** It's always good practice to include instructions about where visitors can download any player needed to view files, but keep in mind that won't work for everyone. Many people surf the Web from offices, libraries, and other locations where they are unable to download and install new players (which is why choosing the popular Flash player or providing multiple versions are the safest options).

Comparing popular video formats

One challenge to working with video on the Web is choosing the best format. This list briefly describes the most common digital video formats and their file extensions and supplies a Web address where you can find out more about each program.

Flash Video: Because the Flash Player is so commonly used on the Web, many developers consider Flash one of the best options for sharing video on the Web. Videos can be converted into the Adobe Flash Video format (which uses the `.flv` extension) with the Adobe Media Encoder (`www.adobe.com`).

Windows Media Video: Developed by Microsoft and popular on PCs, Windows Media Video is another popular format which uses the `.wmv` extension. See `www.microsoft.com/windows/windowsmedia`.

QuickTime: The QuickTime video format, which uses the `.mov` extension, is popular among Macintosh users because the player is built into the Mac operating system (although QuickTime files can be viewed on Windows computers with the QuickTime player). See `www.quicktime.com`.

AVI: Created by Microsoft, the Audio Video Interleave (AVI; `.avi`) format is one the most common video formats on Windows computers, and it can play on most common video players. AVI works well if you're viewing video on a CD or on your hard drive, where the file doesn't have to be downloaded, but you can't optimize AVI files well for use on the Internet. If your files are in AVI format, you should convert them to one of the other formats before adding them to your Web site. Otherwise, you force visitors to download unnecessarily large video files. You can find more information if you search for **AVI** at `www.microsoft.com`.

No matter which player and format you choose, I recommend that you

✔ **Make it easy for people to turn off sound.** Remember that many people surf the Web in libraries, offices, and other places where unexpected sound can be jarring, disruptive, or worse. If you get someone in trouble for surfing the Web in their cubical, they may never come back to your Web site. I recommend you always warn people before you play video or audio, and always provide a way to turn off the sound quickly and easily if necessary.

✔ **Optimize your video for faster downloads.** Optimizing multimedia for the Web works much like it does with images: the smaller the file size, the lower the quality but the faster the file download. One task in this chapter shows you how to optimize a video with the free Adobe Media Encoder.

Working with Adobe Flash

Most of the tasks in this chapter focus on techniques using the Flash video and animation formats because Flash has clearly emerged as one of the most popular technologies for creating animations as well as videos for the Web. Indicative of its popularity, YouTube converts videos into the Flash format for display on its Web site.

Flash animation files use the file extension `.swf`. Flash video uses the `.flv` extension. You can easily insert Flash animations and Flash videos into your pages using Dreamweaver.

Before you choose Flash, though, you should be aware of its few downsides:

✔ Flash isn't supported by most mobile devices, including the iPhone and Blackberry. (Check the iPhone and Blackberry Web sites for updates as this may change in the future, but as of the writing of this book, if you visit a site built in Flash with an iPhone, you just get a blank page.)

✔ Flash doesn't always print well. Many people like to print Web pages, especially pages that include instructions, directions, and other important reference material. If you include that information in a Flash animation which can't be printed, consider including a simple XHTML version as an alternative.

✔ Flash can cause accessibility problems for visitors with disabilities unless you create an alternate text option for Flash files. Similarly, text included in Flash files isn't easily read by search engines (although including alternative text can help with this limitation, too). You can add Alternative text to a Flash file in Dreamweaver by clicking to select the Flash file, and then entering a text description in the Alt field in the Property Inspector.

✔ Some people deliberately block Flash files because they're often used for advertising or to create animated introduction screens that look pretty but don't offer much value to site visitors. (You may want to describe what they're missing.)

Despite these downsides, adding a little Flash video or animation can add a lot of life to your site. And, if you're not designing your entire site in Flash, it's generally a safe format choice for adding a little video, audio, or animation to your Web site.

Inserting a Flash Animation File into a Web Page

Stuff You Need to Know

Toolbox:
- Adobe Dreamweaver
- A Flash file in the SWF format (sample file available for download from www.Digital Family.com/diy)

Time needed:
About an hour

Flash animation files are relatively easy to insert into a Web page when you use Dreamweaver. In this section, I assume that you have a completed Flash animation file and that you want to add it to your Web page. To create a Flash file, you need Adobe Flash or a similar program that supports the Flash format. (If you want to know how to create Flash files, check out *Adobe Flash CS4 For Dummies,* by Ellen Finkelstein and Gurdy Leete, from Wiley.)

You insert a Flash file in much the same way as you insert an image file, but because Flash can do so much more than a still image, you choose from a variety of settings and options for controlling how your Flash file plays. Before you start, make sure to move or save the Flash file into the main root folder of your Web site (see Chapter 6 for detailed instructions about setting up a site in Dreamweaver and identifying the root folder). If you like, you can create a subfolder to store your Flash files inside your main site folder, just as you might create an images folder for images.

To add a Flash file to a Web site, first open an existing page or create a new document and save the file, and then follow these steps:

1. In Dreamweaver, click to insert the cursor where you want the Flash file to appear on your Web page. In this example, I'm inserting it into a `div` tag in the middle of the page. You can read more about `div` tags in Chapter 6.

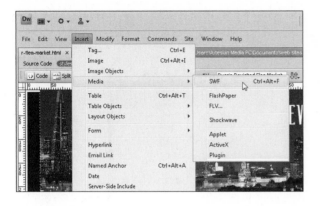

2. Choose Insert⇨Media⇨SWF from the menu. You can also choose Common from the Insert bar, if it isn't already selected, and then choose SWF from the Media drop-down list. (Note, if you are inserting a Flash video file, you would choose FLV.)

3. In the Select File dialog box that opens, browse your hard drive to locate the Flash file that you want to insert in your page, click to select the file, and then click OK. You can also double-click to select the file.

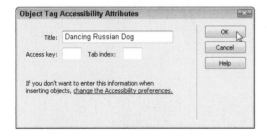

4. If you haven't turned accessibility options off in Dreamweaver's Preferences dialog, you're prompted to add alternative text to describe the Flash file. Enter a short description or name for the Flash file. Use of the Tab Index and Access Key options is optional. Leave these blank unless you want to include a special key command to control the file. Click OK; the dialog box closes, and the Flash file is inserted into your document.

Because Flash is an open standard, you can create Flash files with a variety of programs, including Adobe Photoshop Elements (which uses the Flash format when you create Web galleries in Elements), and Adobe Illustrator (which has an Export to SWF option).

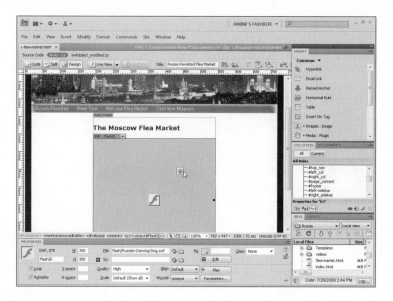

5. Dreamweaver displays Flash as a solid, gray box that represents the width and height of the Flash file. Click the gray box to display the Flash options in the Property Inspector at the bottom of the workspace.

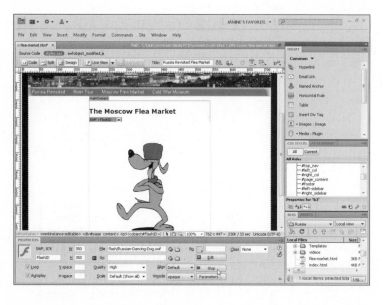

6. Click the Play button in the Property Inspector to play the Flash file. In this example, the Flash file is a dancing dog I purchased from iStockPhoto.com, so pressing the Play button causes the cartoon dog to dance on the screen. (***Note:*** When the Play button has been activated, the button text changes to *Stop.*)

7. Choose File➪Save to save the page. You'll be prompted to also save the related script files. Dreamweaver saves the files into a folder named Scripts in your main site folder. ***Remember:*** You must upload this entire folder to your Web server for your Flash file to work properly when the page is published to the Web.

8. You can make a number of adjustments to the way a Flash file is displayed by changing the settings in the Property Inspector: for example, Loop (replays the file if it's an animation), Autoplay (causes the file to play as soon as the page is loaded into a browser), and Quality (controls how good the file will look, how fast it will play, and how long it will take to download).

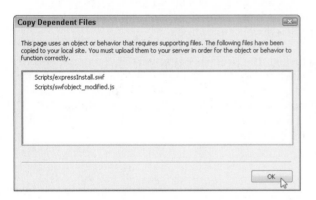

9. When you finish adding the Flash file to your page, choose File⇨Save to save the page. You'll be prompted to also save the related script files. Dreamweaver saves the files into a folder named Scripts in your main site folder. **Remember:** You must upload the entire Scripts folder, as well as the Flash file, to your Web server for your Flash file to work properly when the page is published to the Web.

Scripts to make Flash function better

When you insert Flash or other multimedia files with Dreamweaver, the program automatically creates a JavaScript file that helps the file play automatically. The file, named `AC_RunActiveContent.js`, is stored in the Scripts folder, which Dreamweaver automatically creates inside your root site folder. The first time Dreamweaver creates this file, a dialog box alerts you that you need to upload the script in order for your multimedia file to work properly. Make sure to include this script (and the entire folder) when you publish your site on your Web server. If you don't include it, your multimedia file may not play properly, or visitors might be required to click the Play button twice before the file begins to play.

Converting and Optimizing Flash Video

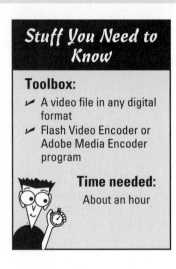

Stuff You Need to Know

Toolbox:
- A video file in any digital format
- Flash Video Encoder or Adobe Media Encoder program

Time needed:
About an hour

You can convert video from one file format to another relatively easily by using most video-editing programs. For example, you can open a video in AVI format in a program such as Adobe Premier Elements (a good video editor for beginners) and then choose File⇨Export to convert the file to any of a dozen other formatting and compression options.

Editing video gets complicated, and optimizing video for the best quality with the fastest download time is both an art and a science. The most basic process of converting a video file isn't difficult, however, after you understand the conversion options.

This task walks you through the process of converting a video file from Windows Media into Flash video (FLV), using the Adobe Media Encoder. In this task, I'm using the encoder that comes with Adobe CS4 Creative Suite. A very similar, but somewhat more limited version called the Flash Video Encoder is also included in Adobe CS3 Creative Suite. Both versions will work fine for this task.

1. Launch the Adobe Media Encoder and click the Add button to load a video that you want to convert into a Flash video file. In this example, I added a short video clip that was saved in Windows Media Video (WMV) format, but you can add video in a variety of formats, including AVI, MP4, and QuickTime. Click the Settings button on the right side of the encoder to launch the Export Settings dialog box, as shown in the next figure.

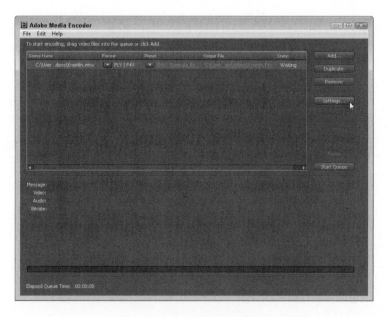

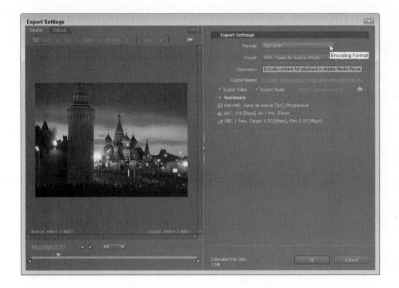

2. In the Export Settings dialog box that appears, leave the Format set to FLV and then choose a Flash encoding profile from the Preset drop-down menu.

3. You can choose from a long list of presets. The later the version of Flash and the larger the size, the better the video will look. However, a trade-off is involved: Not everyone has already downloaded the latest version and not everyone has a high-bandwidth connection to the Internet. If you know many people who visit your site will be using older computers or have slow connections, you may want to use one of the lower presets.

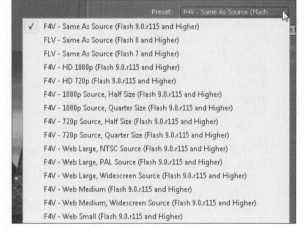

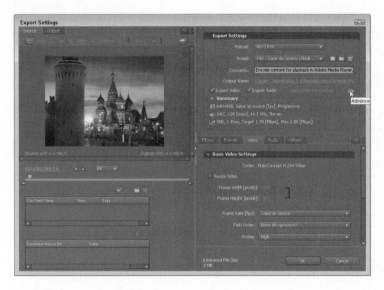

4. Click the double arrows to access Advanced Mode for more specific settings if you want to change any preset options, such as Frame rate, which you can find under the Video tab. To achieve the fastest download time, set the frame rate to the lowest setting that still looks good. If you're encoding a video that has lots of action, you need a higher frame rate — ideally, 24 or better — or else your video loses details and looks fuzzy in places. If you're converting a video, such as this Windows Media file that has already been encoded, your best option is to choose Same As Source from the preset drop-down list and leave the frame rate unchanged.

5. Click the Audio tab to adjust the Bitrate and other options. If your audio file has only a single voice, you can set this option quite low, and it still sounds good. If your audio file has music, special sound effects, or other multifaceted audio factors, set the Bitrate to at least 128 Kbps.

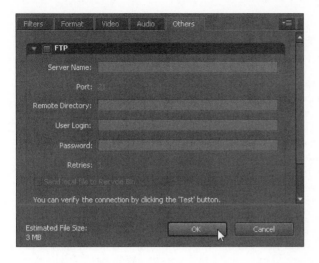

6. Choose the Others tab to enter FTP options; then you can upload video files to a server directly from the encoder. When you have all the settings the way you want, click OK. The Export Settings dialog box closes, and you return to the encoder.

7. After you have everything adjusted, you're ready to begin the encoding process. Click the Start Queue button. *Hint:* The encoding process can take several minutes, even for a short video file. A small preview window in the lower-right corner of the encoder enables you to watch the encoding process in action. A new file is created in the Flash format and is saved in the same folder as the original video file.

Adding Flash Video to Your Site

Stuff You Need to Know

Toolbox:

- ✔ Adobe Dreamweaver
- ✔ A Flash video file (available from this book's companion site; see the Introduction for details)

Time needed:
About an hour

Flash video is fast becoming the video format of choice among many designers. Video on the Web has been problematic for a long time because many different formats are available and you can never guarantee that everyone in your audience can view your videos in any single format.

Although the video players have been fighting it out for years, Flash seems to be winning the game. YouTube offers videos in the FLV Flash video format and millions of people have the Flash player on their computers because it's small, easy to download and install, and free.

Because Adobe owns both Flash and Dreamweaver, you find support for Flash files in Dreamweaver. You can use the Insert dialog box to easily set the many options for how a Flash video plays within a Web page. In the previous task, you find instructions for converting a video file into the Flash format. Follow these steps to insert a Flash video file into a Web page:

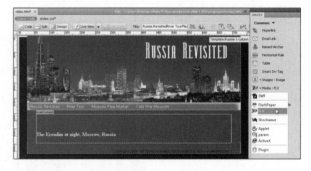

1. Create a new Web page in Dreamweaver or open an existing page, and then click to place your cursor where you want the file to appear on the page. Select Common from the Insert panel; then, from the Media drop-down list, choose FLV for Flash Video. (You can also choose Insert⇨Media⇨Flash Video from the menu.)

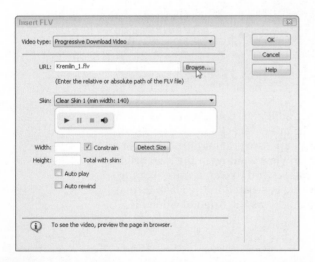

2. At the top of the Insert FLV dialog box that appears, specify streaming or progressive. Note that you must have special server software to stream video. Check with your Internet hosting service or system administrator to find out whether your Web server supports streaming Flash files. If not, select Progressive. Click the Browse button and select the Flash file from your hard drive. If the file isn't in your site's root folder, Dreamweaver offers to copy it there for you. ***Remember:*** The Flash file must be in your site's main root folder and it must be uploaded to your Web server in the same relative location when you upload the page that displays the file.

3. Next you choose a Skin, which creates a player, or Flash controller, for your video. The Skin drop-down list includes a variety of Play, Pause, Stop, and Volume controls in different sizes and designs that can be inserted into the page with the Flash file. When you choose a skin from the drop-down list, a preview of the selected skin is displayed, as shown here, so you can see the size and style of the Flash controller.

4. Click the Detect Size button; Dreamweaver automatically inserts the height and width of the Flash file into the HTML code. If you want the Flash video to play as soon as the page is loaded, select the Auto Play check box. To automatically rewind the video after it has played, select the Auto Rewind check box.

5. Click OK to insert the Flash file and close the dialog box. The Flash file is represented in the Web page by a box that has the same height and width of the video. Click the box that represents the video to select it. You can make further adjustments to the settings in Property Inspector at the bottom of the workspace. Click to select the Flash file to display the Flash properties, such as size, autoplay, and loop.

6. To view the Flash video, preview the page in a Web browser by choosing File⇨Preview in Browser and then choosing any browser from the menu. You must have the Adobe Flash Player installed on your computer in order to view the Flash video in your Web browser. (Note that the Flash controller, created by the skin, becomes visible only when you roll your cursor over the bottom of the video.)

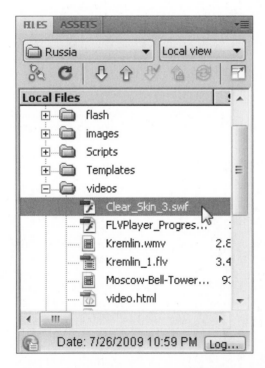

7. When you insert a Flash video file and include a skin for the player, Dreamweaver creates a Flash file with the .swf extension and saves it in your root site folder. This Flash file contains the player controls. It must be uploaded to your Web site when you publish the page with the Flash file for the player controls to work on your Web site. In this figure, the file named Clear-Skin_3.swf contains the Flash controller.

Finding out more about Flash online

One of the best places to find out more about creating Flash files is on the Internet, where a wide range of Web sites offer everything from predesigned Flash files that you can easily customize to useful ideas for getting the most from this award-winning technology. Here's a short list of useful sites to get you started:

✔ **Adobe:** (www.adobe.com) You find loads of tips and tricks for creating and using Flash files (as well as many inspiring examples of Flash in action).

✔ **GotoAndLearn:** (www.gotoandlearn.com) You find many free tutorials on creating Flash files on this site.

✔ **SWiSH:** (www.swishzone.com) If you're looking for an alternative to Adobe Flash, SWiSH is an excellent little program that's more reasonably priced.

✔ **Flash Kit:** (www.flashkit.com) This site has a wide range of resources for Flash developers.

✔ **Flash Arcade:** (www.flasharcade.com) Play some of the best interactive games created in Flash.

To find out more about advanced Flash settings, called *parameters,* visit www.Adobe.com and search for **"Flash parameters"**.

Uploading Videos to YouTube, Vimeo, and Other Sites

Stuff You Need to Know

Toolbox:
- An Internet connection
- A video file optimized for the Internet

Time needed:
About an hour

YouTube has attracted a tremendous amount of attention in recent years as *the* place to find Web videos. You can upload your own videos to www.youtube.com for all the world to see (a great way to garner free promotion), and use the site to host videos. So why not host your videos on your own Web server? Because bandwidth costs money, especially if you get lucky enough to get millions of visits to your video. YouTube, Vimeo, and others also provide streaming video hosting, which many Web hosts charge extra for (or don't provide at all). After videos are uploaded to a site like YouTube, you can then embed them so that they play within a page in your site. The result is that visitors see your video on your site, but you don't have to pay for premium bandwidth.

If you want the greatest possible audience to view your videos, I recommend YouTube. If you want more control over the use of your videos and how they're displayed in your pages, the premium service at Vimeo is a great option. Other video hosting services include Photobucket, Google Videos, and Revver, which offers advertising revenue for videos that attract a large audience.

As you see in this short task, YouTube makes it easy to upload videos and then embed them into your Web pages. Vimeo and other services are similar. The good thing is that most videos can easily work within those parameters. If your video is ready to post, follow these steps:

1. Before you can upload videos, you must first register at YouTube, a free and relatively painless process that simply requires filling out a form on the site.

2. To upload a video you must first log in, then click the Upload link in the upper-right corner of any YouTube page, and then use the Browse button to locate the video file you want to upload from your hard drive. Fill in the fields in the upload form to describe the video and add keywords to make it easier for YouTube visitors to find your video when they search the site.

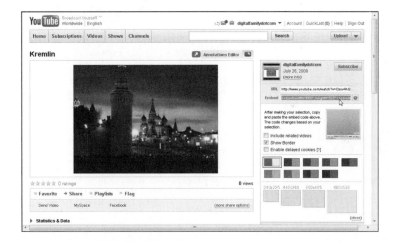

3. When uploading is complete, YouTube displays a confirmation page that includes HTML code you can add to your own Web site or blog to display your video on your own site. You can even choose the size and other display settings. To link to a video on YouTube, copy the URL and create a link in Dreamweaver like you would to any page on the Web. If you want to embed the video so that it plays within a page on your site, click and drag to select all text in the Embed box and then press Ctrl+C to copy it.

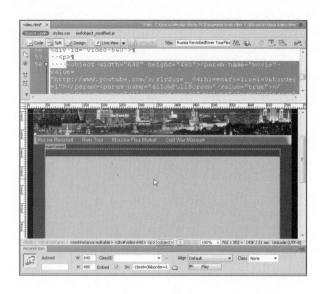

4. To add the code to your Web page in Dreamweaver, click the Split View button at the top of the workspace to view the HTML code of any page, click to place the cursor in the code wherever you want the video to be displayed, and choose File➪Paste to insert the code you copied from YouTube. (You find more detailed instructions for adding code from sites like YouTube in Chapter 6.)

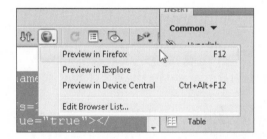

5. Choose File➪Preview in Browser and then select any browser you have associated with Dreamweaver to view your video displayed within the page on your site from YouTube.

TIP

You can always return to the YouTube page to edit your description or keywords and to find the code you need in order to embed the video in your own site: Click the My Account button and then My Videos, and then select the video you want from your list of uploaded files.

Choosing YouTube versus Vimeo

Vimeo offers a free service, similar to YouTube, and also provides a reasonably priced premium service ($69 per year at the time of this writing). Vimeo's premium service enables you to embed videos as easily as you can from YouTube, but with more options for how the video is displayed. For example, with Vimeo's premium service, you can remove the Vimeo icon from the player and remove any mention of related videos on the Vimeo site. You can also prevent other people from embedding your video on their sites.

YouTube is free, but when you upload your videos to YouTube, you give up some rights to your content. (Read the agreement at YouTube.com for more details about copyright and other legal issues.) Also, you can only upload videos that are smaller than 100MB and take fewer than 10 minutes to play. According to the site: "YouTube accepts video files from most digital cameras, camcorders, and cell phones in the .WMV, .AVI, .MOV, and .MPG file formats." You can also upload files in the Flash video format.

Chapter 14

Making Money with Your Site

Question: "How do you make $1 million on the Internet?" Answer: "Invest $10 million."

It's an old joke, but there's still an element of truth in it today. Although you can find many stories about Internet millionaires who became rich with seemingly little effort or investment, the truth is that most good Internet businesses aren't much different from brick-and-mortar ones. You need a product or service that people are interested in, you have to deliver it in a way that's useful and accessible, and you must be able to promote your business so that customers can find you.

Despite the risks involved, many people are making money from their Web sites, by using one of these two primary models:

✔ **Making money from advertising:** You can sell and host ads yourself, or you can sign up for one of the online advertising networks, such as the exceptionally popular Google AdSense. In this chapter, you find step-by-step tasks for creating and integrating advertising using Google AdSense or the affiliate advertising services Commission Junction or LinkShare, which make it easy to add advertisers to your site that pay a commission on any sales generated from your visitors.

✔ **Selling products or services online:** To sell products or services, you need to set up a system for accepting payment. Your options range from the simple (publishing a phone or fax number on your site that customers can call or send orders to) to the complex (a fancy, integrated shopping cart that enables visitors to select items as they navigate your site and automatically tabulates their purchase totals). Somewhere between these two extremes, you can sell products on sites like eBay or Amazon with little investment (or training) or set up a simple shopping cart or order button with Google Checkout or PayPal's one-click service, which you find out about later in this chapter.

PayPal and Google offer the simplest solutions for selling single products — like memberships, tickets, or e-books — via a Web site. If you want a more complicated shopping system, read my recommendations in the sidebar "Adding a shopping cart to your site," at the end of this chapter. I don't cover these services in detail because another excellent book in this series, *Web Stores Do-It-Yourself For Dummies,* by Joel Elad (Wiley), explains this type of sales site in depth.

Because this chapter features live Web sites, some screen shots may have changed since this chapter was written. As a result, you may have to make adjustments to some of the instructions, although the basic concepts and tasks should be similar.

Adding Advertisers with Google AdSense

You can find Google ads on so many different Web sites that the ads seem to appear automatically. And in a way, they do. As you see in this task, you must sign up for an account, select the type of ads you want, and generate a snippet of code to insert into your own site before you can include Google ads on your pages. After you set it up, though, the rest is automatic.

Google has developed an extraordinarily complex system that makes it exceptionally simple to host its ads — and not just any ads, but ads that Google can specifically deliver to your pages based on a number of criteria. The little snippet of code that you place in your pages enables Google to handle several tasks at once, including the ones in this list:

- ✔ **Target ads:** The automated Google system reviews the text on your Web pages and matches any relevant keywords it finds to related ad campaigns.

- ✔ **Deliver ads:** After the snippet of code is on your pages, Google can deliver ads automatically based on keyword targeting and other criteria.

- ✔ **Track traffic:** Google measures the traffic to each page that displays Google ads and tracks the number of people who view the page as well as the number of people who click to view the ad.

- ✔ **Measure effectiveness:** Using a complex system of data collection and analysis, Google can deliver detailed reports to advertisers about the success of their campaigns.

- ✔ **Calculate payments:** The system keeps a running total of the income you've earned from your Google ads and deposits the money into your bank account automatically.

Google makes buying ads as easy as placing other people's ads on your pages. And the two programs have similar names, which makes it easy to get confused. Remember this: Google AdSense pays you a few cents (or a fraction of a cent) every time someone clicks on an ad. Google AdWords makes it easy for you to buy 'words' so that your ads appear on Google and related Web sites.

To sign up for Google AdSense, follow these steps:

1. Open a Web browser with a connection to the Internet, and enter the address **www.google. com**. On the main Google page, click the Advertising Programs link.

2. The Advertising Programs page is split in two sections: On the left side is information about buying ads, and on the right is information about how publishers can make money by placing ads on a site (publishers, in this sense, are site owners who place ads on a site). In this task, I focus on the publisher side of the business, so click the Sign Up Now button, on the right side.

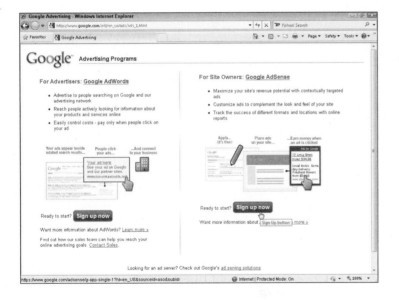

3. Fill in the registration form with your Web site address, your name, and other details. *Note:* Be careful to fill out this form accurately because the address you enter is the one Google sends checks to if your ads are successful.

4. Pay special attention to the Google Policy section, at the bottom of the registration form. You must select all these check boxes to indicate that you agree with the policies and will follow the rules. Google has had problems with site hosts clicking the ads on their own sites in an effort to generate income, a practice Google now works hard to prevent because it devalues the advertising. When you're ready, click the Submit Information button.

5. On the verification page that's displayed, read the form carefully to ensure that your information is entered correctly. If you already have an account with Google (for Gmail or any other Google service), you can either use that account with AdSense or create a new login. Either way, complete the form and click the Continue button.

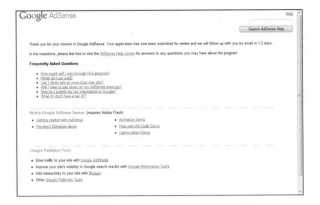

6. If you filled out the form correctly, Google displays a confirmation page, even though you can't get started right away. Google reserves the right to accept or reject anyone who applies for the AdSense program and, as the confirmation page warns, it can take a day or two for Google to review your site and notify you of your acceptance. In the meantime, you can find lots of helpful tips and tutorials for finding out more about how to make the most of Google AdSense.

7. After you receive e-mail confirmation from Google, you have everything you need to log in and create the code for advertising on your site. Follow the link in the e-mail message or enter **www.google.com/adsense** to go directly to the login page.

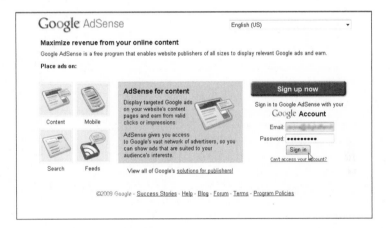

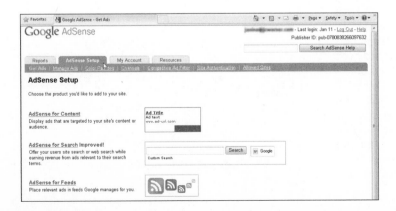

8. Click the AdSense Setup tab at the top of the page and then select the type of ad you want to create. If you want to place advertisements on your Web site, the AdSense for Content section is the best place to start. Simply click the AdSense for Content link to continue.

9. Choose the kinds of ads to display on your pages. For example, select Ad Unit and then choose from the options: text ads, image ads, or a combination of the two, which results in the largest number of advertising options for your site. Alternatively, you can select a link unit, which displays links to more general topics (matched to the keywords on your site) and displays for visitors a page of ads related to that topic. After you make your selection, click the Continue button at the bottom of the screen.

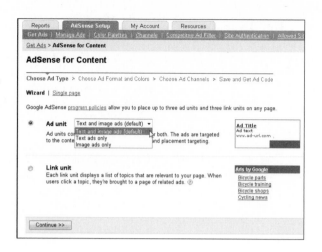

10. Choose the size and colors of the ads to display on your pages. Using the Format drop-down list, choose a size and shape that works best with the design of your Web pages. *Note:* You can repeat this process again to create ads of different sizes for different pages in your site. For now, choose the one you want to start with, such as the vertical 120 x 600 skyscraper that I selected in this example.

11. Choose a color scheme from the drop-down list next to the palettes, or create your own color scheme by selecting the color check boxes next to each of the ad elements, such as Border, Title, and Background. You can also specify the style — rounded or square — of the corners of your ads. Finally, choose the content you want to display if no Google ads match the content of your Web page. For example, you can choose to display public service ads for free if no paying advertisers are available or simply fill the space with a solid color. Click the Continue button when you're done.

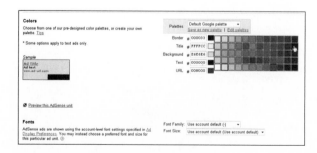

12. On this screen, you have the option to create *channels,* which can help you track the effectiveness of advertising on different parts of your site or across different Web sites, if you manage more than one site. You can create a channel for a specific domain name or create a custom channel to track the effectiveness of an ad size or style that you use across your sites. Channels are a unique concept at Google, but they essentially serve as categories for certain kinds of advertising you want to track.

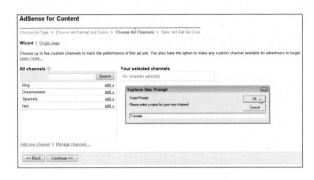

13. Finally, you see the Get Ad Code page, where Google has generated a snippet of code based on your selections on the previous screens. If you change your mind, you can always go back and make adjustments by clicking the Back button at the bottom of the page. If you're ready, simply click and drag to select all code in the AdSense code window, and then choose Edit➪Copy to select the code so that you can add it to your Web pages. You find instructions for inserting code into a Web page in Chapter 6.

Signing Up with Affiliate Programs

Stuff You Need to Know

Toolbox:

- An Internet connection
- A Web browser, such as Internet Explorer or Firefox
- A Web site where you want to add affiliate advertising

Time needed:

About half a day

Affiliate programs are a special type of advertising program designed to pay you a commission on any product or service that's sold if someone clicks on an ad on your Web site. The tasks of signing up for affiliate programs and adding their respective code to your Web site work similarly to Google AdSense, but the way you earn money with them is quite different.

With AdSense, you earn a small commission every time someone clicks an ad on your Web site. If you use affiliate ads, however, you're paid only if someone clicks the ad and then buys something from the advertiser — but you're usually paid much more if your ad leads to a sale. For example, a Google ad might earn you a fraction of a cent when someone clicks on it. But an affiliate link to Total Training (which produces video training programs) can earn you as much as 20 percent of the sale price on purchased videos, and that amount can be $20 or more per video.

Perhaps the most famous affiliate program is the one created by Amazon. Like most programs of this type, including Google AdSense (covered in the previous task), you must first fill out a registration form and wait to be approved, and then generate on the Amazon site a snippet of code that you can add to your own pages. Many companies run affiliate programs themselves, like Amazon does, but other sites serve as virtual matchmakers, making it easy to sign up with several affiliate programs at once. The two largest affiliate networks sites are LinkShare and Commission Junction, which take on the task of managing the relationship between advertisers and publishers.

For advertisers, the advantage of a site like LinkShare is that it handles all the technical details of signing up publishers, delivering ads, and tracking results. The advantage for publishers who want to add affiliate ads to their Web pages is that you can sign up once with a site like Commission Junction and then manage your relationship with many advertisers from one place.

The following steps walk you through the process of signing up for the Commission Junction affiliate program. (The LinkShare program is quite similar, and many Web publishers sign up for both programs to access their combined stable of advertisers.)

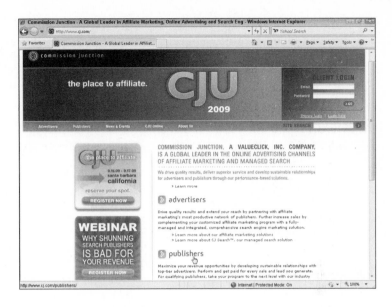

1. Open a Web browser with a connection to the Internet, and enter the address **www.Commission Junction.com**. Click the Publishers link to read more about the program, and then follow the links to the publisher's registration page.

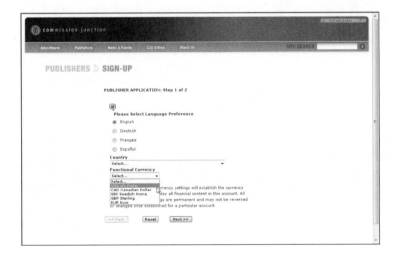

2. Select the language you prefer and your country and currency, and then click Next. (As of this writing, Commission Junction invites participants for most countries in the world but supports currency only in U.S. dollars, EU euros, British pounds, Swedish krona, and Canadian dollars. Check the Web site for specific instructions for currency exchange based on your country, as well as updates and additional currency that the company plans to support in the future.)

3. Review the service agreement. You must scroll to the bottom of the agreement and click the Accept button in order to accept it. Fill in all required fields, indicated with an asterisk (*). Commission Junction asks for a great deal of information on this page, including your Social Security number or corporate EIN, and you must answer all required questions if you want to sign up for this affiliate program. Remember to click the Accept Terms button at the bottom of the page when you're done.

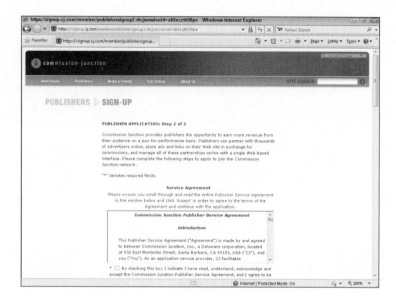

4. When you click the Submit Information button, Commission Junction displays a confirmation page and automatically sends you an e-mail with instructions for completing the registration process, filling out a W-9 tax-information form, and logging in to the site with your new username and password. Enter **www.cj.com** into your Web browser, and use the login and password information from the e-mail to sign in to the site.

5. The CJ Account Manager features a series of tabs across the top of the page, where you can make changes to your account information, run reports to track the success of ad campaigns, and use the Commission Junction integrated e-mail system. Click the Get Links tab to start creating the code to add to your Web pages.

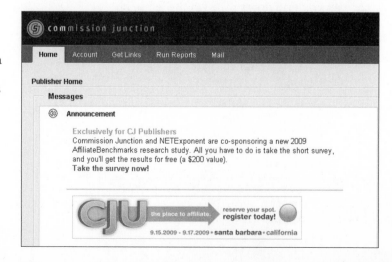

6. On the Get Links page, you find a seemingly overwhelming number of options, but your first step is essentially to choose the advertisers you want to work with. A good way to start is to browse the categories of advertisers to get a sense of the available options. Look for advertisers that sell products or services that are most likely to appeal to the people who visit your Web site.

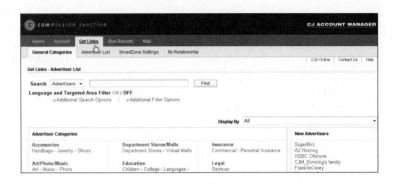

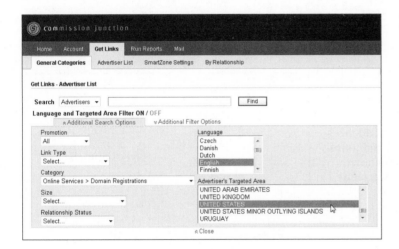

7. To narrow the list of advertisers, you can search for company names, products, or other keywords. Click the Additional Search Options link (shown in the figure for the preceding step) at the top of the Get Links page to reveal more search criteria. You can then search by language, product, and other criteria. Limiting the list to just the advertisers in your primary language and in the geographic area you serve is a good start. In this example, I selected companies in the Domain Registrations category.

8. As you drill down through the list of potential advertisers and start to make your selections, consider the commissions they offer and their overall performance in the network, all of which are listed for each advertiser.

TIP

If you're looking for a specific company, you can enter the name into the Search field at the top of the Get Links page at any time. If the company you're looking for isn't available, Commission Junction provides you with a list of similar companies.

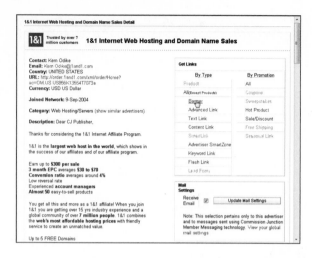

9. Click the name of any advertiser to display a Details page with a description of the company, program highlights, and links to advertising options. Click any of the options in the Get Links box, in the upper-right corner, to generate the code you need in order to add the advertiser to your Web site. In this example, I chose the Banner ad option for 1and1.com.

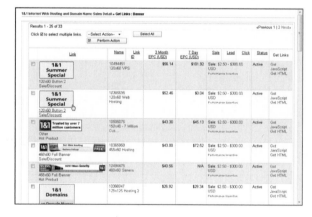

10. Most advertisers offer a collection of ad sizes and designs, and you can choose which ones you want to place on your pages. When you find one you like, simply click it to continue.

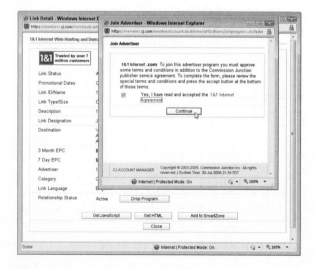

11. If you've never worked with the advertiser, you need to join its program before you can add its ads to your site. Some advertisers require a manual approval process that can take a few days; others accept you into the program right away.

12. After you're accepted into the program, the bottom of the Details page changes to offer options about how you can obtain the code you need to add to your own site. Choose HTML if you want to add the advertiser by simply copying and pasting HTML code into your Web page.

Advertiser	1&1 Internet Web Hosting and Domain Name Sales
Category	Online Services > Web Hosting/Servers
Link Language	English
Relationship Status	Active [Drop Program]

[Get JavaScript]   [Get HTML]   [Add to SmartZone]
[Close]

13. When you're ready, simply click the Highlight Code button to select all code in the code window and then choose Edit➪Copy to copy the code so that you can add it to your Web pages. Then open the Web page you want to add this code to in a program such as Adobe Dreamweaver. You can add the same code to as many individual pages in your site as you want, and you can add the code to a template page in Dreamweaver to update numerous pages simultaneously. (For instructions, see the task "Inserting Code into a Web Page in Dreamweaver," in Chapter 6.)

Hide tracking code in link?	☐ Yes
SID	[ ]
Image URL	http://www.advertiserserver.com/advertiserimage.gif
Destination URL	http://www.1and1.com/?ac=OM.US.US469K02463T2103a
[Update Link Code]	
Code	`<a href="http://www.dpbolvw.net/click-1869587-10505076" target="_top"><img src="http://www.tqlkg.com/image-1869587-10505076" width="150" height="40" alt="Over 7 Million Customers!" border="0"></a>`

[Highlight Code / Copy Code]   [Close]

Finding affiliate programs

This list describes a few of the more popular affiliate programs you can add to your Web site:

⚫ **Commission Junction:** Featured in the task in this chapter, Commission Junction (www.commissionjunction.com) is one of the most popular affiliate networks on the Web.

⚫ **LinkShare:** Similar to Commission Junction, LinkShare (www.linkshare.com) is a network of affiliate advertisers and makes it easy to work with many affiliates at once.

⚫ **Chitika:** Specializing in blogs, this site, at www.chitika.com, offers publishers a service that's part Google AdSense and part affiliate program, by offering ads that pay for clicks and sales.

⚫ **Amazon:** One of the oldest and best known affiliate programs on the Internet, Amazon (www.amazon.com) makes it easy to sell books, computers, and any other products available on the site with links that direct your visitors to the exact product page at Amazon.com.

Check out these popular affiliate programs online, and don't forget to search the Web for affiliate sites.

Adding a PayPal Button

Stuff You Need to Know

Toolbox:

- An Internet connection
- A Web browser, such as Internet Explorer or Firefox
- A Web site where you want to add a PayPal purchase button
- A Web page editing program, such as Adobe Dreamweaver

Time needed:

About half a day

You can sell products and services online in many ways. At the simple end of the spectrum, you can set up an account at PayPal.com and start selling products or services in a matter of minutes, with minimal effort and no upfront investment.

Moving up the scale in complexity and price, you can create a shopping system at any of the dozens of e-commerce sites that offer more complex shopping cart systems.

I recommend, as a general rule, that you start simple and add more complex and expensive e-commerce options as you start making more money. If you're determined to add a full-featured shopping cart right away, the book *Web Stores Do-It-Yourself For Dummies,* by Joel Elad (Wiley), gives you detailed instructions for using some of the most popular online shopping systems. If you want to get started with PayPal right away, follow these steps:

1. Open a Web browser with a connection to the Internet, and enter the address **www.PayPal. com**. Click the Products & Services tab at the top of the window to see a detailed explanation of the many kinds of payment services offered by PayPal.

2. On the Products & Services page, you find links to the many kinds of payment services offered by PayPal. Click the link for any of the services to sign up, watch a demo, and find out pricing information, including fees and commissions. Click Website Payments Standard if you want the simplest options for using single Buy Now buttons or PayPal's simple cart to sell multiple products, services, tickets, and so on.

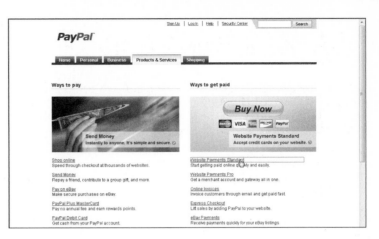

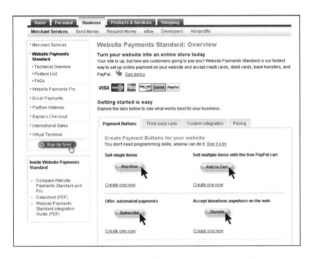

3. The Website Payments Standard page provides an overview of the options, a demo video, and other information about how you can use PayPal to sell one or more items. Click the Sign Up Now link to continue.

4. If you already have a PayPal account (even if you used it only to purchase items in the past), you can log in with your existing account information and continue with the setup process to upgrade PayPal so that you can use its sales services. If you're new to PayPal, click the Sign Up button to continue.

5. You can read about your options and the steps involved on the Getting Started page, but all you need to do is click the Go button in the Sign Up Now area to continue.

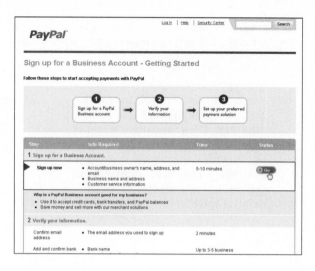

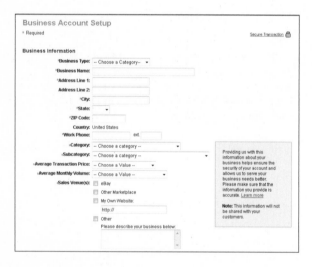

6. Fill in the forms carefully and completely. PayPal uses this information to process payments and to verify your identity when you use its service. When you finish with the online registration process and enter all your bank information, the Get Started page is displayed, where you can verify your information.

Because PayPal is a prime target for fraudulent activity and identity theft, it provides many levels of verification and mechanisms to confirm your information, from your e-mail address to your bank account. Taking a little extra time to verify all your information can help protect you and your accounts.

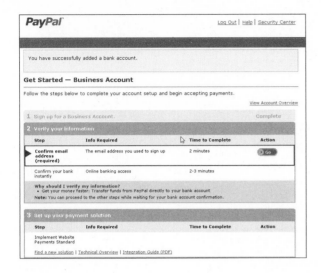

7. To confirm your e-mail address, click the Go button. PayPal sends an e-mail message to the address you entered when you completed the registration form. Open the link in that message in a Web browser and enter your password when prompted to complete the e-mail verification process.

8. When you complete the registration process, and whenever you log in to PayPal, you should see the My Account Overview page, where you find links to the many features offered by PayPal. Next, you should complete the bank verification process, which you can do by scrolling down the page and clicking the Go button, next to Confirm Your Bank Instantly.

9. To ensure that you're who you say you are and that you have access to the bank account you entered when you registered, PayPal makes two small deposits into your account — maybe as little as a few cents. The goal isn't for you to make a lot of money but to ensure that you can prove that the account is yours by entering the exact amount of the deposits into the bank confirmation form on PayPal. Your bank will likely take a few days to record the deposits, so you'll have to wait to find out the amounts and confirm your account. In the meantime, you can continue to set up your account and even begin using the PayPal services, but PayPal won't deposit any money you've earned from sales until you confirm your account by telling PayPal the exact amount that was deposited.

10. Click the Merchant Services tab at the top of the screen whenever you're logged in to your account, to set up or edit any of your payment systems for your Web sites. The simplest payment system uses the Buy Now button. To create one for your site, click the Buy Now Button link near the upper-left corner of the page.

11. Fill in the Create Buy Now Button form with information about the product or service you want to sell and the amount you want to sell it for. Then select the size and style of button you want. (This is how the button will appear on your Web page.) Then choose your shipping and sales tax options. You also have Button encryption options: Select the Yes radio button to enable encryption if you want to create a button that's more secure. (**_Note:_** It cannot be edited again after you create it. Of course, you can always go back and create a new button if you want to make changes.) Select the No radio button if you want to be able to modify the code after it's added to your page. (**_Note:_** Choose this advanced option _only_ if you know how to edit the code yourself.)

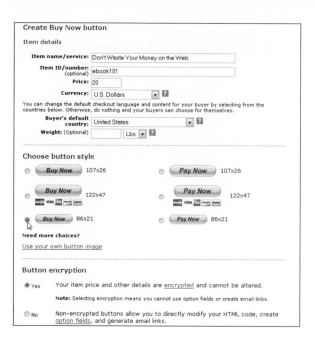

12. Click the Create Button Now button at the bottom of the form. Then click the Select All button at the bottom of the page to select the code that PayPal generated and choose Edit⇨Copy to copy the code. Next, you need to open the Web page to which you want to add this code in a program such as Adobe Dreamweaver. (For instructions, see the task "Inserting Code into a Web Page in Dreamweaver," in Chapter 6.)

Online services, such as PayPal and Google, that handle money are especially vulnerable to unscrupulous spammers and fraud. If you receive e-mails from these services, check them carefully and make sure the domain of the sender and any links you click really are from PayPal or Google.

Adding a shopping cart to your site

Although PayPal offers a quick and easy way to start selling products and services on the Web, you might find many other options superior, especially if you want to sell many products or services on your Web site. Here are a few of the most popular e-commerce options on the Web:

✔ **Yahoo! Merchant Solutions** (`store.yahoo.com`) offers a full line of e-commerce services, including a multi-faceted shopping cart. One of the most popular services on the Internet, Yahoo! is competitively priced, highly customizable, and takes care of every aspect of the shopping cart and transaction services.

✔ **Google Checkout for Merchants** (`https://checkout.google.com/sell`) requires no sign up fee, is quick and easy to set up, and provides buy buttons as well as a simple shopping cart, similar to the one provided by PayPal, which is covered in the final task in this chapter.

✔ **ProStores** (`www.prostores.com`) is an eBay company that offers an all-in-one shopping system and an enterprise-level ecommerce solution that includes supply chain and vendor management tools.

✔ **1&1 Internet** (`www.1and1.com`) claims to be the largest domain registrar in the world. This site also provides Web hosting, e-commerce, and a shopping cart system.

✔ **PayLoadz** (`www.payloadz.com`), is specially designed to sell e-books, software, and other digital products, as well as fee-based services, such as subscriptions and memberships.

For more detailed instructions on working with these shopping carts, read the book *Web Stores Do-It-Yourself For Dummies,* by Joel Elad (Wiley).

Part IV
The Part of Tens

Chapter 15

Ten Cool Services for Your Site

- -

- -

The best Web sites include a broad range of features, from attractive graphics to interactive surveys to detailed reports about site visitors. However, many of the most advanced features are highly complex to create and maintain. Fortunately, a growing list of Web services allows you to easily add specialized options to your Web site, without having to spend a lot of time or money. In this chapter, I introduce you to some of my favorite online resources — sites that can help you take your site beyond the basics without breaking the bank.

Most Web-based services like these make it easy to set up an account and then generate a snippet of HTML code that you can add to your own Web site. You find instructions for adding code snippets to your pages using Dreamweaver in Chapter 13.

Measuring Traffic from Web Visitors

Don't settle for the lame statistics you get from most Web servers. You need to know who is visiting your site. Add your own stat counter and you'll get far more details about where visitors come from and even what they search for in Google to find you. Although most service providers include basic Web traffic reports as part of their hosting services, you're likely to get far better results from a service like Google Analytics or StatCounter.com.

Google Analytics is one of the best traffic counters on the Web, and one of the most popular — and it's free! You just add a little snippet of code to your Web pages, and Google tracks your visitors, creating a comprehensive report full of juicy details.

You'll not only get the numbers of visitors and where they came from, you can even see what people search for on Google before they visit your site.

To sign up, just visit `www.google.com/analytics` and follow the instructions to create an account for your site and generate the code you'll need to add to your pages. Then it's as easy as copy and paste to get your site set up. If you use a template to create your pages, you can simply paste the Google Analytics code snipped into the bottom of your template and it will automatically be added to all your pages.

Creating and Managing E-mail Newsletters

One of the best ways to keep people coming back to your Web site is to remind them of what you have to offer, and one of the best ways to do that is to create an e-mail newsletter.

Managing e-mail newsletters is a complex process. Creating a page design that works well in lots of different e-mail programs is hard enough, but did you know about all the legal requirements regarding what you can and can't do when you send an e-mail letter to a mailing list?

Among other things, you're legally required to make it easy for people to stop getting your e-mail if they don't want to subscribe. If you've ever used the *unsubscribe* link at the bottom of an e-mail message you received, you probably understand why it's important to make it easy for people to get off your mailing list, as well as sign up in the first place. See the nearby sidebar for more about legal requirements.

If you have more than a few people on your mailing list or you want to send messages on a regular basis, you'll be best served by signing up with an e-mail newsletter service. You can read all about such services in *E-Mail Marketing For Dummies* by John Arnold (published by Wiley).

Here are a few of the most popular ones:

- **Constant Contact:** Considered the most popular online newsletter service, Constant Contact has been in business since 1996. As of this writing, prices start at $15 per month for up to 500 e-mails per month. (`www.constantcontact.com`)

- **iContact:** This service is quickly growing in popularity, in large part because it's priced more competitively than Constant Contact and offers more newsletter designs to choose from. As of this writing, prices start at $9.95 per month. (`www.icontact.com`)

- **Benchmark Email:** In this increasingly competitive category, Benchmark offers 600 e-mails per month for $9.95 or a popular $19.95-per-month plan that enables you to send up to 2,500 messages per month. (`www.benchmarkemail.com`)

U.S. law and e-mail newsletters or other bulk messages

If you send bulk e-mail messages of any kind, here are the basics you need to know about U.S. law, as well as generally-recommended netiquette. For more details about how the laws vary from state to state, visit www.mass-emailer.com/bulk_email_info. html. If you live outside the United States, your government Web site likely provides the information you need to stay in good legal standing.

✔ **No false or misleading information in the header area of an e-mail:** Spammers do it all the time (and many get caught, or at least blocked by spam filters for the practice). If you're sending a legitimate message, make sure the address you use in the From field of the message is your legitimate e-mail address, and also that any addresses you display in the To field are real. One of the biggest advantages of using an e-mail service (such as iContact) is that it provides a contact manager with which you can manage all your e-mail addresses.

✔ **Deceptive subject lines:** You can't claim that the e-mail is about dogs and cats in the subject line and then try to sell the recipient guinea pigs via the message.

✔ **An opt-out method:** There must be an easy way for recipients to let you know they don't want to receive any more messages from you — and you must remove them from your list if they do. This is one of the best reasons to use a service, such as Benchmark Email or iContact because all these services enable subscribers to opt-out automatically.

✔ **Compliance with restrictions on distributing addresses you collect:** You cannot sell or transfer e-mail addresses of people who have chosen not to receive your e-mail, and you cannot help any other entity send them messages (even if you don't charge for the service).

✔ **Clear intent:** All commercial e-mail must be identified as an advertisement and must include the sender's postal address.

Downloading Professional Images Inexpensively

Professional photographs and graphics can transform a simple page design into a professional showcase. High-quality images can be pricey, though. For professional, royalty-free images without the high price tag, visit iStockphoto (`www.istock photo.com`) where you can buy — and sell — high-quality photos and other images for $1 to $5 (depending on the resolution).

This searchable site makes it easy to find all kinds of photographs, illustrations, and even animated graphics and videos. Search for **German Shepherd**, for example, and you'll find nearly 1,000 photos of those lovely beasts; search for **dogs**, and you'll find more than 16,000. You can even search for general terms, such as **smile** or **raised hands**, to find images to fit almost any design idea or Web site.

When you find a photo that you like at iStockphoto, you can download a comp version for free. Free images have the iStockphoto logo printed across the middle but are handy to use for mockups. You can also save images to a collection (a *lightbox*) stored on the iStockphoto Web site so you can easily go back and review your favorites later.

When you're ready to purchase images, you can use any major credit card to buy credits on the site. The more credits you buy in advance, the better the price. The cost of each image is based on the resolution: The higher the resolution, the more the image costs, but most images are available in multiple resolutions. Prices can vary by image, but most low-resolution images (less than 400 pixels wide at 72 dpi), which work fine for most Web sites, cost as little as $1. Make sure the read the license agreement for details.

If you're looking for free images, or you like the idea of using images that are provided for free by photographer directly, consider www.sxc.hu, where you find more than 300,000 images from more than 30,000 photographers. Again, make sure to read the contract details carefully because some images on this site require that you work out the right to use the images with the photographers directly.

In Chapter 5, I give you instructions for editing, resizing, and saving images. See Chapter 6 for instructions for inserting images into your Web pages.

Highlighting Links with Pop-Up Previews

The innovative online service Snap-shots (www.snap.com) creates a small pop-up preview of any page you link to on your site. You simply sign up for the free service at Snap.com and use its online tool to generate special code that you can copy and paste into the code in your Web pages.

With the unique Snap.com pop-ups, anytime a visitor rolls the cursor over a link, a small pop-up window appears with a preview that displays the page or site that you linked to from your site. It's a useful way to give visitors a little more information as they peruse your pages and to highlight the links on your site.

WhatTheFont? (An Online Matchmaker)

If you've ever tried to identify an unusual font, you know how challenging it can be — and you'll likely appreciate the character recognition software offered from WhatTheFont (www.whatthefont.com). Using this free online service, you can upload any graphic or enter the URL to any image on the Web, and the program analyzes the image and tries to identify the font.

The system isn't perfect, but even if WhatTheFont can't identify the exact font, it gives you the closest matches it can find, which at least gets you pointed in the right direction. You can also opt for the "human" service, to have your graphic further reviewed by expert font matchers.

And, if you want to buy the font after you use the service to identify it, the site's creators are happy to sell you fonts that you download to your own computer. For more on the best options for using fonts on the Web, see Chapter 6.

Another great place to test fonts . . . www.dafont.com.

Surveying Your Visitors

If you want to know what visitors to your site really think, just ask them.

An online survey is a helpful way to gauge the experience of your audience and to invite reviews. You can also use online surveys as planning tools to poll your audience about how and where they might want an event, for example, or what new features they're most interested in.

You can create a free, online survey from SurveyMonkey (`www.surveymonkey.com`) and link to it from your Web site. SurveyMonkey makes it easy to create the survey by simply filling out a form in a Web browser, and then it automatically tallies the results and presents them in a series of reports and pie charts. The data you can gather and present is an excellent way to impress your board of directors at your company's next annual meeting.

Dressing Up the Address Bar with a Favicon

Have you ever wondered how some sites add those little custom graphics to the address bar, at the top of the browser? For example, Google adds the letter *G,* and Adobe adds its logo. You too can add any image to your site — you just have to get it in the right format.

Fortunately, turning a graphic into a *favicon* (or *shortcut icon*) is easy and free with FavIcon from Pics (`www.htmlkit.com/services/favicon`). Just upload any graphic of your own, and this online tool automatically converts it into a favicon that you can use on your site. After your image is saved in the ICO format, you simply upload it to the main root folder of your Web site, and your image is automatically displayed on the address bar in a browser.

Favicons also appear in the list of bookmarks, or favorites (which is where the name comes from) when a visitor saves your Web site in a browser. Thus, including a favicon can make your site stand out from a list of saved Web addresses and can help build and strengthen your brand.

Protecting Your E-Mail Address from Spammers

Spammers gather millions of e-mail addresses from Web sites every day by collecting e-mail addresses from links on Web pages. Web designers commonly include e-mail links so that visitors can easily contact them. Unfortunately, those simple e-mail links make it even easier for spammers to gather e-mail addresses automatically.

To help counter this problem, the programmers at AddressMunger (`www.addressmunger.com`) have come up with a special way of "hiding" e-mail addresses from the automated bots that spammers use. When you add this special code to your Web pages and use AddressMunger to create the e-mail links on your Web pages, your visitors can still e-mail you easily, but spammers can't read your e-mail address. It's an easy way to cut down on all that spam in your inbox.

To use this service, you need two snippets of code:

- ✔ One that you insert into the top of a Web page
- ✔ Another that you add wherever you want your e-mail address to appear

You can find instructions for adding code to your pages in Chapter 13.

Setting Up Free Conference Calls

Want to set up a conference call for free? Really, for *free*. Well, you do have to pay any long-distance charges you incur if your call to the conference center requires dialoging a long-distance number, but if you have an unlimited calling plan with your phone company, you're already covered on that front. You can pay extra for an 800 number, but if you're willing to let the service pick the number, all you pay are any necessary toll call charges.

To use the service, simply visit FreeConference at `www.freeconference.com`, sign up for the free account, and immediately start scheduling conference calls. You can invite as many people as you like into the call. FreeConference even includes a handy system for managing contact information and sending out invites on your behalf.

I use the service on a regular basis to schedule conference calls with clients and students. You can even add desktop sharing for $9 per month, making it possible to simultaneously share information on your computer or use the service. That makes it ideal for Webinars, review sessions, or other kinds of collaborative meetings online.

The company makes money by charging for specialized services, such as the use of an 800 number, or if you want FreeConference to record or transcribe your calls.

And like most things that are free, FreeConference can't guarantee availability, so scheduling in advance is always wise although I've rarely had any trouble setting up a call, even at the last minute.

Sharing PowerPoint Presentations

Online training, teleconferences, and virtual seminars are increasingly popular, thanks to services like SlideShare (`www.slideshare.net`). To use this innovative service, just upload your presentation to the site and point visitors to your special address, where they can view your slides and use the simple controls at SlideShare to move forward and back through your presentation.

Combine SlideShare with a service like FreeConference, and you're ready to host a professional teleconference or online seminar — without spending a cent.

Chapter 16

Ten Ways to Promote Your Site

What if you build a Web site, and nobody comes? Unfortunately, that's an all-too-common problem on the Internet. And, that's why I can't end this book without at least pointing you to a few places where you can promote your Web site. Driving significant traffic to the pages of a site requires a significant amount of time or money or an incredibly compelling message. If you can manage all three, you should do very well indeed. In this chapter, you find tips and online resources to help bring people to your Web site.

Scoring High in Search Engines

The buzzword here is *search engine optimization,* or *SEO,* a highly complicated science that involves getting search engines like Google, Bing, and Yahoo! to list your Web site higher on the page than your competitors.

Thousands of companies and services promise to "get you in the top 10 matches" on search engines for as little as $19.99. Be wary of these services. The truly good ones charge hundreds or even thousands of dollars per month (with good reason), and the bad ones can get you delisted from search engines for breaking the rules with old tricks like inserting the word *sex* into your code when you're site is really about car maintenance. Most SEO experts agree that the best way to score high in search engines is to provide useful information on your site and to use appropriate keywords effectively.

Scoring high in Web searches is complicated because millions of sites vie for the top spots and search engines use complex formulas to determine which Web site should match any given key word search. Search engines also guard their formulas for how they prioritize Web sites more carefully than Coca-Cola guards its recipe. And if that doesn't make it complicated enough, most search engines change their formulas regularly. (*How* regularly is also secret.)

The reason for all this secrecy is that the people who run sites like Google and Bing want to deliver the best results when someone conducts a search — not just a list of the sites that smart Web marketers figured out how to trick their way into top position. Because there's much money to be made at the top, Web marketers spend countless hours testing how search engines work to come up with their best guesses about the criteria that search engines are using and how best to move their sites up the list.

The result is sort of a cat-and-mouse game, with search engines changing the rules to thwart the most calculated efforts of specialist's in SEO, and people who specialize in SEO charging big bucks to figure out the secret formula that can put you on top.

For the most part, search engines score sites based on the words and images on Web pages and on how well their content matches the keywords that are searched. For example, if you own a B&B in Point Reyes Station, California, you should include *at least* the name Point Reyes Station on your Web site because the term B&B has many competitors and people searching for lodging in the area are likely to include the town's name in their search.

A great way to determine how best to make your own site search engine friendly is to search for keywords that you want to lead people to your site and then study the Web sites that match those words already. Often, the best way to move your Web site up the ranks in search results is to emulate the strategies of other sites that are already doing well.

Achieving the best placement, especially for popular keywords, is a full-time job, but here are a few tips that most SEO specialists agree are likely to help you score better in search engine searches.

- ✔ **Invite other sites to link to you.** It's widely believed that Google rewards people who attract the most links to their sites, especially if those sites already have good rankings themselves. It makes sense: If lots of other Web sites consider your site good enough to send their visitors to you, you probably have something of value to offer.

- ✔ **Fill your site with fresh, original content related to your business or industry.** Include tips, articles, tutorials, and other content that's valuable to your visitors, and don't stop there. Keeping your content updated by adding fresh information on a regular basis is another great way to keep search engines — and visitors — interested.

- ✔ **Develop a list of keywords and a good description for your site.** The trick to writing a good Web site description is making it concise (every word counts), packing it with your most important keywords, and phrasing it so that it reads like a sentence (not just a list of words). Include this description toward the top of your home page in the *meta description tag,* which is a special tag that can be used to add information just for search engines. (You find instructions for adding Meta descriptions and keyword content in Chapter 6.)

✔ **Include your most important keywords in the title of your Web page and the name of the file.** The title doesn't appear in the body of a Web page; the title appears at the top of the browser window. You can add or edit the title of a page in Dreamweaver by changing the text in the Title field at the very top of the workspace. Similarly, including keywords in the filename of each page in your Web site can also boost rankings.

✔ **Include keywords in the headlines on your Web page.** Most search engines place higher priority on keywords that appear in the headlines on a page, but only if you use XHTML heading tags to style those headlines. Heading tags, which include h1 (the biggest) through h6 (the smallest), identify text as headlines in a way that search engines easily recognize.

✔ **Don't expect instant (or permanent) results.** Even if you do everything right in the search engine search game, you might still have to wait for the results of your efforts to be recognized. Some search engines can take weeks or months to reflect changes to Web pages on the Internet. Search engines, such as Google, generally update the most popular sites very quickly while lagging weeks or months behind in updating less-visited sites.

A great place to learn more about how search engines work and how to achieve the best ranking is www.searchenginewatch.com.

Buying Traffic (Yes, You Really Can!)

In addition to the "natural" results that search engines deliver when someone does a keyword search, buying keywords on search engines helps to ensure that your site is listed when someone searches for words that are relevant to your site, although the process is far more complex than most people realize. Search engine ads generally appear at the top and right side of most search-result pages.

Not all keywords sell for the same price. Using a complex bidding process, most search engines charge significantly more for the most popular keywords. Adding to the complexity, the results of those keywords for your site can vary dramatically based on a dizzying array of factors. For example, the expensive keyword *Hawaii* may bring the most amount of traffic to your site, but the lower-priced keyword *luau* may result in more reservations to your hotel. Because it's possible to measure not only the traffic from a keyword search but also the actions of the person who clicks on that keyword, you can measure and compare the effectiveness of nearly every aspect of search engine advertising.

Again, this process can be highly complex. Just developing a list of keywords worth purchasing seems easier than it really is at first. Sure, if you have a B&B in Point Reyes, you can likely make a list of a few dozen obvious words quickly. But the real art of developing a list of keywords for search engine advertising requires more than just brainstorming a few words related to your business. The best SEO companies come up with hundreds or thousands of keywords and phrases and then track the results to find the best return on dollars spent for paying customers. Thus, running a campaign with 10,000 words might not cost much more than running a campaign with 100 words, and might prove much more effective over time.

Add to that strategy the importance of landing pages and sales messages. The most sophisticated ad campaigns involve creating special Web pages to go with each keyword ad. For example, you can create a special page (often called a *landing page*) on your Hawaiian hotel site for people who click the search term **scuba diving** that is different from the page for those who click the search term **health spa**. You can learn more about how to make the most of your keyword ads by carefully reading the instructions and tips on any site where you plan to advertise.

Google AdSense offers the largest online advertising program for keywords. Just click the Advertise button at `www.google.com` to find detailed instructions and a number of tips and tools to help you develop the best campaign and measure the results.

In addition to buying ads on Google, you can include Google Ads on your own Web site to earn advertising income. In Chapter 14, you find tips on how to earn income from your site with Google Ads.

Using Social Networking Sites for Promotion

Social networking, the art of meeting and building contacts on the Web, is an increasingly popular way to increase your personal and professional contacts, make new friends, develop professional relationships, and even find a new job. You can also use social networking sites to promote your personal or business Web site. *Netiquette* (Internet etiquette) calls for a subtle approach to promoting your site in these kinds of environments, but simply including your Web address in your online profile can help drive new people to your site.

Here are some of the most popular social networking sites and what you can expect to find there:

- **Facebook:** (`www.facebook.com`) Facebook wins top place as the fastest growing social networking site on the Web, and its broad appeal makes it an excellent place to promote your Web site. Facebook was originally considered a vanity site and a place for college students, but its professional power is growing with its ever-expanding audience.

- **LinkedIn:** (`www.linkedin.com`) This is *the* site for professional connections and online business networking. If you're online to develop business contacts with other professionals, especially if you're job hunting or trying to attract new business clients, this is a powerful place to promote yourself and your Web site. Unlike Facebook and MySpace, LinkedIn is all business.

- **MySpace:** (`www.myspace.com`) One of the all-time most popular social networking sites, MySpace makes it easy to create a profile site, add music, write a blog, and post as many photos as you want to share with the world. Although the site has dominated the social networking landscape on the Internet, at the time of this writing, it was rapidly falling behind its biggest competitor, Facebook. Still, its huge online audience is a popular place for musicians, performers, and many others to promote themselves and their Web sites.

✔ **Ecademy:** (www.ecademy.com) Similar to LinkedIn, Ecademy is a site where professionals network, seek new clients, hunt for jobs, and recruit employees. What makes Ecademy different is that it's much more international, with an especially strong audience in Europe and Asia.

✔ **Ning:** (www.ning.com) You can create your own social networking site at Ning and invite your friends and colleagues to create profiles there in your own exclusive social network environment.

Getting Ranked on Social Bookmarking Sites

Social bookmarking sites rank the popularity of Web pages by the number of votes they get. The result is that these sites are excellent resources for people who want to keep up with what's popular online. Most offer special software that makes it easy for anyone to vote on a site.

Getting your site listed on social bookmarking sites is a highly effective way to increase traffic. Dozens of these sites and services exist, with more sure to come, and they feature catchy and unusual names, like Digg (http://digg.com), delicious (http://delicious.com), StumbleUpon (www.stumbleupon.com, and reddit (www.reddit.com).

Although you can submit your own pages on any of these sites, it's generally frowned upon and if you do it too frequently, you can be banned. Besides, your one little vote won't make much different anyway. A better method is to add a button to your site from each of these services that makes it easy for your visitors to vote for you. If you're a blogger, you can add a button each time you post. You can get the buttons (chicklets) for free and add them to your pages by simply inserting a little code you generate on the social networking site. (Find instructions for adding code to your pages in Chapter 6.)

Enticing Visitors to Return for Updates

One of the best ways to improve traffic to your site is through repeat visitors, and regular updates to your site can make all the difference. If you want your visitors to know when to look for updates, consider making regular changes to your Web site. Add a post to your blog every Thursday morning, for example, or post your newest photos to the site on Saturday mornings. Regular updates help get people in the habit of visiting your site.

Gathering Ideas from Other Web Sites

One of the best ways to create good habits in Web design is to visit other people's Web sites and study what works and what doesn't on their pages. While you're there, check out the title of the page, any descriptive text, or keywords that are used throughout the site. As you look at related Web sites, ask yourself what you like about the site and why you like it. Also, determine whether you can easily find the information you're most interested in and how easily you can navigate around the site.

Sometimes the best way to discover the problems in your own Web site is to look for problems on someone else's site and then return to yours with a fresh perspective.

Marketing a Web Site to the Media

Attracting traditional media attention to your Web site is not unlike attracting it to any other business. The trick is to tell a good story and get the attention of someone who can write about it in a publication that's read by your target audience. If you're looking for press coverage, make sure to include a Press section on your Web site with contact information, story ideas, and any other press coverage you've received.

Don't wait for journalists to come to you! You should never pester a reporter with a barrage of e-mail, press releases, or phone calls, but a well-timed or well-pitched message can get the attention of a reporter *and* the desired result — your Web address in the press. One good way to find journalists who might be interested in your site is to visit related sites and study their Press sections to find out who has been writing about them. Note not only the publication but also the writer. Then send a note directly to that person with a message that starts like this:

> Dear *fabulous journalist* <insert *that person's name,* of course>:
>
> I enjoyed reading the article you wrote on the XYZ company and thought that you might be interested in what we're doing.

Keep your message brief, and try to include a news hook and story idea that go beyond just promoting your business. For example, rather than tell a reporter that you have the best B&B site in northern California, pitch a story about the best hikes in the area. With any luck, the article on great hikes will include a quote from you and a mention of your B&B's Web site (especially if the reporter can send readers to your online list of hiking tips).

Unleashing the Power of Viral Marketing

Viral marketing is another of the marketing industry's new buzzwords in the digital age. The idea is that a message (a video, an article, or a photo, for example) is so exciting, fun, and compelling that people want to share it with each other, passing it on to their friends, who then pass it on to their friends, until it spreads like a virus. Such messages are often sent via e-mail, blogs, or chat, which can make the ever-expanding impact happen at an almost instantaneous pace.

Tap in to the power of viral marketing, and you can become an overnight sensation. Humor seems to be the most effective strategy. Among the mainstays of the viral phenomena are those silly photos of cats with clever sayings. Known as the LOL cats, these photos have spawned several Web sites, like Icanhascheeseburger.com.

Funny video clips, the kind you would expect to see featured on a show like *America's Funniest Home Videos,* are also highly viral because they're shared around the Web.

To use viral marketing to attract traffic to your Web site, include a section with funny photos, industry jokes, or a Top 10 list, and you might just get visitors to tell their friends about your site.

Blogging, Blogging, Blogging

Creating a blog and adding it to your Web site makes it easy to add fresh content because blogs are designed for frequent updates. When you become a blogger, you also join the ranks of a prolific group of writers who regularly refer their readers to each other's Web sites.

 Don't launch a blog just to "do it." Make sure that your blog features interesting, relevant information for your audience and that you update it regularly. And, if you want your blog to serve as an effective marketing tool, take the time to participate in other people's blogs. Adding relevant tips and thoughtful comments to other people's blogs is an excellent way to get their visitors to come back to your Web site.

Instructions for creating a blog and integrating it into your Web site are in Chapter 11.

Using Twitter to Promote Your Site

One of the most popular new forms of social media can be found at `www.twitter.com`. Described as *micro blogging,* Twitter makes it easy to register and start sharing your words of wisdom, but you have to keep it brief. Twitter limits users to 140 characters (about a sentence) of text per post. At first, many users complained that Twitter was a trivial place where people shared too many boring details, such as "I'm going to lunch at Red Lobster now."

But as Twitter has evolved, it's become an incredibly popular way for friends to stay in touch, and for businesses, actors, and others to promote themselves. Just visit `www.twitter.com` and register for a free account, and you can start posting short messages about what you're doing, what you're thinking, or questions you're pondering. Anyone who uses Twitter can subscribe to the *Twitter feed* of anyone else who uses Twitter and receive all their comments, called *Tweets.*

Telling Everyone You Know

It might seem obvious, but many people are either too shy or too busy to reach out to their friends, family, and personal contacts when they launch a Web site. Don't overlook your most obvious supporters. Launching a new Web site, or redesigning an existing site, is an excellent excuse to e-mail personal and professional contacts. To make the announcement even more fun, consider sending an e-card with a colorful character, animation, or music to dramatize your announcement.

Hallmark.com is one of my favorite e-card sites because it has lots of free cards with clever sayings, professional designs, and interactive animations. Most of its free e-cards even include sound. BlueMountain.com is another useful e-card site, but you have to pay for the pleasure of sending its professional greetings. When choosing an e-card to announce your Web site, look for blank cards or the Friendship and Any Occasion sections, where you can find messages that are easily personalized for nearly any kind of Web site.

Make sure you include your URL on all your marketing and other materials, too. Your Web address should be prominently displayed on your business cards, brochures, stationery, and anywhere else you promote your business.

Index

• N •

• O •

• P •

(continued)

Do-it-yourself.
Easy.

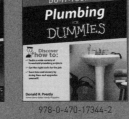

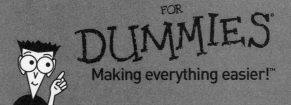